Woody Guthrie
L.A. 1937 to 1941

For Michelle

Woody Guthrie
L.A. 1937 to 1941

Darryl Holter
and William Deverell

Foreword by Ed Cray

Take a walk
in Woody's
LA.

(signature: William Deverell)

(signature: Darryl Holter)

ACP
ANGEL CITY PRESS
SANTA MONICA

Published by Angel City Press
2118 Wilshire Blvd. #880, Santa Monica, California 90403
+1.310.395.9982
www.angelcitypress.com

Opposite: Woody and Mary Guthrie with their children in Los Angeles, 1940.

For our children . . .

for their future.

—D.H. & W.D. 2015

Maxine "Lefty Lou" Crissman and Woody Guthrie promote their *Woody and Lefty Lou* radio show.

CONTENTS

INTRODUCTION

Ed Cray

It would be hard to overestimate the impact upon popular culture and the arts of Woodrow Wilson Guthrie.

Consider that he composed our unofficial national anthem, "This Land Is Your Land," and two official state folk songs, Washington's "Roll, Columbia, Roll" and "Oklahoma Hills." He wrote some three thousand songs in all, writing almost one a day, though we have the musical score for only half of them. The others are only verse, some of them quite poetic, others barely a cut above doggerel.

Woody was unpretentious. Though named after the twenty-eighth president of the United States, he was simply "Woody" to everyone. Woody demonstrated to any number of singers that one didn't have to wait for well-known songwriters Sammy Kahn or a Jimmy Van Heusen to turn out a new song. Singers could write their own songs and perhaps even make a living from it. Woody created singer-songwriters, key components in the development of rock bands.

Evaluating Woody's contributions is a rather difficult task given his staggering output. Three characteristics mark Woody's oeuvre, a word I imagine he would snort at: his unfailing sense of humor, his optimism, likely learned from father Charley, and his love of his country.

Even in his protest songs, there were often a pointed line or two that was wryly wrought. In "Pretty Boy Floyd," Woody wrote:

> Yes, as through this world I've wandered
> I've seen lots of funny men,
> Some will rob you with a six-gun;
> And some with a fountain pen.
> And as through your life you travel,
> Yes, as through your life you roam,
> You won't never see an outlaw
> Drive a family from their home.

Opposite: **Woody Guthrie, Shafter Labor Camp, 1941**

Or these lines from "Do Re Mi":

Lots of folks back east they say
Leavin' home every day.
Beatin' a hot and dusty way,
To the California line.
'Cross the desert sands they roll
Getting out of the old dust bowl,
They think they're going to a sugar bowl,
But here is what they find:
Now the police at the port of entry say:
You're number fourteen thousand for today.
Oh, if you ain't got the do re mi, folks,
If you ain't got the do re mi.
Why you better go back to beautiful Texas,
Oklahoma, Kansas, Georgia, Tennessee.
California is a garden of Eden,
A paradise to live in or see.
But believe it or not,
You won't find it so hot,
If you ain't got the do re mi.

The second characteristic of Woody's work was optimism. It is likely the reason he struck a sour verse from his draft of "This Land." It read:

One bright sunny morning in the shadow of the steeple,
By the relief office, I saw my people,
As they stood hungry, I stood there wondering if
God blessed America for me.

Optimism. In an essay Guthrie wrote, "The note of hope is the only note that can help us or save us from falling to the bottom of the heap of evolution, because, largely, about all a human being is, anyway, just a hoping machine, a working machine, and any song that says the pleasures I have seen in all of my trouble, are the things I can never get—don't worry—the human race will sing this way as long as there is a human race."

The third characteristic is an unquenchable love of this nation; its grand variety of people; and the stunning beauty of its mountains, rivers, and canyons. This quality is apparent in two stanzas from "Pastures of Plenty," written in 1941, before the attack on Pearl Harbor, but with a European war blazing in skies over London and the Wehrmacht sweeping across the continent:

> Green pastures of plenty from dry desert ground,
> From that Grand Coulee Dam where the water runs down,
> Every state in this union us migrants have been.
> We work in this fight and we'll fight till we win.
> Well, it's always we ramble, that river and I,
> All along your green valley I'll work till I die.
> My land I'll defend with my life if it be,
> 'Cause my Pastures of Plenty must always be free.

As fine as these songs are, they would have been lost or forgotten were it not for the House Un-American Activities Committee, HUAC, in the U.S. House of Reprentatives. On August 16, 1955, the committee subpoenaed Pete Seeger, ostensibly to investigate Communist influence in the entertainment industry. Seeger refused to answer any questions about his political beliefs or groups he had sung for. He was blacklisted—with a wife, Toshi, and three kids to support. Slowly, he and Toshi put together a living: former radicals, sometime liberals, children always, pass-the-hat concerts, house parties, eventually touring the country making music. And wherever he sang, Seeger included songs written by his friend, Woody Guthrie.

In an obituary for Woody in the *Journal of American Folklore,* John Greenway—incidentally the first academic to write about the importance of Woody—sadly wrote, "The poet has ten years." (The reference, of course, was to Percy Bysshe Shelley.) Woody had his ten years, from about 1937, when he left Pampa, Texas, for Los Angeles, to 1947, when the symptoms of Huntington's disease first appeared. In that period, Woody produced a huge inventory of songs, poems, essays, biographical musings, artwork, and three books. It is a mammoth archive, and undoubtedly, in that trove there are gems of value still to be mined.

Woody himself never copyrighted his songs. He took the attitude that if you sang one of his songs, you did him a favor. He has given us a great gift.

WOODY

TH' DUSTIEST OF TH'

DUSTBOWLERS

KFVD 215-245

One

WOODY GUTHRIE IN LOS ANGELES 1937–1941

Darryl Holter

We know Woody Guthrie as the Dust Bowl vagabond who rode the rails during the Great Depression. We know him as the radical folksinger who boldly scrawled "This Machine Kills Fascists" across his guitar. We know him as a pioneer in the folk music revival of the 1950s and as a role model for Bob Dylan, Phil Ochs, and other young singer/songwriters in the 1960s. And we know him as the author of one of America's greatest songs, "This Land Is Your Land."

We know so much that we might think we know it all, or that we know enough. But there is so much more to know.

What happens when we push beyond Woody's iconic image to try to understand how an unemployed hillbilly singer in the late 1930s transformed himself into something else? We learn that transformation started in, and started because of, Los Angeles, a place key to Woody's evolution. His years in L.A. were important years—vastly important. This uniquely American musician/songwriter brought southern folk music to urban intellectuals in Los Angeles just before the coming of the Second World War. And he brought his sound, and his words, and his spirit to the masses.

The few years Woody spent in Los Angeles were years of rapid professional, musical, and political development. In L.A., Woody became a minor celebrity on KFVD radio, wrote more of his own compositions for live performances, met novelists John Steinbeck and Theodore Dreiser, performed agitprop skits with actor Will Geer in support of striking cotton workers, and shaped his unique "political Okie" persona and public image. The songs he wrote and sang are the core of his achievement and defined him in the public eye. A close examination of the lyrics, themes, and political content of Woody's songs from 1936 to 1941 reveals a musical journey from amateur hillbilly singer to professional musician/songwriter and poet of the people, and it shows his parallel political evolution from a Dust Bowl Democrat with populist leanings to a streetwise radical, a staunch supporter of the Communist Party, and as a figure rising in American popular culture and history.

More than anything, Woody's songs reveal his growth and evolution. Woody was a collector as well as a composer. His first collection of songs, entitled the *Alonzo M. Zilch's Own Collection of Original Songs and Ballads*, in April of 1935, was a small, mimeographed pamphlet. Guthrie compiled three song folios during his Los Angeles period: *Woody and Lefty Lou's Favorite Collection* [of] *Old Time Hill Country Songs* in 1937 (reprinted in 1939), *Woody and Lefty Lou's One Thousand and One Laffs* in 1938, and *On a Slow Train through California* in 1939. Examining these songbooks, with special attention to Woody's introduction of new songs, his elimination of old songs, and revisions of lyrics of existing compiled songs, allows us to trace a profile of Guthrie's evolving musical growth and his enhanced political consciousness.

EARLY MUSICAL INFLUENCES

Woody's father sang square dance songs and African-American blues songs he had learned from black laborers. Woody's mother Nora preferred the sentimental Hill Country narratives, popular parlor songs, and old Scottish-Irish ballads.[1] As a teenager, Woody learned to play the harmonica from George, an older black teenager who played "lonesome songs" in front of an Okemah barbershop.[2] Woody followed the minstrels, medicine shows, and traveling musicians when they came through town, and he listened to folk and hill country music from KVOO, a radio station in nearby Bristol, Oklahoma. In 1927, following an incident that left his father hospitalized with serious burns and his mother committed to a state hospital, Woody and his older brother Roy were left to fend for themselves in Okemah. Woody took to the streets, playing his harmonica and singing for food and tips. In high school, Woody shared musical interests with Matt Jennings, who also played harmonica, and soon Woody began to play chord progressions on a guitar. Woody stayed at the Jennings house, playing Carter Family songs on their Victrola. Woody, Jennings, and another boy named Cluster Baker formed a group called "The Corncob Trio," which brought its rough-hewn old-time music to weekend house parties in the poor section of town. Guthrie

Opposite: Teenaged Woody in Pampa, Texas.

PAMPA, Texas

Woody and Jack Guthrie, left, 1937.

also began playing with his uncle Jeff Guthrie, a fairly accomplished fiddler who arranged for the group to play unpaid radio broadcasts at small stations in Pampa, Texas.

The end of Prohibition offered new venues for Woody to entertain, at parties, dance clubs, bars, and saloons. He sat in with other musicians to improve his skills on guitar and harmonica, and tried his hand at mandolin, drums, and violin. Left without an instrument, Woody would pull out a couple of spoons or the wooden sticks he called his "bones," or an available washboard. Or he would simply tell stories and jokes, usually copying his favorite radio entertainer, Will Rogers.[3] During these early years, Woody began to view himself as a musician and entertainer, one who had to make ends meet by working odd jobs, especially painting signs.

Woody's marriage to sixteen-year old Mary Jennings (Matt's younger sister) in October 1933 took place just as the dust storms intensified, businesses collapsed, and unemployment soared. Since he spent the bulk of his time playing songs, Woody soon learned hundreds of hillbilly and folk songs. He added new lyrics to old songs or substituted his own lyrics. In 1935 Woody described black dust enveloping and choking the town in one of his earliest songs, "The Texas Dust Storm." Similar themes were developed in another original song, "Dusty Old Dust" (or "So Long, It's Been Good to Know You"). These early compositions exhibited characteristics that marked Woody's own brand of music. He created narratives with specific details about events, places, and people. He also wrote in a voice that echoed the language used by ordinary people. While he developed his musical skills on the guitar and other instruments, he was not interested in learning complicated chords or advanced fingering techniques. As Joe Klein wrote in his biography of Woody, "The music was usually an afterthought. The words were most important." Mark Allen Jackson agrees, noting "almost all of his lyrics simply ride on the back of someone else's music, both folk and commercial songs. For Guthrie, the emphasis was on words, and any easy-to-sing tune could be their vehicle."[4] This characteristic of Woody's writing—his emphasis on the accessible melodies, lyrics worth listening to, and a willingness to make changes in the song whenever he wanted—was reinforced by his expanding experience with small audiences in rather unlikely venues: coffee shops, bars, street corners, and barbershops. Woody quickly learned that to make money or attract tips in these public spaces, he had to find a way to grab the attention of his listeners. His repertoire of songs was not purely an artistic act; it was an economic necessity. As he learned to develop his unique entertainment style, Woody concluded that the way the audience reacted to the song was more important than the song itself. The songs themselves transcended art to become instruments of survival.

CALIFORNIA AS THE GARDEN OF EDEN

As Woody told Alan and Elizabeth Lomax in a 1940 interview, the allure of California offered a powerful incentive for residents of the Dust Bowl towns to leave their old homes behind and seek new lives on the West Coast. Jimmie Rodgers' song, "Blue Yodel #4" (also known as "California Blues"), written in 1927, became one of the staples in Guthrie's repertoire, partly because so many people were familiar with it and so many identified with it. Guthrie's 1940 version of Rodgers' song shows how his views of California had moved away from simple glorification. Rodgers' narrator flees to California to escape a love affair gone sour, and then Guthrie altered the lyrics to describe Dust Bowl residents heading to California to escape poor living conditions.[5]

As a young father, Guthrie exhibited a habit of wandering off from his family for days at a time, supposedly searching for work, but more likely to see more of the world. Then, in March 1937, Guthrie told Mary he was leaving for California and would send for her once he found work. He thumbed rides and hopped freight trains following the path of Dust Bowl refugees who took Highway 66 west to California. He settled at his Aunt Laura's house in Glendale in May. His cousin, Leon Guthrie, who went by the name of Jack (or "Oklahoma" or "Oke")," soon joined him. Three years younger than Woody, Jack was nevertheless a polished guitar player and singer with dreams of becoming a singing cowboy in the movies. Jack was taller than Woody, with a strong tenor voice and good guitar skills. Jack had learned how to yodel and knew all the songs that were popularized by Gene Autry and Jimmie Rodgers.

The two Guthries joined forces and looked for work in a place that seemed to have a lot of opportunities for the newly popular western music. Jack soon scored a one-night show playing on a bill with the Beverly Hillbillies, a popular local group (not to be confused with the TV show by the same name of the 1960s and early 1970s), at the Strand Theater in Long Beach. Woody played for tips at various Skid Row saloons and cafes and rented a cheap room on Main Street in downtown Los Angeles. Jack suggested the two try to get a show on KFVD, a local radio station that had opened its studio to western singers and musicians. An audition in July went well; *The Oklahoma and Woody Show* went on the air for fifteen minutes starting at eight in the morning on July 19, 1937. Jack took the lead, playing his Washburn guitar and singing from his repertoire of popular singing-cowboy songs. Woody played the loyal sidekick, sometimes playing his harmonica, adding back-up vocals, or providing comic relief. Woody wrote the show's theme song, "Lonesome Road Blues," a song that was very familiar to the large Dust Bowl population with its refrain, "I'm a-goin' down the road feeling bad . . . and I ain't gonna be treated this a'way."

In August, Woody and Jack asked Maxine Crissman, the daughter of one of their friends, to join

Woody in a couple of duets. Twenty-two year old Crissman overcame her stage fright and performed Woody's version of "My Curly Headed Baby." She sang low, while Woody sang high. The combination worked well. As Crissman became part of the show, J. Frank Burke Sr., owner of KFVD and a Democratic Party activist, offered the group a second show at eleven at night. When Jack opted to leave the program in search of other work, Woody renamed it *Woody and Lefty Lou*. (He gave Crissman the name Lefty Lou because she was left-handed, and it rhymed with "Ole Mizzou," after the state of Missouri from which the Crissman family had migrated). In contrast to the popular cowboy songs on the airwaves, Woody and Crissman favored the old-time, traditional songs, the kind with timeless melodies and familiar narratives. The large migrant population who had left the Dust Bowl regions quickly tuned in. "KFVD had 1,000 watts," said Crissman. "It wasn't too big, but it went all across the country to other states in the Dust Bowl regions."[6] Soon *Woody and Lefty Lou* was the most popular show on KFVD.[7]

Nearly five hundred fan letters poured into KFVD during the first month of *Woody and Lefty Lou*. Burke clearly understood the connection between the new popularity of *Woody and Lefty Lou* and the large population of Dust Bowlers who arrived in California during the Depression years. From 1935 to 1940, nearly 100,000 Dust Bowlers arrived in Los Angeles.[8] Many of the "Dust Bowl Refugees," as Guthrie dubbed them, lived in trailers and tents in the working-class suburbs of southeastern Los Angeles, such as El Monte, Bell Gardens, and Lynwood. Others with more skills and work experience moved to apartments in the low-income areas of middle-class towns such as Burbank and Glendale, or to places like Long Beach and Signal Hill, which were located near oil refineries. The poorest Dust Bowlers camped along the banks of the Los Angeles River, along Tujunga and Topanga Creeks, and beside other rivulets and washes that fed the river from outside the city limits. Others, including Woody, inhabited Downtown's Skid Row. Despite their varying degrees of poverty, the Dust Bowlers had easy access to the radio.

THE RADIO SONGS

The success of *Woody and Lefty Lou* convinced Burke to pay the duo twenty dollars a week—a hefty amount during the Depression. Fan letters continued to stream into the station telling the pair that their songs reminded them of their hometowns in Oklahoma and Texas and captured the old days, the church picnics, and local ice cream socials. Crissman started singing solos, with Woody on guitar and harmonica. The duets were especially popular as Crissman's sweet voice complemented Woody's rough vocals. The biggest problem was coming up with enough songs. "We were so desperate for songs," said Crissman.[9] "We would sing anything we could think of. When we couldn't think of any new songs, we would do religious songs."[10]

Woody and Crissman played all the songs they knew. In 1970, Richard Reuss examined the 272 songs compiled by Woody during his L.A. years and found that about half were written or adapted by Woody while the rest were folksongs, parlor ballads, or religious songs.[11] Writing in 2003, the historian Peter La Chapelle noted that of 155 songs whose origins can be verified, more than 60 percent had tunes or lyrics—or both—that had been already professionally recorded or published as printed sheet music.[12] La Chapelle argues against an overly simplistic interpretation of Guthrie's development by challenging the common notion that Guthrie evolved easily from a homespun folksinger to a sophisticated protest songwriter without any compromise to commercialism. Rather than relying on folk ballads to reach their target audience, Woody and Crissman initially drew predominantly from Tin Pan Alley, minstrel songs, and popular hillbilly recordings.

The shortage of songs led Woody to write more of his own compositions or, more frequently, to write new lyrics for old songs. "Woody had about half-a-dozen songs that he had written to the tune of 'Little Green Cottage,'" said Crissman. "When we ran out of songs, Woody started putting his own words to old ones. When we ran out of them, he started writing his own lyrics."[13] And in order to keep track of the songs they were singing, Woody reverted to his old practice of compiling song folios. His folios contained lyrics, but no musical notations, and were often accompanied by comments about the songs. Woody used a typewriter at the offices of KFVD, typed in the content himself, duplicated the folios, and then sold them to interested listeners. A typeset song folio called *Woody and Lefty Lou's Favorite Collection [of] Old Time Hill Country Songs*, adorned with the logo of KFVD, appeared in late 1937.

In an effort to drum up interest in *Woody and Lefty Lou,* Woody wrote a theme song that opened and closed the show.

> Drop whatever you are doing,
> Stop your work and worry, too;
> Sit right down and take it easy,
> Here comes Woody and Lefty Lou.
> We're easy goin' country people
> Plain ole Woody and Lefty Lou.
> If you like our kind of singing,
> I'm gonna tell you what to do,
> Get your pencil and your paper
> Write to Woody and Lefty Lou.[14]

The theme song reveals that Woody approached his audience very seriously. Unlike much live radio of the time, *Woody and Lefty Lou* was broadcast from a small studio with no audience. Woody intended the theme song to attract an audience, to encourage listeners to allow Woody and Lefty Lou to join them via the airwaves. "We're easy goin' country people," they sang. "Sit down and take it easy" . . . and listen to the show. Further, Woody urged listeners to write letters to the show, understanding that their support was key to its survival.

During his two-year stint at KFVD, as he cultivated his radio audience, Woody developed the unique persona that distinguished him from other artists. He spoke and sang as a "country boy" with an exaggerated Oklahoma accent and purposefully mispronounced words, projecting an image of an uneducated, simple person. But despite a simplistic, almost childlike delivery, his comments made common sense and often had double meanings that implied his deeper understanding. As Thomas Conner observed, "Though he was known and is now remembered as an authentic representative of a particular segment of downtrodden Americans struggling through the Great Depression . . . Guthrie's image was partly a persona constructed . . . as a radio personality in order to maintain a certain kind of relationship with his listening audience . . . Guthrie himself carefully chiseled out this identity and successfully hammered it into public consciousness."[15]

Woody's original compositions from this period shed light on the issues that were being discussed by the listeners of *Woody and Lefty Lou*. He penned a song about the powerful rainstorm that suddenly turned the Los Angeles River into a raging torrent of water, mud, and boulders one New Year's Day. Bridges, roads, and homes were destroyed, but no group was hit harder than the hundreds of poor people who lived in encampments of tents and shacks along the banks of the river. He wrote a song about a fire in the Los Feliz area. Unemployed workers were sent to fight the fire and several of them died when the wind suddenly shifted. One of the best-known songs from this period, "Do Re Mi," offered a warning to people from the Dust Bowl areas who naively believed everything they have heard about the wonders of California:

> California is a Garden of Eden
> A paradise to live in or see
> But believe it or not
> You won't find it so hot
> If you ain't got the do re mi.[16]

Woody relates how the Los Angeles Police Department sent officers to the Arizona border to set up checkpoints to interrogate people and slow the movement of Dust Bowl refugees into the state. His song urges folks to think twice about migrating to California: "You better go back to old Kentucky/Oklahoma, Kansas, Georgia, Tennessee." Despite the reference to the police checkpoints, "Do Re Mi" has a droll, humorous feel and a cheerful singalong melody that projects thoughtfulness rather than anger.

Woody liked to describe the problems that migrant families faced in transitioning to the new set of realities in Los Angeles, the big city. In his never-ending search for new songs, Woody drew upon his own experiences and described the difficulties migrants faced as they learned how to survive in L.A. "Fifth St. Blues" warns of the dangers people encounter in the Skid Row section of downtown Los Angeles. A sailor, a soldier, and a little girl from Hollywood all meet their demise on "old Fifth Street."

> If you go down on old Fifth Street
> Keep your money in your jeans
> 'Cause the peaches down on 5th St.,
> They ain't got a bit of cream.
>
> You can go down on old 5th St.
> Where the people hit it hard
> But if you've got a little money
> It's the Wilshire Boulevard.[17]

Woody wrote the song "Downtown Traffic Blues" after he and Crissman were involved in a car accident on the way to the radio station one morning. Crissman recalled, "We were going to the station on Wilshire and a lady made a left in front of us. Woody put that song together in a few minutes.[18] . . . We were desperate for songs."[19] Woody narrated the story as follows:

> A drivin' yore car by night or day
> In the downtown Traffic of old L.A.,
> It's piece by piece they'll take it from you
> And leave you settin' on top of the frame
>
> Hey! Hey! Mister! Hold out yo' hand!
> Somebody will knock you to the Promised Land;
> When you git to Heaven, wont be no Drivin',
> There'll be no Downtown Traffic Blues!
>
> 'Twas on the Corner that I lost my wheel;
> He ruined my Paint Job, was a purty bad deal;

I walked home packin' my gasoline tank, and
A singing them Downtown Traffic Blues!

O' blow yo' Whistle, Mr. Policeman!
I come to town in a New Sedan—
I come home rattlin' an old Tin Can
And a singin' them Downtown Traffic Blues![20]

In "Them Big City Ways" Woody offers a cautionary tale of how Dust Bowlers can fall into bad habits in the big city. ("Big City Ways" is now the copyrighted title.)

Brother John moved to town
Rented a flat and settled down
Brought his wife and his kids along
But fifteen dollars don't last long
Law! Law! He's a-gettin' them big city ways

Unfortunately, John had moved next store to a liquor store that "got his wages and some more." He also bought a car and some furniture on credit, but soon fell behind on his payments and lost them to the finance company. John's oldest son married "a downtown honey" but "now he's paying alimony." Meanwhile, the sister took up with a gigolo. Pestered by his landlord, John gets his family on relief and is rewarded with a job with the WPA. Reflecting the widespread view, even among working-class people, that WPA jobs were make-work or boondoggling, the narrator says of John:

Got him a job on the WPA
Woke up to eat about twice a day

In other words, John slept most of the time at work in his WPA job. In the last verse, Woody warns "Eastern refugees" of the dangers of scheming Los Angeles women:

These Jellybeans and Sheba Queens
Will trim you quicker than a mowing machine
If you . . . go to . . . a-gettin' them big city ways.[21]

"Them Big City Ways" exhibits the tradition in hill country songs to offer warnings against worldly evils such as alcoholism, gambling, and infidelity. In "Stay Away From Home Brew," Woody urges listeners to abstain from "home brew, wine and liquor, too."[22] A warning against men who chase other men's wives was a central feature of one of Woody's more famous songs from his Los Angeles period, "The Philadelphia Lawyer" (initially called "Reno Blues").[23]

If Woody's songs often criticized policies that made it tough for migrant families uprooted by the Dust Bowl debacle, he could also praise the state of California for its natural beauty and largely progressive attitude toward people. In "California California," Woody captured the hope felt by Dust Bowl migrants when they arrived in the bright sun and green valleys of California. He pointed out to his Okie listeners:

> You've all sang your glories
> Of the country back home
> But searching for sunshine
> To California did roam.

Guthrie extolled Southern California's mountains, the "golden poppies in the land of the sky," the "wide peaceful ocean," "bright-colored sand," and "sun-kissed green valleys." Waxing euphoric, he added:

> If you want to see beauty
> And progress abound
> Just open your sad eyes
> Take a look allaround
> Her people are healthy
> All happy and free
> When heaven's on earth
> This is where it will be[24]

"That song was a real original," said Crissman. "He talked about entering it in a contest."[25] Unlike any of his other songs from this period, Woody registered the lyrics and a crude musical score of "California: Land of the Sky" with the Library of Congress in 1937. Guthrie scholar Will Kaufman offers that the lyrics suggest not a paean to the Golden State, but rather a sarcastic, bitterly ironic song. It is just as likely that Woody intended the song to be upbeat and positive about the new life in California. He drew another similarly favorable view of the life and the people of the state in an upbeat poem written around the same time in 1937:

A Poem
A sunny sky
And mountains high,
That's California.
A grassy spot
On which to flop,
That's California.
A friendly face most everywhere,
A friendly somethin' in the air
That helps a feller forget his cares,
That's California.
Upon a mountain layin' down
In California.
I hear the sounds of a booming town
In California.
And I wonder how many people below
Like Hillbilly music on the radio,
Some yes, some no, some just so-so,
That's California.[26]

The popularity of *Woody and Lefty Lou* forced Woody to face, for the first time in his life, the possibility of commercial success. Woody confronted a quandary as he sought to find a path between commercial survival as a singer/songwriter and his reluctance to compromise with commercial values he couldn't accept. Woody and Crissman tried to generate fan mail to show that they were reaching an audience and deserved to be paid by the station. "He loved to read the letters," said Crissman. "He waited every day for the mail to come, and then he would read all the letters."[27] When Crissman complained about Woody's conduct on the show, saying that he spent too much time talking and telling jokes, Woody's response was to spin even longer tales and stories. He also bristled when she said that he was bringing too many relatives onto the show. In Crissman's view, Woody was reluctant to do what was necessary for commercial success. "We blew so many chances to make good money. We were asked to play at the Hollywood Barn Dance. People were interested in having us play. But when we got into the big time, Woody didn't want any part of it."[28]

"MY PEOPLE"

Woody and Lefty Lou came to an end in June 1938. Crissman suffered from severe anemia and was unable to hold up under the demands of two shows a day, six days a week. Burke wanted to send Woody and Crissman on a bus tour through rural California in an effort to drum up support among agricultural workers for Culbert Olson's campaign for governor. But Crissman's poor health forced him to cancel his plans. Burke then suggested that the two suspend the program for six weeks while Crissman recuperated. Meanwhile, Woody could work as a roving correspondent for Burke's new newspaper, *The Light*, a media vehicle for Olson's campaign. Burke asked Woody to write about the difficulties facing agricultural workers. He agreed and spent a month visiting the Hoovervilles and campsites that migrant workers had erected along the banks of the Sacramento River and other rivers and streams. He rambled from campsite to campsite, living among the migrant workers, trading his music for food, and working only sporadically. He spent time in the skid row sections of Sacramento, Tracy, and Redding, and in the shantytowns near railroad stations.

According to plan, Woody met up again with Crissman and her parents in Chico on July 25. The group camped on the Sacramento River, along with other Okies and Arkies, the people Woody began to describe as "my people" in his writing and songs. They lived off trout caught in the river and peaches stolen from a nearby orchard. It was a hard life. Woody hit the road again, hopped freights, and was arrested in Reno, Nevada, for vagrancy. "The jail in Reno is so dirty and filthy that the disease germs turned in a complaint to the city health inspector," wrote Woody, released after a day spent behind bars.[29] He traveled to Barstow, California, where he was stranded for two nights on the side of the road in the Mojave Desert with a small army of unemployed men and nowhere to go. "These people," Woody reported in an article for the progressive newspaper *The Light,* "are mostly the ones who have tired of marching with the starvation armies of wandering workers and grown weary of the smell of rotting fruit crops."[30] He decided to ride the rails back to Oklahoma. He talked with migrants along the way, and many of them were familiar with *Woody and Lefty Lou* ("Where's Lefty Lou?" they would sometimes ask). Others expressed surprise that a radio personality would be riding the rails and sleeping in hobo villages. Woody then hitchhiked back to California, by way of Okemah, Oklahoma, and Route 66, and ended up in Kern County in the midst of a strike by cotton workers. It was during this trip that Woody experienced the violence of roughnecks and vigilantes, who attacked a group of migrant workers with guns and clubs.

Woody's summer on the road in 1938 seems to have altered his view of the world and his place in it. He catalogues some of his activities in a song called "A Watchin' the World Go By":

I been a catchin' them freight trains.

I been ridin' them railroads.

I been a sleepin' in a box car,

    And a watchin' the world go by.

I been a walkin' them highways.

I been a hittin' them back doors.

I been a sleepin' in a haystack,

    And a watchin' the world go by.

I been a pickin' your lettuce.

I been a pickin' your maters

I been a livin' on taters

    And a watchin' the world go by.[31]

Rootless and on the road, Woody experienced prolonged hunger for the first time in his life. He lived with a bedraggled crowd of poor migrants squeezed in ramshackle huts and leaky tents, mired in poverty and disease. Woody saw how badly his people were treated, not just with poor pay and working conditions, but by open discrimination: many hotels, retail outlets, and other establishments posted signs saying "No Mexicans or Okies."[32] As Charles McGovern observed, "Guthrie showed that the experience of displacement, movement, homelessness, and transit was not simply a condition but a fundamental fact of American life."[33] Woody experienced first-hand a union-led strike in the town of Shafter in Kern County, north of Los Angeles. He connected with radical labor organizers and interacted with "his people" in a new and exciting musical way as a participant as well as a performer. He had experienced the poverty and displacement of the migrant workers and how they seemed to be up against insurmountable obstacles, but he also had seen how the union and radicals were able to organize the agricultural workers to raise their voices in protest.

Woody's limited involvement with organized labor in the cotton workers' strikes in the San Joaquin Valley expanded to include a number of picket lines and rallies in Los Angeles as the movement for industrial unionism took hold in Southern California. He saw a concrete demonstration of how the government could take positive action in a way that might resemble socialism in the Farm Security Act work camps. Woody expanded his repertoire almost effortlessly by altering the lyrics of a certain song to fit the local situation—the particular union, the issues, the bosses—so the song resonated with the audience, albeit steelworkers, garment workers, or auto workers. The old hillbilly songs, traditional ballads and

religious songs disappeared from Guthrie's repertoire and were replaced by songs built around social justice and union organizing themes. But even as he honed his ability to craft instant picket line sing-along
songs, Woody's lyrics, perhaps strengthened by his recording experiences, radio shows in New York, and
months of writing his autobiography, became richer and deeper. The powerful imagery of the poetic
"Hooversville," reaches far beyond the simple lyrics of many of his early songs.

> Ramblin', gamblin', rickety shacks
> That's Hooversville
> Rusty tin and raggedy sacks
> Makes Hooversville . . .
> Down where the big rats run and jump
> In Hooversville
> Hot swamps steam in the old hot sun
> That's Hooversville
> Kids that ain't knowed too much fun
> Makes Hooversville
> Kids that bed on the old wet ground
> An' eat old rotten grub they found
> Diggin' the great big dumps around
> Hooversville
> Maybe you just didn't know
> That's Hooversville
> Guess you didn't ever go
> To Hooversville
> Maybe you ain't never seen
> The little girls around fifteen
> Sold for the price of a bowl of beans
> In Hooversville.[34]

Others were taking notice of Woody's activism as well: Carey McWilliams wrote *Factories in the Fields* in
1939, and John Steinbeck released *The Grapes of Wrath* the same year. Guthrie had also witnessed the work
camps established by the Farm Security Administration (FSA) and had seen how a benevolent government

Opposite: Woody Guthrie Singing at Shafter Labor Camp, 1941

As the Depression deepened, public health officials documented the distress of the Los Angeles homeless living in their Hooverville encampments.

Photographer Seema Weatherwax brilliantly captured both the destitution and the valiant hopefulness of California's Depression-era migrants, the very same people John Steinbeck and Woody Guthrie also brought to the world's attention.

program could protect his people. As Linda Gordon pointed out in her biography *Dorothea Lange: A Life Beyond Limits*, the great photographer who documented the lives of the migrant workers in California and elsewhere, for the agricultural workers and their families,

> The FSA camps seemed to them like paradise. The typical camp provided metal shelters or tent platforms arranged around utility buildings. Clean water came out of numerous outdoor faucets; the central buildings featured flush toilets, hot and cold running water, showers, and laundry and ironing rooms. There were garbage cans. . . . The camps operated day-care centers, infirmaries, and first-aid centers. . . . Families typically paid ten cents a day and were required to contribute two hours of work a week.[35]

CIO organizer Dorothy Healy, a communist leader representing the United Cannery, Agricultural, Packing and Allied Workers of America, CIO, remembered how Woody came across. "He was just another Okie," said Healy. "He had no pretensions. But when he finished singing a song, there was a love affair between Woody and the workers."[36] As Ed Cray wrote, "The Okies and Arkies, the Texicans and Jayhawkers, had become Woody's people. They were rootless, ground down, stripped of farms and jobs back east, shorn of their dignity in California. Even the coined name 'Okie' had become a snarled epithet, a euphemism for the shiftless and the unemployed."[37] Although Woody had never liked the term "Okie" (recalling handwritten signs in stores saying "No Okies Allowed"), he began to use the term to brand himself.

When he returned to KFVD in January 1939, Woody painted a new portable stand-up sign advertising himself and his radio show, and prepared new business cards calling himself "Woody, th' Dustiest of th' Dust Bowl Refugees" with the telephone number of KFVD in the lower right-hand corner. The same description adorned the cover of *On a Slow Train through California* when it appeared in 1939.[38]

Looking more closely at the Guthrie song folios also tells us a good deal about the themes expressed in Woody's early, prolific songwriting during the Los Angeles years.

WOODY, THE LONE WOLF

Woody reclaimed his radio show in January 1939. Burke doubted the show could survive without Crissman, but he agreed to give *Woody, the Lone Wolf* a thirty-minute show, at 2:15 in the afternoon, but with no pay and a dollar a day to cover meals.[39] Woody would have to find sponsors and sell songbooks to bring in revenue. He returned to the airwaves, this time with more commentary and a batch of new songs. He wrote a new theme song for the show. In the afternoons, Woody stayed around the KFVD offices to use the typewriters and mimeograph machines to produce his new songbook, *On a Slow Train Through California*. He typed and made mimeographed copies that sold for a quarter and distributed them by hand and through the mail. The songbook was a takeoff of an old joke book called *On a Slow Train Through Arkansas*, which had been sold in railroad trains and stations.[40] Woody's new songbook also included a number of little stories and jokes that highlighted his droll, country humor, now laced with a new class consciousness. The booklet contained the lyrics for fifty-six songs, about a third of which were Woody's originals or adapted songs. The stories and comments reveal how Woody was beginning to assess world affairs and day-to-day life in political terms. In addition to *On a Slow Train*, a "second edition" of his earlier songbook, *Woody and Lefty Lou's Collection* [of] *Old-Time Hill Country Songs*, was underwritten by a sympathetic listener named Buck Ackerman whose friend owned a printing shop.[41] Woody worked the food markets and street corners for tips and songbook sales. Often he worked the bars and honkytonks in Skid Row and didn't return home at night.

Woody, the Lone Wolf did not have the same impact as its predecessor. Part of the problem was the absence of Crissman, whose sweet-sounding lead vocals on the old traditional songs had charmed the migrant audience. And their duets had partially masked Woody's thin, raspy voice and uneven instrumentation. With the *Lone Wolf*, listeners received pure, unadulterated Woody. Music began to give way to social and political commentary as Woody, benefiting from what he had learned from labor and political activists, spoke more confidently on current events and controversial issues, trying to fulfill his self-appointed role as a tribute for the Dust Bowl refugees.

The *Lone Wolf* also changed, as Woody shifted the type of songs played on the show. Many of the popular old hill country songs and gospel tunes were dropped in favor of new compositions or new adaptations of old songs. Woody used the airwaves to introduce a new set of political songs, usually oriented to the progressive wing of the Democratic Party and progressive electoral initiatives, including "I'm Looking for that New Deal Now," "Give Us an Old-Age Pension," "Ham and Eggs Is Marching On," and "Roosevelt-Olson." In addition, several new songs about the Dust Bowl were added to older ones to form the main body of material for Woody's first album, *Dust Bowl Ballads*, in 1940.

Crissman was surprised by the changes in the show, particularly the shift to more overtly political songs. "None of our songs were Dust Bowl songs except for 'Do Re Mi' and 'Pretty Boy Floyd.' 'Talkin' Dust Bowl Blues'? That was new to me. When we were on the radio there were no unions, no organizers, nothing like that. . . . The political stuff began after he went into the camps. I never heard that before he went up to the labor camps."[42]

Substituting leftwing politics for traditional country music limited his audience and probably kept sponsors away. Struggling to keep the *Lone Wolf* show alive, Woody attempted to cross-market the show by plugging it in the articles he wrote for *On a Slow Train* and for papers like *The Light* and, a month or so later, *The People's World*. Woody toted his portable sign promoting his KFVD show around Skid Row and other public venues where he played for tips, probably a more secure revenue stream than the quarters he received for sales of *On a Slow Train*.

Shortly after returning to the radio station, Woody introduced himself to Ed Robbin, a fellow KFVD radio host whose thirty-minute news show followed the *Lone Wolf*. Robbin, a political activist and Los Angeles editor of the *People's Weekly*, a daily published by the West Coast Communist Party, had never listened to Woody's show, assuming it was just another country and western show. "I had just assumed that he was singing run-of-the-mill western songs, full of 'run little dogies' and 'hosses in the sunset,'" explained Robbin.[43] Woody asked Robbin a lot of questions about Tom Mooney, the San Francisco labor leader who had been framed for the Preparedness Day bombing in 1916 and was serving time in prison. Robbin listened to Woody's show the next day and was surprised to hear Woody introduce a new song, "Mister Tom Mooney is Free." Then he sang some of his Dust Bowl ballads with easy, rambling, homey talk between songs. Impressed, Robbin asked if Woody wanted to perform his song at a big event that evening to celebrate the news that Mooney had been pardoned by the new governor and was out of prison. Woody agreed.

At the downtown rally, the speakers talked on and on. Finally, near eleven o'clock, Woody was introduced. He ambled to the stage, dressed in his ragged Dust Bowl attire, his guitar hanging on a rope on his back, and offered a rough introduction in his Okie argot. Then he captured the attention of the audience with his Mooney song.

> Way up in Frisco town
> Mister Mooney and Billings
> Accused of a killing
> And railroaded, jailhouse bound
> But the truth can't be tied with a chain
> Mr. Olson said, 'O' let Tom Mooney go!
> I'm a-breakin' that long, lonesome chain
> Mister Tom Mooney is free.[44]

The audience responded enthusiastically and Woody played more songs, including "Do Re Mi" and "Vigilante Man," the poignant protest against the thugs Woody had seen beating migrant workers in the San Joaquin Valley. Ever the enlightened hillbilly, Guthrie recited off-the-cuff little stories about "my people, the Dust Bowl Refugees" while casually retuning his guitar. Robbin felt the electricity. "I was deeply impressed with the wonderful lyric descriptions of all his experiences as a migratory worker and his songs about the dust storms that he had experienced in Oklahoma and Texas, and by the many outlaw songs that he had already written at that time."[45] With his performance that night, Woody reached a new audience of urban intellectuals and political activists who had never before seen a political Okie.

Woody had tapped into the new public interest in the issue of agricultural workers in California, which had emerged as a hot-button issue in the 1938 election. "The migrant workers," wrote Robbin, "were oppressed, beaten, and exploited. They lived in shacks, dumps, under bridges, their kids running dirty and half-naked in the fields." The audience was captivated by Woody's unusual, down-to-earth personality. "Here was this skinny guy on the stage, the very embodiment of these (the migrant) young people, speaking their language in bitter humor and song, with the dust of his traveling still on him, a troubadour, a balladeer, a poet."[46]

After his performance at the Mooney rally, Woody was invited to perform a series of political and union events in the L.A. area. He became a phenomenon for local activists. "Prior to the time Woody encountered the Left," wrote Richard Reuss, "he held no special status within society other than that of another 'good' hillbilly songwriter. Later, after radical publicity brought him to the attention of urban intellectuals, he became a symbol of the Okie trauma and the turmoil experienced by millions of anonymous Americans during the Depression."[47] Woody's new friend Robbin found him work. "I became an informal booking agent for him," wrote Robbin. "In those days there were so many causes that each night he was asked to sing at some fund-raising party in the homes or union halls. He would get five or ten dollars for each gig, if he remembered to appear."[48]

Woody had spent a good share of his last ten years jobless and practically homeless. When he sang his song, "I Ain't Got No Home," the lyrics weren't far from the truth. But in 1939, his connection with Robbin and the Communist Party served as a useful new "home" for the Lone Wolf. Following his performance at the Mooney event, Woody went to Robbin's home in Edendale to spend the night. Soon Woody began spending nights on end at the small home owned by Robbin and his wife, Clara. Often Woody borrowed their typewriter and wrote nearly all night, falling asleep on the kitchen floor. As he attracted more political friends, Woody frequently crashed at their homes rather than returning to the one-room shack (a former motel room) in Glendale where his wife and children lived a tenuous, day-to-day existence.

More than providing a roof over Woody's head, Robbin offered Woody an intellectual and cultural place in the "Movement," the vibrant leftist community of liberals and radicals in Los Angeles in the late 1930s. Robbin's home was located in the Edendale area of Echo Park, a center of political and cultural activity that allowed Woody to move beyond the Okies and Arkies who had formed the base of his support.[49] The movement's political network provided a community for Woody. Robbin introduced him to the intellectuals, writers, and actors who supported the anti-fascist agenda, including Theodore Dreiser and the young actor and political activist, Will Geer. In turn, Geer introduced Woody to notables such as John Steinbeck, Eddie Albert, and John Garfield.[50] Geer also connected Woody to Harry Hay, a Communist Party activist (who later founded the Mattachine Society in Los Angeles, the nation's first advocacy group for homosexuals[51]), Waldo Salt, a screenwriter who had agreed to chair the committee that drew Hollywood support to the striking cotton workers,[52] and progressives around the Hollywood scene.

Greater exposure also led to more work for Woody at political and educational events, which brought in some greatly needed income. Politics also offered Woody a new, explicable ideological framework for understanding the larger issues of the nation and the world. And the movement's emphasis on the working class, "ordinary" people, and the underdog also conformed to Woody's own visceral feelings about inequality and class. Most important, as Guthrie scholar Reuss noted, Woody "found an intellectual climate within one segment of the Left where he was accepted essentially on his own terms."[53]

While the weeks Woody spent with the migrant workers in the San Joaquin Valley led him to see himself as a representative of "my people, the Dust Bowl Refugees," his adoption by the movement brought him into contact with activists and union organizers, and he began to broaden his musical concerns to other types of workers or to working people in general. Toward the end of 1938, in his introductions, songs, stories, and radio commentaries, Woody began to use the term "refugee" to refer to a broad range of oppressed peoples. As Mark Allen Jackson points out, "Beginning in the spring of 1939, Guthrie first included terms and phrases such as 'worker,' 'working man,' and 'workin' folks' into his songs and moved away from his earlier focus on agricultural workers."[54]

Woody's songs also began to change as his politics evolved. Some of these changes involved subtle alterations in lyrics. "Them Big City Ways" is a case in point. In the first version, Brother John's proximity to a liquor store had led him to spend his money unwisely ("Licker store is right next door/Got his wages and some more.") But in subsequent versions, with the title shortened to "Big City Ways" the liquor store was removed and it is the "finance company" that takes John's wages. Likewise, in the first version, John finally gets a cushy job with the WPA that allows him to "boondoggle" and sleep most of the day while getting paid. In later versions, however, we hear that John is a victim of layoffs by the WPA. Also, in the earlier version, the listener is instructed to beware of dangerous Big City women described as "Jellybeans and Sheba Queens," who "will trim you quicker than a moving machine." But a later version drops the reference to Big City women altogether, warning instead that the "Finance Man he runs the town/And the working man, he gets run down."[55]

A more dramatic evolution appeared in Woody's paean to the country life: "I'm Goin' Back to the Farm." In his radio song of March 1939, Woody's narrator lamented his hunger and the long distance to a job site.

> Been eatin' 'bout like a canary bird
> A huntin' and a pickin' and a peckin'
> Ever time I get a job I got to walk six hundred blocks
> I done wore a hole in the seat of my pants
> Wore out my shoes and socks

The second and last verse of the March version include descriptions of the wonders of rural life:

> I'm a goin' back to my forty-acre track
> Where cotton blossoms bloom
> Hitch my old plug hoss to a rickety hack
> Where a man's got elbow room
> Gonna plow them rows with a buzzard wing
> And lay with a Georgia stock
> And make my beer with elegant cheer
> In a fifteen gallon crock. [56]

In his October 1939 version, however, the situation had changed:

> Every day I look for a job
> Huntin' and a pickin' a peckin'
> Somebody's got the money
> And won't give me a job
> I wish I could get back
> To that good old farm again

The second verse of the October 1939 version scaled back the superlatives of rural life offered in the original. And in his new version, Woody added a third verse with more class-conscious political commentary:

'Bout everywhere you look
The rich folks own the land
And it looks like they just can't find jobs
For ten million workin' men
I hope and pray the government
Will give me a house and barn
I'll find myself a pretty little girl
And get back to the farm.[57]

Woody expanded his vision to other types of workers, gaining a fuller understanding of issues such as race, poverty, and crime. His experiences in Los Angeles forced him to confront deeply rooted prejudices and attitudes towards race that were part of everyday life in Pampa, Texas, and Okemah, Oklahoma, where African Americans were treated as second-class citizens. An indication of Woody's evolution on racial issues is revealed in his first professional recording for the Library of Congress when Alan Lomax interviewed him in March 1940. Commenting on how he had learned the harmonica song "Railroad Blues" from "a colored boy that was playing when I walked past the barbershop door," Woody added,

> The common everyday feeling in that country was, for some strange reason, that some people are born better than others and some are supposed to work pretty hard and others are supposed to just coast through. . . . But I wanted to say that I never hardly pass either an Indian or a colored boy, I'm telling you the truth, I learned to like 'em, especially since I been hobo'in' and freight trainin' too.[58]

He also attributed the most well-known Okie song of all, "Goin' Down the Road Feeling Bad" (which was used by John Ford in the film version of *The Grapes of Wrath*) to a "colored slave that escaped to the north."[59] As Lomax has noted about Woody's attitudes toward race issues, "These encounters with Communist Party members, writers, and propaganda gave Guthrie some education on the complexities of race relations beyond what he had been able to formulate on his own."[60] Woody's sensitivity to racial issues increased after he spent time in New York City and met Lead Belly, Sonny Terry, and Brownie McGhee. These personal encounters would lead to a number of his compositions attacking Jim Crow laws, lynching, and racism as a whole.

Woody's songs about outlaws and bandits also evolved during his years in Los Angeles, enhanced by his experiences on the road and riding the rails, where local policemen, sheriffs, and railroad guards meted out a rough and capricious justice against train-hoppers and hoboes gathered in encampments near rail stations and stops. When Guthrie watched local police and private security guards violently confront striking cotton workers, he lost whatever respect he had for authority figures. Soon, Woody expressed the notion that if the "good people," those who were supposed to uphold the laws, were actually the villains, then perhaps the "bad people" were actually the heroes. His composition of "Pretty Boy Floyd" in March 1939 (the song was probably written in 1938, however, since Crissman says she recalls singing it on the radio show) is a clear example of how Woody's pen transformed outlaws, thieves, and bank robbers into backcountry Robin Hoods who stole from the rich and gave to the poor. To make his point more explicit, Woody used the last verse of the song to suggest that banditry and other crimes committed by Floyd and other country outlaws paled in comparison with the injustices and lawlessness of "respectable" people like lawyers and bankers who used more sophisticated ways to swindle ordinary people:

> I've seen a lot of outlaws, I've seen a lot of men
> Some will rob you with a six gun, and some with a fountain pen
> I'll tell you what I'm thinking before the story's end,
> A fool robs with a six gun, a coward takes the pen.[61]

A few months later, Woody altered the last two lines again to make his class-conscious point more direct:

> But as through your life you'll travel, wherever you may roam,
> You won't ever see an outlaw drive a family from their home.[62]

Just as the outlaws in Woody's new songs evolved into socially conscious bandits, hoboes became heroes and Skid Row denizens emerged as some of the nicest people around. In "Fifth Street Blues," from *On a Slow Train Through California*, Woody tells the sad story of the soldier, the sailor, and the little girl from Hollywood—all of whom met their fate on "Old Fifth Street," Fifth and Main in downtown Los Angeles. The narrator laments in a blues vernacular: "Oh, Sweet Mama, Daddy's got them Fifth Street Blues" and repeats the line again. And Woody dedicates the song "in respect and honor to Fifth Street, Los Angeles, California, for the Spirit that abides there, and for the people who go there, by the forces of an unbalanced social order, or by their own free will. . . . I love the Spirit and the people that walk there." As for hoboes: "Billionaires cause hoboes, and hoboes make billionaires. Yet both cuss the other and say they are wrong . . . but personal I ruther trust the hoboes. Most of what I know I learned from the kids and the hoboes. Kids first. Hoboes second. Rich folks last—and I don't give a dam if you like it or not."[63]

It was also during this period that Woody lost interest in eastern mysticism and the theories of Kahlil Gilbran, topics that had intrigued him when he lived in Pampa, Texas. He became more critical of religious songs if they implied that the poor and oppressed should accept their fate on earth knowing that they will gain their reward in heaven (or, "You'll get pie in the sky when you die," as Joe Hill wrote in "Long-Haired Preachers."). He rearranged the old gospel song "I Can't Feel at Home in This World Anymore," widely popularized in 1931 by the Carter Family, and came up with "I Ain't Got No Home in This World Anymore." The song recalls how the narrator's family lost their home and farm and eventually became homeless wanderers. Woody then connects that bitter reality to the existing economic and political system. It concludes:

> Now as I look around it's very plain to see
> This wild, wicked world is a funny place to be
> The gamblin' man is rich while the working man gets poor
> I ain't got no home in this world anymore.[64]

Commenting on the song's origins, Woody wrote: "I seen there was another side to the picture. Reason why you can't feel at home in this world any more is mostly because you ain't got no home to feel at."[65]

Back in L.A., after his experiences in the San Joaquin Valley, Woody reworked the Carter Family's version of "No Depression in Heaven." Some of the religious songs that had been popularized in the West during the 1930s had suggested that the black dust storms were God's punishment or even the beginning of the end of the world (thus, the reference to the "latter days"). The Carter Family song drew upon that imagery by suggesting in its lyrics that while the Great Depression made life on earth almost unbearable, it was important to remember that the afterlife would be wonderful:

> Oh fear the hearts of men are failing
> These are latter days we know
> The Great Depression now is spreading
> God's word declared it would be so
> I'm going where there's no Depression
> To a better land that's free from care
> I'll leave this world of toil and trouble
> My home's in heaven, I'm going there

Woody altered the Carters' lyrics to give the song new meaning. Acknowledging that life in heaven would indeed be wonderful, Woody redefined heaven as a place where there was no more hunger, no more poverty, and "no more songs in a minor key." In a note below the lyrics, Woody took liberties with the Lord's Prayer to state that the goal of the politicians should be: "Thy Kingdom Come, Thy Will be Done, Down here on earth so it'll be jest like Heaven (perfect government)."[66] In a later version of the song, Woody further redefines heaven in specific economic terms that were familiar to people living through the Depression era:

> No debts and no burdens in Heaven,
> Nor mortgages and loans to repay
> And never a landlord in Heaven
> No rent to take from you each day.

In this version, Woody attacks the banks for foreclosing on peoples' homes. He also ended the song with a new verse suggesting it would be better if people did not have to wait until death to enjoy such basic things as a pension and a job:

> There's a job for us all up in Glory
> With a work and a wealth you can share
> Let's make it here like you dream it up there
> Then there's no disappointment . . . down here.[67]

For Woody, the social and humanistic aspects of Christianity trumped the notion that suffering on earth is justified by the splendors of heaven.

FROM POPULIST TO RADICAL

Woody's politics evolved from Democratic/Populist in the 1930s to Radical/Progressive in the 1940s. His introduction to radicals began in 1938 at a time when the Communist Party pursued its "Popular Front" strategy that sought to build a broad following among liberals, intellectuals, writers, and musicians. This approach opened more political space for artists like Will Geer and the many others who gravitated to the party and its affiliates. Much has been made of Woody's association with the Communist Party. He was labeled "a Stalinist" by Stephen Whitfield who contended, "Woody Guthrie had proudly cultivated an ardent pro-Communism in the late 1930s and did not waver thereafter." Whitfield reminds the reader that Stalinists were "enemies of civil liberties," and "mini-totalitarians."[68]

Was Woody Guthrie a Communist? It depends upon the criteria for membership. A person did not join the party by merely filling out an application and turning it in. Membership was more rigorous than typical political parties where party involvement was chiefly relegated to electoral activities. The Communist Party required its members to defend its positions, support it financially, and regularly attend weekly meetings. Pete Seeger said that Woody was a communist with a lower-cased "c", but not really a party member because he was not especially disciplined and certainly could not tolerate the long, turgid political discussions that dominated weekly meetings. Woody was never involved in party debates or decision-making. When Ed Robbin asked him to list the most important historical figures in the world, Woody deviated from the usual Communist choices like Marx and Lenin, and named Jesus and Will Rogers. Yet Woody defended the party as the underdog as international forces and then Cold War repression weakened the party and began its long and steady demise. Accused of being a Communist, Woody often replied: "I ain't necessarily a communist, but I've been in the red all my life." In *On a Slow Train*, Woody defended the party with a reference to Jesus: "I never am overly attracted by anybody till everybody else goes to jumpin' on 'em. Strikes me they framed up a Carpenter that same way, back over in Jarusalem." The more the media and the politicians attacked the party, the more Woody felt the need to defend it.[69]

WOODY, THE WRITER

Woody's brief stint as a reporter for *The Light* stimulated his interest in writing.[70] In 1939, he authored several articles in the *Hollywood Tribune*, offering his impressions of Hollywood Boulevard, Downtown's Skid Row, the beach in Santa Monica, and what happens on a movie set.[71] He asked Ed Robbin if he could write some articles for the *People's World*, a request that surprised Robbin who had bought the unfinished, proletarian image that Woody projected to his friends on the Left. The next day, Woody handed Robbin a sheaf of clever, one- or two-paragraph articles. Impressed by what he read, Robbin convinced Al Richman, the editor of the paper, to run a new series of daily columns written by Woody. His Woody Sez series began on May 12, 1939, and continued on nearly a daily basis until January 3, 1940, for a total of 174 pieces. Woody modeled his column after the well-known Will Rogers Says series. His witty little stories commented on daily life, people, work, and current events. As Guy Logsdon wrote, Woody "deliberately used misspellings in an effort to recreate the speech patterns of the common people—those he knew best."[72] Woody complemented his column with two-inch by two-inch, simple-but-arresting cartoons that usually related to his narrative. He attempted to promote his radio show in his Woody Sez articles, encouraging readers to tune in to KFVD to listen to *Woody, the Lone Wolf*.

Once Woody met Will Geer, the Shakespearean actor and political activist, the pair hit it off immediately, and Woody joined in Geer's portable "agitprop" shows for the Hollywood crowd. Later, they went on the road to migrant worker camps in the San Joaquin Valley where Woody again motivated "his people." Geer had come to Los Angeles to star as a doctor who runs a prenatal clinic for poor women in a film entitled *The Fight for Life*, and he was able to land Woody a small part in the movie, playing a husband whose wife is about to give birth. There was even a part for Geer's pregnant wife Herta and for Woody's wife Mary, who was carrying their third child.

On the surface, the financial situation for the Guthrie household had improved. Woody had his radio show, he performed at various events around town, the film was being shot, and mingling with novelists like Dreiser and Steinbeck, as well as Hollywood writers and actors was exciting. "Woody is just Woody," wrote Steinbeck. "Thousands of people do not know he has any other name. He is just a voice and a guitar. He sings the songs of a people and I suspect that he is, in a way, that people. . . . But there is something more important for those who will listen. There is the will of a people to endure and fight against oppression. I think we call this the American spirit."[73]

As summer came to an end in 1939, even Mary Guthrie, who had experienced six difficult years of marriage, began to feel more positive about the family's future. But those hopes were soon dashed, in part by international events that quickly overtook politics at the local level. News of the Non-Aggression Pact between Russia and Germany shook the foundations of the anti-fascist movement. It forced many members to question the Communist Party or to leave it altogether, and it drove a wedge between party members and their former allies, the liberals, radicals, and intellectuals. Woody, however, seemed to draw closer to the party, defending it—in his own dogged "country" way—against detractors and fair-weather friends. Indeed, during this period, Woody seemed to take pleasure in needling those he considered to be wishy-washy liberals. He flaunted his working-class language and appearance, his subtle put-down to those "weekend radicals."

Instead of tiptoeing around the issue of the Pact, Woody met it head-on in his songs and radio commentary. When the Soviet Union grabbed the eastern third of Poland in September 1939, Guthrie penned a new talking blues song, "More War News," which celebrated the Soviet invasion and saw it as a liberating moment:

Stalin stepped in, took a big strip of Poland,
And gave the farm lands back to the farmers.

If I'd of been a-living in Poland then
I'd been glad Stalin stepped in—[74]

Woody found it easy to connect the party's new call for peace with the deeply rooted strains of isolationism that existed in the country, especially in the western states. And while, as Seeger has emphasized, Woody was not a pacifist;[75] he offered a down-to-earth application of Lenin's contention that imperialist wars were fought by the working classes for the ruling classes when he wrote in his *Woody Sez* column: "Locate the man who profits by war and strip him of his profits—war will end."[76]

Burke, a progressive Democrat who tolerated many political views, had allowed Robbin and Woody to continue to state their political views without interference. But their rigid support for the Pact and the other political gyrations that flowed out of its logic soon proved too much, even for Burke. Robbin was the first to go. Meanwhile, Woody came under sharp criticism from another country music radio host at KFVD, Stu Hamblin, who referred to Woody as "the Communist Cowboy." After Woody crossed the line and mocked his boss's leftist politics on the air, Burke pulled the plug on the *Lone Wolf*.

The end of the show coincided with a big decline in demand for Woody to entertain at party-affiliated events and fundraisers, and Geer had left for New York to star in a Broadway production of *Tobacco Road*. So suddenly, those jobs—and dollars—that were once streaming in, were no longer. There wasn't much left for Woody to do in Los Angeles except sing for tips on Skid Row. Around Thanksgiving in 1939, he packed Mary and the kids into an old Plymouth, and they drove to Pampa, Texas. Within a month, Woody boarded a bus for Pittsburgh, Pennsylvania (which was a far as his money would take him), and then hitchhiked the rest of the way to New York City.

By the time Woody arrived in New York in February 1940, his music and political philosophy had evolved and solidified. Like many young artists, Woody felt a need to define his music, to locate it within the larger world of musical endeavor. In *On a Slow Road Through California*, Woody noted that the editor of *People's World* had recently referred to him as "a progressive hillbilly singer and a writer of 'Folk Songs.'" Woody called this characterization "just a shade too deep for me," but went on to focus his music more clearly than he had to that point.

The old songs on one side arise from the hardships and suffering of my people—the working people and the poor people—brought upon them by hard times, and hard work, and rich grafters and profiteers. . . .The broken hearts, the broken love affairs, the sadness of the old love songs—obtain a spiritual 'something' that no creation of sexy jazz can ever surpass. Folks songs are songs which reflect the conditions of the lower classes down through the pages of time."[77]

The writing techniques employed by Woody—writing the way ordinary people talked, using the verbal rhythms and bad grammar, the long, wandering, run-on sentences, the cataloguing of names of people, specific details of places, and dates of events—became more pronounced in Woody's songs and prose. Some elements of his music also hardened, particularly his resistance to fancy guitar chords, elaborate guitar picking, and complex melodies.[78] As Seeger noted, "Woody sometimes played a ten-verse song without changing chords."[79] And he maintained his antipathy to more modern variations of popular music, including country and western and jazz, preferring instead the older and simpler treatments of vocals, melodies, and instrumentation.[80] Most important to Woody was not the song itself, but rather the specific connection made between the song and its audience at that particular performance.

The wide variety of themes that had comprised the radio songs of *Woody and Lefty Lou* were narrowed to reflect Woody's enhanced social and political consciousness. After his first extended trip to New York City in 1940, Reuss noted, "[Woody] consistently used his talents to describe concepts, events, and political causes that were not central to the experiences of the groups he had previously represented in California."[81] His months and weeks in the San Joaquin Valley had produced a new body of songs that made up most of the *Dust Bowl Ballads* collection for his RCA Victor recordings of 1940. Religious songs built on themes of sin on earth and redemption in heaven, which had been so prevalent in the early music, gave way to his new interpretation of Christianity. "Jesus Christ" or "They Laid Jesus Christ in His Grave," one of the first songs he wrote after returning to New York, portrayed Jesus as a social radical. Songs describing the difficulties Okies and other migrant workers faced in the big city were changed to emphasize that working people of all occupations were exploited by an economic system based on class and by bankers and land speculators. A handful of songs that displayed insensitivity to African Americans were dropped in favor of new compositions that took aim at racism, discrimination, and lynching. Hoboes became unsung heroes of the lost highway, while cops and security guards were depicted as vigilantes. Bank robbers were transformed into Robin Hoods.

Woody's unique persona and radical politics defined him for his audience, but his songs propelled him into the pantheon of great American songwriters. Two decades after Woody left Los Angeles for New York, those songs had a profound influence on Bobby Zimmerman, a young, marginal figure in the emerging folk music scene in the Dinkytown area of Minneapolis, Minnesota. The man who dubbed himself Bob Dylan would later write:

> I put one on the turntable, and when the needle dropped, I was stunned. I didn't know if I was stoned or straight. What I heard was Woody singing a whole lot of his own compositions all by himself. . . . All these songs, one after another, made my head spin. It made me want to gasp. It was like the land parted. . . . I couldn't believe it. Guthrie had such a grip on things. He was so poetic and tough and rhythmic. There was so much intensity. . . . The songs themselves, his repertoire, were really beyond category. They had the infinite sweep of humanity in them. . . . Woody Guthrie tore everything in his path to pieces. To me it was an epiphany."[82]

In New York, Woody stayed for a time with Geer and then moved to a hotel on 43rd Street. He connected with musicians and local political activists and, as had been the case in Los Angeles, saw his reputation grow when he was asked to perform at a benefit for refugees of the Spanish Civil War. His well-oiled "Political Okie" image was perfect for a performance at an event for Steinbeck's Committee to Aid Farm Workers. Folk musicologist Lomax was greatly impressed with Woody's unique musical talents and arranged for Woody to record a raft of songs for the Archives of Folkways at the Library of Congress and Woody's first commercial recording of *Dust Bowl Ballads*. Woody soon landed a job performing on CBS's broadcast for the American School of the Air in April 1940. Several months later, he was hired as a singer and host for the Model Tobacco Company. Woody bought a new Pontiac on credit and sent for Mary and the children to come to New York City in November 1940. But family life, a good income, and an apartment on 101st and Central Park West did not satisfy Woody. After seven shows, he abruptly quit the Model Tobacco show and packed his family into the Pontiac and left New York.

The Guthries returned to Los Angeles in January 1941. The family arrived in the middle of the night at the Robbin household in Edendale. Making use of Robbin's typewriter, Woody spent long hours tapping out pages of material for what would become his autobiographical novel, *Bound for Glory*.[83] He convinced Burke to let him restart his radio show at KFVD, but was unable to recapture the excitement and popularity of

Woody and Lefty Lou. Political rallies and events had dried up. Relations with his wife Mary were strained, and his drinking increased. Woody traveled once more to the San Joaquin Valley work camps, but he couldn't help but notice that most of the old shantytowns and Hoovervilles had disappeared. The Okies and Arkies were finding new jobs in the burgeoning war industries that were springing up in the booming industrial suburbs of Los Angeles. The population that had formed the basis of support for *Woody and Lefty Lou* only a few years ago were reinventing themselves in Los Angeles at the same time as Guthrie moved beyond hillbilly and migrant worker themes and toward larger national and international political themes. Playing for tips at his old haunts on Skid Row also lost its allure. Woody scribbled the following:

> 4-4-41,
> Los Angeles.
> Broke, feel
> Natural again,
> But it ain't
> Natural to be
> Broke,
> Is it?[84]

One afternoon, Woody put his family in his soon-to-be-repossessed Pontiac and headed north for what turned out to be a one-month job writing songs about the building of the Grand Coulee Dam in Washington.

Woody's formative Los Angeles period had come to an end, but his musical development, public persona, and political orientation had evolved decisively. The Los Angeles years solidified and shaped Woody's subsequent work. Perhaps more importantly, his songs, popular image, and politics formed a legacy that evolved through years of terminal illness and expanded exponentially after his death. When we think of the Urban Folk Revival, Greenwich Village in the late 1940s comes to mind. But its real origins were in Los Angeles where Woody Guthrie brought the folk music message to urban intellectuals and political activists.

Okemah High School, 1926–27. Woody is at center, front row in the light pants.

Two

RAMBLIN' IN BLACK AND WHITE

Dan Cady and Douglas Flamming

By his own admission, Woodrow Wilson Guthrie rambled.[1] Chronically restless, Woody rambled around the country on rail lines and in the backseats of hitched rides. As an entertainer, he spun tales in verse, song, and impromptu monologue on any and all subjects—to the delight of many and, if he rattled on for too long, the frustration of more than a few. When he cohosted a radio show on Los Angeles's KFVD, listeners who tired of his verbal ramblings asked him to "sing more and talk less."[2] Guthrie was known to spend hours on borrowed typewriters furiously pounding keys throughout the night only to toss dozens of single-spaced pages into the morning trash. Even his pen-and-ink sketches suggest a restless rambling. His hundreds of doodles, cartoons, and paintings reveal a man grappling with swirling visions of America's other half in strokes that were as honest as they were spontaneous. The sum of his work maps a commoner's Homeric journey across a landscape of uncertainty.

Beginning in the hardscrabble oil fields of Okemah, Oklahoma, Woody tumbleweeded back and forth across the nation. In the process, he saw an America mired in the Great Depression and then emboldened by war. He soaked up what he saw and heard—the emotions, language, and songs of impoverished folk. Ultimately, he seemed almost a living, breathing embodiment of the nation's dispossessed working stiffs and tramps. Never quite at home anywhere, yet somehow able to get by everywhere, Woody's journey ended only when Huntington's disease stopped his rambling and ended his life, quietly and tragically, in New York City—a very long way, in every sense, from Okemah.

As he rambled, Woody made some unexpected turns—none more so than his startling move from a predictably racist southerner to a homespun activist fighting for racial equality. Woody's journey from the familiar landscape of southern (and American) racism to the rocky and unmapped terrain of civil rights activism marked a great divide in his epic storyline. More than three-quarters of a century has passed since Woody made his crossing, and still the United States has a difficult time confronting the issue of race, much less racism's troubled historical relationship to American freedom. To cross the color line, Woody had further to travel than most Americans. When he finally did so, he crossed the line emphatically, and he made it his mission to try to scrub it out of the American soul. His remarkable change in racial values came at a time when racial equality was not yet part of the white liberal agenda. Born into a violently racist family and culture in the "Little Dixie" section of Oklahoma, Woody none-theless crossed over to embrace a pluralistic democracy. That alone compels us to give his racial journey serious contemplation.[3]

Fortunately, Woody's paper trail of songs, prose, and sketches contain clues to his singularly im-probable transformation. From the late 1930s to the end of his creative days, Woody penned dozens of songs, opinion pieces, and autobiographical accounts on the subject of race and racism in America. He condemned American law for its near total racial blind spot and regularly drew parallels between Nazism and Jim Crow; he wrote heartfelt ballads for African Americans killed by white police officers or lynched by white mobs. And his personal correspondence shows a man who exhibited genuine frustration with the lack of racial progress in America. By the time he wrote "This Land is Your Land," that critical word "Your" included all Americans, including African Americans.

Anyone who engages Woody's eclectic writings and art from the late 1930s and 1940s might well as-sume that his embrace of racial egalitarianism was never particularly difficult. Yes, one might suppose, this populist troubadour saw beyond the color line as a matter of course; his rambling ways and big heart showed him the way. Yes, one might add, his move to the political left naturally meant he saw an Ameri-can working class undifferentiated by race. But it was not so easy. His transformation was neither obvious nor preordained. Just the opposite. His enthusiasm on the issue gives a subtle hint. Woody's later work on racial equality rang out with the fervent faith of a newly converted believer.

To read Woody's 1943 autobiography, *Bound for Glory*, is to meet the man who had already seen the light. The very first line of the book reads: "I could see men of all colors bouncing along in the boxcar." And indeed he could. "We stood up. We laid down. We piled around on each other. We used each other for pillows." Interracial togetherness came with the conditions. One seasoned tramp standing next to Guthrie bemoaned their luck and reckoned that there were "pretty close ta sixty-nine" men crammed into the "bastardly boxcar." Space was tight, to say the least, and, to make matters worse, the floor was covered with a thick layer of cement dust, which burned the skin and lungs. Tempers were on a knife-edge. The train was a fast-running east-bounder, crossing Minnesota and bound for Chicago, but not getting there anytime soon. Young and old; restless and weary; healthy and sick; sober and drunk; singing or sleeping—their skins were black or brown or white, and all covered with sweat and cement dust. In Woody's vivid prose, the story that follows in Chapter 1, "Soldiers in the Dust," is surely one of the finest hoboing scenes in American letters and a lively start to his memoir.[4]

There was more to Chapter 1 than a gripping beginning, however. As the opening line suggested, the chapter offers a morality tale: racial discord vs. racial cooperation, with a bit of cosmic justice in the end. Early on, Woody meets and becomes pals with a young black man. Trouble began when two young white thugs in overalls gave a "hot foot"—in this case, with gasoline—to an old black man who was sleeping in the dust. Neither Woody nor his young "Negro friend" found this funny. Shortly thereafter, Woody heaved the bottle of gasoline out of the boxcar door, which outraged the white thugs. Then, in Woody's words, "my colored friend" asked the thugs "how long you been goin' 'roun' cookin' people's feet?"

One of the gasoline gang yells, "Keep outta dis! Stepinfetchit!" A fight was narrowly avoided, but only temporarily. The tinderbox of humanity soon erupted into violence from an unrelated source and spread to envelop every passenger, willing or unwilling. Seeing their common interests quickly intersecting, Woody and the young African American linked arms and found a space near the door where they could sit with their backs to the fight and keep his guitar safe from the sprawling, flailing humanity. But in the chaos, the gasoline thug sees a chance at revenge. He kicks Woody out the boxcar door, which would have meant death—flying onto the cinders at sixty miles per hour. But John (we do not learn his name until the end of the book) holds on tight (with his left arm—or Left arm, if you will), holding Woody above the cinders and leaning back hard to fend off their attacker. Just as all seems lost and Woody is about to lose his grip, the train begins to slow. Then, just as

"He turned a flip out into the lake" by Woody Guthrie. Woody's sketch of the train scene described in *Bound for Glory* was not included in that book. Drawn circa 1940, it was first published in *Woody Guthrie Folk Songs* in 1963. Artworks Series 7, Item 59.

the thug puts everything into one last shove to push the black man out, fate intervenes. The air brakes suddenly jerk hard and the thug is flung out of the car, "jumping like a frog . . . over me and the Negro both," landing on a steep slope and tumbling into a cold Minnesota lake.[5]

But the story is not over. With the train slowed enough, John and Woody exit the boxcar and hit the cinders. They want a fresh start and tighter hold on the same train. But Woody stumbles and, in a scramble to get back into the boxcar, loses his grip on his guitar and can't make it back in. Suddenly, John calls to him; his black ally had made it safely on to a ladder at the back of their boxcar. "Pass me yo' guitah!" Woody sees the plan. With the train still moving slowly, he passes his guitar to John, who then climbs up the ladder to the top. This clears the way for Woody, who swings onto the ladder and follows John to the top of the boxcar. From there they see, in the receding distance, the gasoline thug crawling out of the lake. The two watch him: "Both of us was standing side by side, propping each other up,"[6] and they watched with pleasure, black and white united, with justice served properly.

Then, out of the blue, the future joins them. Two young white boys clamber out of a car behind them and make their way to join John and Woody. The oldest was maybe fifteen years old, Woody reckoned; the youngest was way too small to be riding the rails: "couldn't be over ten or eleven."[7] As they conversed, he considered the boys.

> I'd seen a thousand kids just like them. They seem to come from homes somewhere that they've run away from. They seems to come to take the place of the old stiffs that slip on a wet board, miss a ladder, fall out a door, or just dry up and shrivel away riding the mean freights.

They were, in short, the next generation of hard travelers. But it might be said, given Woody's politics at the time, that these boys also represented the next generation—the Popular Front for the years that lay ahead.

Talk among the four turns to a coming rainstorm and whether the water will ruin the guitar. Then the youngest boy, an innocent where innocence seemingly had no place, gives Woody the sweater off his back to cover his guitar: "'S all I got! Wrap it aroun' yer music! Help a little," the ten year old yelled out. Woody pulled the sweater over the guitar; then he took his own shirt off and buttoned it around the sweater. Then John gave Woody his shirt. The fifteen year old, who had been acting tougher than he really could be, put his shirt in Woody's lap. Touched by the gesture, Woody wrapped it around the neck of the guitar. Bone-chilling rain pelts them hard—the train going 60—and the four hunker down, the boys freezing, the little one trembling. Woody called him over: "Not much of a windbreak, but it at least knocks a little of th' blister out of that rain. Roll yer head over here an' keep it ducked down behind this music box!" This lifted the boy's spirits, and Woody cradled him against the wind, letting the boy use his arm as a pillow. The little one snuggled in, asking, "'T'ink I could eva' play one uv dem?"[8]

And so they rolled into the cold, stormy night—John, Woody, and the two young boys—black and white united in common cause, and the future riding with them. They had acted in unison to save Woody's guitar. And, by 1942, his guitar was not merely a musical instrument, not merely his "meal ticket."[9] It was a machine that killed Fascists. In an undated drawing, not included in the autobiography, Woody illustrated this parable of racial cooperation. This train did carry some racists, but they were thinning out, and the day might yet come when this train *didn't carry no racists*. In Chapter 1 of the book, freight cars carried the possibility of equality based on mutual respect and shared interest. The tale was surely apocryphal—or at best an amalgam of stories wound into one, but it made for good reading and offered a clear political lesson.

It was also too pure by half. The story only relates Woody's fully evolved views on racial equality. It suggests he never really had a racist past, and that the white thugs on the train were alien to folks like him. It suggests that overcoming any ideas about white supremacy, if he had ever had any, were easily overcome in a moment of interracial "all for one." Neither suggestion was anything close to accurate. Instead, the story hid an uncomfortable truth about Woody's racial past. It may be understood, at least partly, as his attempt to minimize his personal participation in the enforcement of white supremacy. From the sum of his creative production, one would reasonably assume that Woody's racial attitudes were the consequence of his early appreciation of black culture and black suffering, combined with the slow but ever-progressing awakening of a creative genius who could see genius across the color line.

According to Woody, notions of common humanity across the color line were part of his youth. In his later writings, he said he had been moved toward tolerance during his Oklahoma childhood by the pleas of a soon-to-be lynched black mother and the confessions of a maternally insightful black neighbor.[10] Unfortunately, there is no corroborating evidence for any of these incidents. There is much to suggest that each was a product of Woody's personal historical revisionism. Indeed, a significant amount of evidence points toward the contrary: Woody himself participated in acts of cultural white supremacy throughout his youth and early adulthood. In this respect, he was—as a child and young man—a typical white Southerner. This, however, should not serve to delegitimize his contribution to civil rights and racial equality. In fact, it should enhance his reputation as a racially progressive pioneer. From where he began, Woody's journey of the mind and of the heart placed him on a much longer road to pluralism than he was willing to admit. Very few figures in American history have traveled such a distance.

Woody Guthrie was born in 1912, a product of white southern racial ideology. Named after Dixie's presidential champion, Woodrow Wilson, Woody cut his teeth on the race-baiting Democratic politics in the age of Jim Crow. Both parents came from southern stock, and the Guthries have rightly been referred to as "fervent Confederates."[11] Woody's brother was named Jefferson Davis Guthrie. Woody's father, Charley, involved himself intimately in the politics of the local Democratic Party, running for office, losing elections, and fistfighting his way through the county. Claimed by some to be a Klansman, Charley worked to disenfranchise the

Woody's racial inheritance: the lynching south of Okemah.

small local black community and penned racist anti-socialism screeds such as "Socialism Urges Negro Equality."[12] Most notoriously, Woody's hometown of Okemah was the site of a vicious lynching a mere two years before his birth. In that episode an African American mother and her thirteen-year-old son were hanged seven miles south of Okemah from a bridge crossing the Canadian River. According to the patchy story, the son fatally shot a white deputy during an altercation over allegedly stolen livestock. While the deputy lay dying, the mother refused the lawman a last drink of water. A photograph, later turned into a postcard, shows the lynch mob's handiwork. Indistinguishable, yet visibly proud, whites stand posed along the bridge, distinctively above the two black bodies hanging off the bridge in the broad daylight. Rumors circulated that the mother's second child, still an infant, was lynched as well. It was later determined that the baby was just simply left at the side of the road to die.[13] If the picture were cropped, one might mistake it for a family reunion or church picnic. Most likely, Charley Guthrie stood amongst those men. If not, he was certainly an admiring observer. Woody learned racism on his daddy's knee, he heard the stories, he probably saw the postcard photographs, and he loved his father.

In his official memory, Woody recalled Okemah as a diverse town where whites, African Americans, and Native Americans came into close contact in an integrated but unequal community. Census data and anecdotes suggest otherwise. Okemah was dominated by whites, with a Cherokee and Creek population as well. African Americans, who outnumbered Native Americans statewide, lived in small communities outside of town and rarely entered the city limits.[14] They were essential laborers for harvesting the cotton crop in southeast Oklahoma, a section of the state nicknamed "Little Dixie" for good reason. This is not to say that black faces were uncommon in Okemah. Quite the contrary, according to the town's residents, white children sometimes dressed in blackface and performed minstrel acts. One such youthful troop was so persistent that locals called them the town's "black family." At the forefront of this group sat the slightly small, highly energetic class clown Woodrow Wilson Guthrie. Friends and teachers recalled Woody's black-face masquerading and escapades. One childhood friend, Glenn Dill, recalled one of Woody's youthful songs "about a nigger gal that took a leak," only to find herself violated by a patch of rapidly growing jimsonweed.[15]

Granted, by the time Woody paraded through town in blackface and wrote ribald racists songs, Okemah had evolved from a dusty Podunk to an even dustier but bustling oil town (though not much oil was found there, it remained a hub). Oil brought fortune for few, but filled the community with countless young roustabouts (exclusively white men), who captivated young Woody with tall tales, old songs, and reckless behavior. The statewide social dynamic had also shifted toward recklessness in Woody's early years. The massacres of African Americans by whites during Tulsa's racial uprising in 1921 swelled the ranks of the Ku Klux Klan, further dividing already unequally separated black and white worlds. Not without its critics, Oklahoma's embrace of racial violence prompted outrage from the black press. "When you get as far down as humanly possible to go," one editor said, "remember that the next place to go is Oklahoma. They have the meanest Jim Crow system I have met yet."[16] Yet among the state's white population, the hardening of these categories only moved them toward more reactionary politics. For example, in 1923, when Oklahoma governor Jack Walton attempted to crack down on Klan activity, he was quickly impeached. This certainly pleased Charley Guthrie. For his part during the Klan controversy, Charley submitted a political cartoon to an Oklahoma City newspaper. It showed Governor Walton being skewered in the rectum by a large fishhook. The paper returned it, remarking, "It was very good, but, unfortunately, unprintable."[17] The concept may have been crude, but the artwork undoubtedly proved itself simple yet provocative. The cartoon was drawn, as it happened, by Charley's eleven-year-old son, Woody.

As Woody grew into adulthood, guitars rather than art supplies were his constant companions. Born with a good ear, an excellent memory, and an uncanny ability to improvise, Woody honed his musical genius in bars, on street corners, and inside crowded railway cars. His approach to music, particularly throughout the 1930s, clung closely to his affinity for white southern culture. He discovered that audiences responded better to old familiar songs than to the day's current hits. Broke, hungry, and intuitive, Woody tapped into his people's shared past for the pleasure of moving audiences and the satisfaction of getting fed.[18] Early country music, performed at fiddling contests, strummed in living rooms, and plucked on back porches, was deemed "hillbilly" by both his supporters and detractors. For Woody's people, hillbilly song unified and comforted the like-minded, especially in times of trouble. For instance, Woody describes the power of "Columbus Stockade," played by two young girls, in lifting the spirits of two thousand desperate white workers at a Redding labor camp.[19] His drawing of a multigenerational group admiring a young guitar-playing woman evokes a sense of well being, despite the visual suggestions of hard life and hard labor.

"Some drunks run up" by Woody Guthrie. Woody often illustrated scenes depicting informal performances in common settings. Circa 1940. Artworks Series 7, Item 29.

In the first half of the twentieth century hillbilly music also attracted the attention of musicologists and music business interests alike. Academics, like John Lomax, sought to celebrate and preserve this truly American sound, and Henry Ford believed it to be America's Great White Hope in a time of declining morals. Salesmen such as Ralph Peer saw it as a way to generate a few bucks off the nasally crooning of the purveyors of the "bozarts." From Appalachia to the Ozarks and the flatlands in between, the bozarts, the music of common whites, credited as born in the British Isles and animated by the richness of the American experience, conveyed a genuine white experience, and was collected and packaged that way. Regardless of the elasticity of the term "hillbilly," folks like Woody wore the label with pride. For them, it signified white cultural authenticity in song, attitude, and demeanor.

In 1937, a twenty-four-year-old Woody rambled away from his pregnant wife and child in Pampa, Texas, and headed toward California. He eventually arrived in Los Angeles, a self-proclaimed "hobo hillbilly."[20] Woody's chain of family connections led him to a little bungalow in Glendale, California, where he attempted to forge a new life. Always unconventional yet exceedingly common, Woody settled among like-kind common folks uprooted from the country's center, scrambling for work in daylight, and commiserating with fellow migrants in rented lodgings at night. They spoke a common language and shared their affinity for the similar foods, similar songs, and similar ideologies that marked them as former residents of those states where the South looked West. Displaced by a lethal mixture of economic despair and environmental disaster, they landed in the West's largest city with tens of thousands other "dustbowl refugees."

Whatever the name—poor whites, plain folk, hillbilly, Arkie or Okie—this group adhered to a social order that prized the common experience, yet privileged white over black, regardless of the economic or educational status of either. When Woody Guthrie set foot in Los Angeles, he was no exception. As a dyed-in-the-wool hillbilly performer (with his partner Missouri-born Maxine "Lefty Lou" Crissman) on radio station KFVD, Woody attracted a large audience of other psychologically homeless white migrants. The duo tapped into the collective subconscious of a displaced population, longing for the familiar amongst the metropolis's daily chaos. They began each program with their "Woody and Lefty Lou Theme Song":

> Drop whatever you are doing,
> Stop your work and worry too
> Sit right down and take it easy
> Here comes Woody and Lefty Lou
> You just drop a card or letter
> We will sing a song for you
> We're easy going country people
> Plain ole Woody and Lefty Lou[21]

In less than a year, "plain ole" Woody and Lefty Lou received ten thousand letters from listeners. Those who wrote wanted to commiserate on life's difficulties, request songs, or—on occasion—invite Woody and Crissman to visit their homes and get a home-cooked "chicken dinner."[22]

Woody's conventional Southern attitudes on race fell on sympathetic ears. It was not uncommon for he and Crissman to sing songs about "darkies" and "niggers." None of his white listeners wrote to complain; none, indeed, thought it unusual enough to comment on. Amid the startling racial and ethnic diversity of L.A., the songs were doubtless a comfort to his homesick audience. Woody's lowest moment in his own personal history of racist reaction stemmed from an episode he and Crissman experienced on Santa Monica Beach. One evening, the Guthrie and Crissman families packed hot dogs and blankets and drove in a little caravan from Glendale to Santa Monica's sprawling beach. It was a familiar scene; the families often rounded up kith and kin to frolic on the beach, light bonfires at dusk, and sing old familiar tunes to the surf and the stars. Sometimes Woody and his cousin Jack "Oke" Guthrie would perform one of their impromptu "Negro dances."[23] On any given night, the sand would be dotted with family groups circling small fires into the early morning hours.

On this particular evening, about forty African American men arrived in a couple of trucks to have their own good time at the beach. Santa Monica Beach was racially segregated; there was an "Ink Well" section there for blacks. We do not know whether Woody's group was close to, or perhaps had transgressed onto, the Ink Well section; we do not know whether the African American group had had enough of segregated beaches and simply hit the sand where they pleased. Either way, the Guthries and Crissmans felt threatened. According to Crissman, the black men began "throwing things" in an attempt to harass the white families and scare them from their places around the campfires. Woody, with Crissman's father in tow, promptly ran to the closest payphone and called the police. Upon arrival, the police removed the threat, and segregated peace was once again restored.[24]

With the incident fresh in Woody's mind, he quickly authored a satirical (if not rambling) headline. Using the format of an article intended to mimic and belittle African American newspapers, he wrote:

> *The Santa Monica Social Register Examine 'Er*
> De Beach Combin' Repo'tah
> Dear Rufus: Hit might in'rest you to know dat de 100 yard dark record was broke
> fo'teen times in fifteen minutes at Santy Monica Beach.

This, he followed with a poem from his own white point of view:

> We could dimly hear their chants
> And thought the blacks, by chance
> Were doing a cannibal dance
> This but dimly we could see
> Guess the sea's eternal pounding
> Like a Giant drum a sounding
> Set their jungle blood to bounding
> Set their native instincts free.[25]

For modern Guthrie admirers, it is difficult to reconcile such writings with the man who devoted so much of his life to the plight of the underdog. Indeed, it is hard to reconcile such writings with Chapter 1 of *Bound for Glory*. The persistence of static racial categories embraced by Woody's people, fueled by the fears and sense of privilege that lay at the marrow of white supremacy ideals, proved too much for Woody to overcome—at least for the time being. According to Crissman, the Woody she knew in those days retained much of "his old Southern perspective." She claimed he always used the word "nigger" in those days; he never used the term Negro.[26] None of the Guthrie clan did. For instance, when Woody's uncle Jefferson Davis "Jeff" Guthrie headed a police department in New Mexico, his frequent use of the term drew ire from a black police officer stationed in an adjacent segregated township. By his own admission, Jeff "exploded in anger and said he was raised to call them niggers, meant no harm by it or ill to anyone, and damned well was going to continue to call them niggers." Ramblin' did not necessarily alter racial views.[27]

But then something happened that changed Woody's life—and more specifically his views on race. In October 1937, Woody was behind the microphone at KFVD, letting fly in full folksy style. On this show, he entertained listeners with a rendition of Uncle Dave Macon's "Run, Nigger, Run." The song—initially recorded in 1925 and described by Macon as a "good ol' southern" standard—employed the word "nigger" frequently. If Woody stayed true to the original, he broadcast the term no fewer than ten times in less than three minutes. As usual, his white readers sent no written response; they didn't mind, didn't register anything unusual. Neither had Woody—but soon he would. Soon after this show, Woody received a letter from Howell Terence, an African American resident of Los Angeles. A local college student who wrote in sincere and measured prose, Terence chastised Woody to the same degree that he illustrated the project of black civil rights in the West. He also suggested the relative backwardness of white southern migrants in California. And he was wise enough to know that his letter might prompt a violent response from Woody and his ilk; Terence refused to disclose his real address. The letter in full reads:

> You were getting along quite well in your program this evening until you announced your "Nigger Blues." I am a Negro, a young Negro in college and I certainly resented your remark. No person, or person of any intelligence, uses that word over the radio today.
>
> May I call your attention to the fact that a news announcer over KHJ [now KNX] was barred from announcing when he used that word about a year or so ago.
>
> I don't know just how many Negroes listened to your program tonight, but I for one am letting you know that it was deeply resented.
>
> If you wish to reply, the above is not my residence.[28]

Terence's letter impacted Woody to such a degree that one might daresay it altered his life's trajectory. First, Woody apologized to Terence and Negroes more generally on the air. This action itself, from the point of view of white Southerners, was a deep violation of racial mores. To apologize to an African

American—in public (and therefore, a matter of honor)—was to be guilty of being a race traitor. Had he used airtime to mock Terence's letter, he would surely have increased his white audience. Instead, by apologizing, he probably lost some listeners: such was the power of cultural rules in a white-supremacy world. His brother Jeff probably found out; doubtless he flew into a rage. By bowing to a colored person, Woody had disgraced the Guthrie name and had rejected all their father had stood for back in Oklahoma.

After Woody's on-the-air apology, his audience never heard him use the "n" word again. Woody changed his mind about race, and his behavior followed his change in outlook. Sometime between his radio apology in Los Angeles and his arrival in New York in 1940, he altered his worldview on race relations dramatically and permanently. Chapter 1 of *Bound for Glory* was probably penned late in the book's development. His early draft chapters—the ones first read by New York editors—centered on his childhood in Oklahoma.[29] But in the end, his black-and-white-unite adventures in the boxcar both open the book and close it, as he returns in a little chapter at the end to the boxcar adventure with which he began—ramblin' atop a westbound with his "Negro friend"—who now has a name: John. With the radio show transformation in mind, the name might well have been Howard. But the essential point is this: In less than five years, Woody moved from a radio huckster performing an untroubled version of "Run, Nigger, Run" to crusader for racial equality and a kind of American pluralism that was, in his time, rare among white Americans.

In doing so he was fully out of step with the times. For a white working stiff to get political in the Great Depression was commonplace; to commit to union labor and the labor movement was also common. But for white folks to cross the color line, and then try to erase it—no, that was not common in the late 1930s. In this, Woody was well ahead of his time. Woody, initially on his own in his conversion, faced the race issue head on.

Once he made his decision, and rambled back to the East Coast, he found himself among leftists who were accustomed to racial equality as a matter of policy. Among them, he could become bolder, more outspoken. He could sharpen his views, place them in a larger political context. That Woody dove into the project head first was typical Woody. That he would stick with it—sticking with things was his serious shortcoming—that was not typical Woody. For the bohemian Left and Fellow Travelers in New York City, embracing the idea of racial integration and racial equality seldom involved any emotional trauma, seldom involved the loss of family or friends, seldom involved the difficult business of giving up one's traditional culture to imbibe another. Not so for Woody. To embrace an outlook that undermined *the* most important part of his family's culture, that was something altogether different. Woody lost many friends as a result. One family member in Mississippi, hearing Woody's views on interracial marriage, threw him out of the house. Woody lost relationships with most of his family. He paid the price and seemingly did so without regret.

But to return briefly to Woody's reaction to Terence's letter, and the long-term impact it had on Woody's views and behavior, one is compelled to ask: Was it really as simple as that? A Road-to-Damascus moment? Possibly. He would not be the only historical figure to have experienced a blinding-light experience. Perhaps, too, the early and tragic death of his beloved sister, and the institutionalization of his mother, created a grief deep enough to alter his view of the world. Woody always loved an underdog, but perhaps his childhood heartaches made it possible for his adult soul to finally side with the underdog among American underdogs. Perhaps Jim Crow culture did trouble him early in life, deep beneath the skin, and it had to gradually work its way out, like a stubborn splinter. Perhaps when he saw his Santa Monica poem in print, he felt he had gone too far somehow, and that, followed by Terence's letter, jarred his sense of self. In any event, his racial "self" did change, and, unlike most other things in his life, he did not leave it stranded.

Soon after Woody's rejection of his father's ideology, he rambled again, but this time with purpose. By throwing in with American leftists and dedicating himself to their causes, he funneled his frenetic genius into pointed political action. And, while he jettisoned many of his old beliefs, he held to at least one significant expression of his Southern white culture. In short, Woody kept the music and threw away the white supremacy. He retained the melodies and common-man ethos of hillbilly music, but purged it of its racist content. "Radicalized" in Los Angeles, by the time he hitched his way to New York City, Woody had graduated from just another hillbilly to common-man activism in order to tackle America's most pressing midcentury problems.

A changed man, Woody publically revisited the subject of race in his Woody Sez column, published in New York's Communist newspaper, *Daily Worker* (later, *People's World*). At the behest of his new leftist friends, Will Geer and Alan Lomax, he toned down his hokum and much of his idiosyncratic spelling (i.e., figgered and microbephones). The Communists thus gained an "authentic" voice from the hardscrabble heartland—a kind of Will Rogers draped in red.[30] With racial equality as a pivotal part of the American Communist agenda, the column provided a venue for Woody to express his race-crusading views without losing his twang. Woody wrote anti-lynching pieces and championed black musicians. One Woody Sez offering lauded the National Negro Congress, a Popular Front civil rights organization: "You're goin' in the right direction," he wrote, still clinging to the remnants of his folksy tongue, "and you got the right idea in your mind, and you're right, dead right, and if you meet with opposition or people who disagree with you, well, that's a darn good sign that they're wrong."[31]

Woody's most powerful message of hope and reconciliation, however, came in song. Perhaps the most biting—and certainly the most personal—song concerning race penned by Woody in this period was

"Slipknot." One of several antilynching songs Woody composed after his conversion to racial equality and civil rights, "Slipknot" marked his first attempt to cleanse himself of his compromised racial past. His handwritten lyric sheet reveals the obvious care he took in getting the words down on paper; the careful script, even the carefully placed ditto marks. On the lower left-hand corner of the sheet, he wrote a singularly powerful statement:

Detail of Woody's "Slipknot" lyric marks a decisive moment in his shift towards racial egalitarianism.

> Dedicated to the many Negro mothers, fathers, and sons alike, that was lynched and hanged under the bridge of the Canadian River several miles south of Okemah, Okla., and to the day when such will be no more.[32]

Woody's coming to terms is punctuated with his sketching of a lynching, which he also labeled "Slipknot." Like the lyric sheet itself, the drawing exposes a genuine seriousness not seen in his earlier contributions. The lines are thick and deliberate with the supporting crucifix bending from the victim's weight. For a white Southerner whose own family was implicated, an actual hometown lynching, the song and sketch reflect an unprecedented illustration of (secular) repentance.

Those familiar with Woody's words and deeds have every reason to trust the authenticity of this profound transformation. In a letter to his second wife, Marjorie, he forcefully advocated the "killing of Jim Crow." In one notorious incident, he trashed a hotel banquet in Baltimore when the hotel staff asked black musicians to eat alone in the kitchen. According to Pete Seeger, Woody screamed, "This fight against Fascism has got to start right here and now!"[33] The Nazi invasion of the Soviet Union had sent Woody and other American leftists headlong into the fight against Fascism. Woody would join the Merchant Marine and would play special concerts for the troops at home and abroad. In the process, he butted heads with the American military and its segregationist policies by insisting that the band play to interracial audiences. He played benefits for black victims of white crime, as in the case of Isaac Woodward, who was beaten blind by cops in South Carolina for washing his hands in a "white" restroom. Woody characterized Joe Louis's beatings of white boxers as a punch-by-punch victory over white supremacy.[34]

Yet for all his talk, songs, drawings, and trashed banquet rooms, his true baptism came at the hands of

SLIPKNOT

Did you ever see a hangman tie a slip knot?
" " " " " " " " "

Yes, I seen it a many a time, and he winds, and he winds,
And after thirteen times, he ties a slip knot.

Tell, ^{me} Will that slipknot slip? No! It will not!
" " " " " " " " " " "

It will slip down round your neck, but it wont slip back again,
That slipknot. That slipknot! O' That slipknot!

Did you ever lose a brother ⁱⁿ on that slipknot?
" " " " " " " " "

Yes. My brother was a slave,.... he tried to escape......
and they drug him to his grave with a slipknot.

Did you ever lose your father in that slipknot?
" " " " " " " " "

(Yes.) They hung him from a pole, and they shot him full of holes.
And they left him hang to rot in that slipknot.

who makes the laws for that slip knot?
" " " " " " " "

who says who will go to the calaboose —
and get the hangman's noose, get that slipknot?

I dont know who makes the law of that slip knot.
" " " " " " " " "

But the bones of many a men are a whistling in the wind.
Just because they tie their laws with a slipknot.

* Dedicated to the many
negro mothers, fathers, and sons
alike, that was lynched and
hanged under the bridge of the   Woody G—
Canadian River, seven miles   2-29-40 N.Y.
south of Okemah, Okla., and to
the day when such will be no
more.

Woody's carefully hand-written lyrics to "Slipknot."

a man whose rocky road made Woody's path seem relatively smooth. In terms of pure admiration in Woody's eye's, Huddie "Lead Belly" Ledbetter was paramount. Arguably one of the most significant artists of the twentieth century, Lead Belly brought the sounds of the black South to a national audience. From the Depression to his death in December of 1949, Lead Belly sang the Delta Blues on national radio and in concert. With a fiery temper and the prison record to prove it, the Louisiana-born singer and self-proclaimed "king of the twelve string guitar" embodied the southern experience more so than any popular artist of the time. Once a comrade of the legendary bluesman, Blind Lemon Jefferson, and twice an inmate of the South's notoriously brutal Angola Prison Farm in Louisiana, Lead Belly's wartime resume included a regular stint on CBS radio's *Back Where I Come From*, which was broadcast from New York City. It was there in New York that Woody's and Lead Belly's paths crossed. Black Louisiana and white Oklahoma, blues and hillbilly—two creative iconoclasts segregated by a haunting past—they sang together in a crowded East 10th Street apartment. Their lives overlapped in important ways. Unpredict-

Woody's illustration for the song "Slipknot."
Pencil, pen and ink on paper. Circa 1944.

able geniuses, both were hopeless ramblers. But, most significantly, there was synchronicity in their sacred and secular musical traditions. They played the same instruments, sang for the fleeting pleasure of the dispossessed, and knew many of the same familiar songs (albeit, often different versions). When Woody listened to Lead Belly's "Midnight Special," he most likely recalled hearing it as a child at Okemah's Crystal Theater while watching Otto Gray's Oklahoma Cowboy Band.[35] Undoubtedly, Lead Belly's version of "Stewball" took Woody back to the Oklahoma oil fields. As an eleven year old, Woody would sit on the grass near an oil worker's shack and listen to him play guitar and sing about the noble horse "Stewbally."[36]

Here, perhaps, was the real epiphany. Woody had been reared to believe in the supremacy of all things white. But in New York, he not only acknowledged the African American contribution to his own cultural

Woody Guthrie accompanying Lead Belly in Chicago. Circa 1940.

history, but he also eventually deferred to it—inverting what his father and uncle would have deemed the natural order of things. In their relationship, Lead Belly was clearly the master and Woody the novice. In 1941, Woody gushed about Lead Belly's guitar instruction on a particularly difficult Jefferson tune. "I am on the edge of playing them One Dime Blues," he wrote friends, "and if I spent ten years on them I'll figure the time pretty well spent. Who besides me in this century has had the honor and privilege of studying under the one and only Lead Belly?"[37]

A photograph from a 1940 radio broadcast illustrates this dynamic. Lead Belly, with his oversized twelve-string guitar sings alone while towering over his Oklahoma sidekick. Lead Belly looks dapper in his pinstriped suit. Woody is dressed in ordinary garb, and he subordinately follows the headliner's lead, watching his hand for the chord changes, and strumming in support of Lead Belly's unequaled prowess. The same can be heard on a recording from the very same year. Together, Lead Belly and Woody sing "Stewball"—not the ballad recorded by Woody, but the blues call-and-response favored by the former. In it one can easily discern Lead Belly's piercing lead vocal and Woody's staggered, nasally response. "You bet on Stewball," they harmonize on the chorus, "you might win, win, win. Bet on Stewball, you might win."

In that moment, and for many years to come, their ideal of racial egalitarianism did not win. But they helped coal up the engine that would pull the train. By the time the southern civil rights movement began to gain traction in the mid-1950s, Lead Belly would be dead, and Woody would be suffering the physical and mental disabilities that come with Huntington's disease. By that time, too, the Cold War had chilled American Communists and fellow travelers, and organized labor had made its transition from radical activism to Big Labor bureaucracy. But on the racial front, Woody had made a break from his conventional Southern past and converted to an ideal of racial equality—and he had done so far, far ahead of virtually all white southerners; he had done so far ahead of most white Americans, period. In his final years of sane and productive writing, he tried again to work through his singular racial transformation, tried to reconcile the full-blown racism of his childhood and of his family with the man he had become. In the end, it was too painful, too overwhelming. Some things were simply too hard to say.

A caveat is needed here: We must not put Woody Guthrie on a pedestal. For one thing, he would not appreciate it. Too confining. Too much like a *pol-ee-tish-ee-un*. For another, Woody was not, in the final analysis, a very good person. All told, it might be difficult to say whether he helped more people or hurt more people during his adult life. If you were down and out on Skid Row, he'd go out of his way to help you; if you needed an uplifting song in a hard-luck labor camp, Woody was your man. So long as he didn't have to know you for very long, it was good to know him. But his compassion for the mass of humanity did not extend to those close to him. If you were part of his family, or a close friend, or a musical associate, he could be dismissive, ill-tempered, even downright mean—and unpredictably so. Even by the standards of his own era, he treated women very badly, including his first wife and three daughters, who did a lot of hard travelin' with Woody and were abandoned by him several times—and not mentioned in *Bound for Glory*. Yes, we may tip a hat to artistic temperament, but on a certain level, Woody simply refused to grow up. The only person who had the combination of creativity, grace, and wisdom to successfully play the role of Wendy to Woody's Peter Pan, was his second wife, Marjorie; even that proved a hard go for Marjorie. But to her, we owe a great debt: She made it possible for Woody to finish *Bound for Glory*; she passed her good graces to their children, who would, as we know, also inherit their dad's wit and populist politics.

It has been suggested that "Woody failed" to honestly spell out the depth of racism in his family and his youth. The implication, then, is that he failed in his own racial transformation. This suggestion has it backwards. Woody failed on many fronts, but not on race. He changed his mind; he changed his behavior; he spoke out, sang out, stood up—and did so at considerable personal cost, including a kind of exile from his family and his past. Precisely because he came to feel so deeply about the sins of his fathers, precisely because he came to see the evil in the culture he inherited—and, as a young adult, openly espoused; precisely because he was haunted: There were personal doors he had to keep shut. In the 1950s, working on a new memoir, he wrote out a version of the Okemah lynching, blending, as he always did in his autobiographical writings, fact and fiction and memory and message. He thought hard about it. In the end, he cut it out of the draft manuscript. Because he succeeded in his own personal transformation—well ahead of the nation, especially the South—he could never quite put into words to the horrors of Okemah. The song and sketch, "Slipknot," seem, in retrospect, more than enough for one person to create.

In the final chapter of *Bound for Glory*, Woody brings the narrative back to the boxcar episode with which the book opened. All the tramps on the train are found out and rounded up by the local police—Woody and John along with the rest. A cop shoos the young boys off the scene. The cops are shocked at the condition of the men in the boxcar, who, after the very long brawl, look like they had been at war. They find it funny that Woody has his guitar bundled in soaking wet shirts. The cops are in no mood to be harsh or to haul them to jail. Suddenly a beautiful westbound eases by on the next track, bound for Seattle. One tramp yells: Hey, boys, there're jobs in the Seattle shipyard. In small groups, the hobos—including Woody and John—decide to take the westbounder, which will take them right back where they started from. There are boastful yells all around—they're off to fight the "Japs," to help defeat the Fascists. Woody and John hop on top, and out of nowhere, the young boys are back. John tells them where they are bound. "Wit cha," confirms the little ten year old. One suspects Woody, in writing this scene, could hardly have kept from wondering what his life would have been like had a couple of friends—one black, one white—taken him under their wing when he, Woody, was still a boy. It would have saved him an awful lot of personal trial and pain. Woody could not change his childhood, but perhaps the boxcar story could reach some folks who otherwise would never get the message.

Lead Belly—who perhaps inspired Woody's "John"—died days before the dawn of the 1950s. Woody played his mentor's memorial concert. Lead Belly's Communist affiliations drove some folk artists, such as Burl Ives, to forgo the event.[38] But for Woody, this was not an option. The two, according to Lead Belly's niece, "just played like they was born together."[39] In a sense, they had been. Born into Jim Crow, Southern culture, and a volatile world, the two eventually integrated politically, musically, and racially. Alone, Woody integrated his songs and his artwork—and added his new politics to both. With Lead Belly, he understood music itself as an integrated force in the world, one with singular political potential. Southern music—the very sound of his own life—was drawn from common sources, both black and white. At a time when radio and record labels segregated white "hillbilly" music from black "race records," Woody and Lead Belly literally and figuratively linked arms in defiance of such easily defined categories. Ramblin' in black and white, ahead of their time.

ON A SLOW
TRAIN
THROUGH CALIFORNIA

BY

WOODY

TH' DUSTIEST
OF TH'
DUSTBOWL
REFUGEES

To: VIRGINIA RICE
Box 816
Chula Vista, Calif.

Thank
you

WOODY!

CLIP
THIS COUPON
AND 50 ¢
GOOD FOR 3
COPIES THIS
BOOK

Woody's handmade pamphlet, with handwritten thanks, about his eyewitness observations of Depression-era California.

Three

SLOW TRAIN THROUGH CALIFORNIA

JAMES FORESTER
The Hollywood Tribune
Monday, July 3, 1939

I'm going to write a book review, and I know that I'm not cutting into anyone's racket because if I don't review this book nobody will.

I'll bet that everybody who reads *The Hollywood Tribune* has either read or heard a lot about *[The] Grapes of Wrath* by John Steinbeck. But there probably aren't ten people who have ever seen a book called *On a Slow Train Through California* by Woody, th' dustiest of th' dustbowl refugees.

Steinbeck's book has a fine jacket and is well gotten up. Next to it Woody's book would look like a very poor cousin. But they are relatives just the same.

Woody's book was written in longhand first, then painfully typed on a stencil, and then run off on a mimeograph machine and stapled. Now Woody sells it to his listeners every day over KFVD at 2:15 p.m. when he sings with his "geetar." He gets two bits for the book. And the people who write to ask for a copy of it, send long windy tales in their letters and tell about the days back home in Oklahoma or Arkansas or Texas and ask Woody whether he has any folks in this town or that.

If Steinbeck ever needs a witness in a court of law to prove that history about the Joads is true, I think he should take Woody.

For Woody is really one of them and at the same time he's a poet and a singer. He's the troubadour of those who are condemned to the other side of the fence.

Woody has been thru the mill, was one of the dustbowlers, has tramped the roads, and ridden the jalopies, and hung from freight trains, seen California inside the jails, looking out and outside looking in and he always had a tune in his head. He's full of the peculiar drawling humor and wisdom of that western country and every time he talks, a kind of folk wisdom comes out like something that has been long mellowing.

I'd like to tell something about who Woody is and where he came from but he tells it better himself in one of the chapters of the book—

"When a feller takes to writin' about his self he might as well quit," reads one of the chapters of his book.

I was born just like you was born, only in a different place.

It was the little town of Okemah, Oklahoma, July 14, 1912, let's see, now, that makes me 27.09 years old, compared to 26.09 in July a year ago. I married a girl by the name of Mary Jennings, in Pampa, Texas, some years ago, I fergot just how many. Anyhow we got two of the youngest daughters you ever seen, Teeny 3½ and Sye 1½. We been married ever since.

My wife has got two brothers, one I owe $30, and one I owe $440. The $440 is a butcher by trade, but he woodent cut down a cent. The other is a racehorseman and he was willin' to take the chance. I am five feet and some inches in my brothers socks feet. My hair is wavy when I'm two haircuts behind, and plumb curley when I'm four. I ain't got any bad habits except my own, and never take a drink unless I am by myself or with somebody.

Woody likes to tell stories about himself and other people in a kind of talking chant. He has one that he calls Talking Dustbowl Blues. It goes like this (in your own mind you have to try to fit in the deep strums of the guitar and the changing rhythm of the chant):

"Back in 1927 I had a little farm that I called Heaven. Prices up, the rain come down, hawled my crops all in to Town, got the money, bought clothes and groceries, fed the kids and took it easy.

"But the rain quit and the wind got high, and the black old dust begin to fly. I swapped my farm for a Ford machine, filled it up with gasoline, and started, up mountains, crost Deserts, to California.

"Away up yonder on a Mt. Road, hot motor and a heavy load; was a ridin' pretty fast, wasn't even stoppin.

"Bouncin up and down like popcorn a poppin, had a breakdown, nervous bust-down, engine trouble.

"Flyin along that mountain road. I wasn't feeling so dog gone good, I give that rolling Ford a shove, gonna coast just far as I could—commenced rollin, picking up speed. Hairpin Turn, and I couldn't make it.

"Man alive! I'm tellin' you, the fiddles and the guitars really flew. That Ford took off like a Flying Squirrel flew ½ way around the world, wives and children all over the mountain.

"Got to old Los Angeles broke, so dawgone hungery I thought I'd choke. I hustled up a spud or 2, wife cooked up tater stew—mighty thin stew—cood read a magazein through it. Fed the kids a bait of it—to keep from starvin."

Woody has seen the jails and so he's written about them and he's got a song about Lincoln Heights Jail that ought to be sung before the City Council.

> You drunken drivers come listen to my tale
> Your drinkin' and drivin's gonna get you in jail
> You got to go slow if you want to go free
> You're bound to get lousy in Lincoln Heights Jail.

Woody has a few droll comments on another jail he has experienced.

The Jail in Reno Nev. is so filthy that the disease germs turned in a complaint to the city health dept. The lice had a board of directors meetin' and migrated to the city dump where it was at least decent. The disposal which shood of been disposed dont dispose so well, an over a period of several months you got a good bit of disposal to dispose of. Well, I don't know how the devercees is in Reno, but the jail is rotten, an' I got 3 circus side showmen, one male robber, one dope fiend, one drunk indian, 1 drunk swede, 1 lumberjack, an 13 vagrants to help me prove it. (After all, they cood tell you more than the health officers.) They jest found a feller that dident know nothin about health an elected him to overlook it.

There's never any bitterness in Woody but his laughter just digs its hooks into the upper crust that has pushed his people around. And you can see that Woody and the people he talks for, though they were kind of muddled at first and didn't know just who to strike out at, now point their fingers in the right direction. Woody is down on bankers, millionaires, loan sharks, big landowners, and Congressmen. In a ballad about Death Valley Scotty, he winds up:

> Now, if it's a plan to get dough from the rich man,
> To Death Valley Scotty I take off my hat—
> To the best of my knowledge, the best I can figure
> He's done more than the boys up in Congress at that.

Woody has a chapter about Stockton where he learned who were the right guys and who weren't. He even picked up the word reactionary and got wise to what it means.

He starts by saying that "Stockton is as good a town as you can go hungry in." Then toward the close:

> Longshoremen are purty thick around Stockton, and are a swell bunch of boys. They are great big husky boys, about so broad and so high and big shouldered and muscles, you just caint beat em. They stay broke most of the time, but when you can catch a longshoreman with four bits, you can dern shore get a meal off of him.
>
> That's something you caint do with a politician. When you are playing a guitar in a salloon, and ½ a dollar hits the kitty, it's a longshoreman. If neither half dollar hits the kitty, its a logger.
>
> If you play nine pieces right in a row and a fellar throws a penny in and wants 9 more, he's either just out of a state office, or just agoin in. Of course if you play half the night, till you fall in your tracks, and some feller stands over there and just grins, he's a reactionary.

I have spent all this time quoting Woody because I think Woody is a new voice straight from the heart, a kind of Will Rogers, only still closer to the pain of his own folks than Rogers was.

There are so many hillbillys who sing over the radio, so many voices that just drum on through night and day that this voice might be lost to some of us, which would be a shame, wouldn't it?

four

THE GUTHRIE PRESTOS
WHAT WOODY'S LOS ANGELES RECORDINGS TELL US ABOUT ART AND POLITICS

PETER LA CHAPELLE

R uggedly nonconformist, Woody Guthrie pioneered an unvarnished, political approach to music making, which has lingered on, half hidden, in our electronic age. He also was, to be sure, a complicated figure. He cared deeply about the common man, but sometimes less so about the people in his immediate vicinity. Biographers from Joe Klein to Ed Cray have noted the long absences and infidelities that interfered with Woody's family life.

He complained about the commercialization of music and yet his personal writings reveal an individual deeply frustrated with the Left's inability to sell itself effectively. He criticized the music industry as a centralized, homogenizing "Monopoly on music" whose "fonograft records" put live musicians out of work, but he also hoped political activists and performers would follow his lead by using "every trick and device of the trades of salesmen, showmen, P. T. Barnums, Flo Zeigfelds, [and] Jimmie Rodgers" to get Angelinos fired up about labor organizing and politics.[1]

Although he was a prominent and active member of the political Left for more than two decades, even his political standpoint could prove difficult to nail down. While in Los Angeles in the late 1930s, he flirted with the Townsend and Ham and Eggs pension movements, populist campaigns generally frowned upon on by the Left.[2] He also wrote simultaneously for two newspapers—the liberal anti-Soviet *California*

Progressive Leader and the Communist *People's World*—at a time when their editorial boards were fiercely sparring over such issues as the Molotov-Ribbentrop Pact between Stalin and Hitler and the invasion of Finland.[3] He famously deflected inquiries into his political identity with humor—"I ain't a Communist necessarily, but I been in the red all my life"—or obfuscation—"Left wing, right wing, chicken wing—it's the same thing to me."[4]

Perhaps it is because of this complexity that Woody's Los Angeles recordings—his earliest known—are so revealing. The four tracks, recorded most likely in 1939 on lacquer-covered aluminum "Presto" discs, provide a snapshot of the songwriter at a key period of political and musical transition. They capture, perhaps more than any other group of Guthrie recordings, a moment when Woody was moving from writing topical songs that merely document injustice to crafting lyrics and music that was infinitely more political. They also demonstrate that this process occurred somewhat unevenly, with Woody writing some protopolitical songs before returning to songs that merely document, and later returning to more political takes on songwriting. They similarly offer some clues to his thoughts as a young man about the role of the marketplace in the creation and dissemination of political art. And finally, they give support to the idea that Los Angeles, not New York, served as locus of Woody's political transformation, and that it was in Southern California that he really began to blend the folk and commercial music-making traditions of his home region with the kind of politics that he would eventually be associated with.

The story of Woody's Presto recordings begins with a key figure in the history of gay politics and some dumb luck on my part. I stumbled upon the two discs in 1999 when doing research for what became my first book, *Proud to Be an Okie: Cultural Politics, Country Music, and Migration to Southern California*. I was a young graduate student in the history department at the University of Southern California formulating a plan for dissertation research and had decided that it would include examining Woody Guthrie's time in Los Angeles. I wondered whether Woody had left behind a radio transcription disc, or another kind of recording or two, while in Los Angeles.

Initially I approached librarian-archivists Sarah Cooper and Mary Tyler at the Southern California Library for Social Studies and Research, located some three miles south of USC, about whether they had any Woody Guthrie materials in their collection. The library has its own illustrious history rooted in the Red Scare of the late 1940s and 1950s. Founder Emil Freed had allowed Southern California leftists to store records and reading material in his garage during the McCarthy era because many feared such materials would implicate them. Eventually these materials became the genesis of a labor college library which in 1963 was transformed into a community library and as a repository of materials related to the histories of regional labor, civil rights, and the women's and the immigrants' movements.[5] I viewed some of the library's materials, but I didn't uncover anything solid. Cooper, however, suggested that I interview veteran activist Harry Hay, who had helped promote the library in a variety of ways over the years.

In Stuart Timmons' biography, *The Trouble with Harry Hay*, Hay was credited with founding the Mattachine Society, an early gay rights organization. Although there are some who contest the claim, many scholars and activists, in fact, consider Hay to be a founder, if not, *the* founder, of the modern-day gay rights movement. Hay had led an illustrious life, cutting his teeth as a union organizer, joining and then later parting ways amicably with the Communist Party and the People's Songs movement, and founding the Radical Faeries, a gay movement focused on Native American spiritualism, in the 1970s.[6]

During an interview at Hay's home in West Hollywood, he mentioned that he met Woody through a mutual friend, actor Will Geer of *The Waltons* fame. Hay had been active in the Communist Party in the 1930s and 1940s, during which time he had taught a music appreciation class at the California Labor College for workers. During our conversations, Hay remembered that he had donated two discs among a larger of collection of commercial 78-rpm phonographs to the Southern California Library for Social Studies and Research several years prior. Hay said he had hung onto them from Guthrie's stay in Los Angeles and had played them for years for his students and at cocktail parties for members of the Los Angeles Left.[7] I trudged back to South Central and spent a few hours looking through stacks of dusty records.

There, lo and behold, I found two lacquer-covered aluminum discs, both adorned with bright orange labels emblazoned with the words "Presto U.S.A." The imprint referred to the Presto Recording Company, a New York–based manufacturer that in 1934 began making both the easy-to-use pregrooved lacquer-coated blank recording discs and schemata for building the Presto lathe, the large, heavy machine that cut the record. A few years later, Presto began mass-producing the lathes themselves because it turned out that most of their customers were not adept at building their own recording equipment. Once recorded, a Presto disc could be played on a standard 78-rpm phonograph player. This "instantaneous-recording" technology soon became the radio industry's standard way of recording broadcasts whether for future airplay or for archival and legal purposes. It also became a standard way for folklorists at institutions such as the Library of Congress to record folk songs. By the late 1930s, Presto had begun to produce less-expensive home versions of the recorders and discs.[8]

The Prestos I discovered were of this home-version variety, but, as I would later find out, they appear to have been cut by an expensive professional lathe that in the era would most likely be owned by a radio station or university. The titles to four songs were scratched into the lead out, the innermost grooves of each side of each disc, and, perhaps most tantalizingly, one of the lead outs also had the word "Woody" etched into it in a handprint that closely resembles Woody's writing among documents in the Library of Congress and the Woody Guthrie Archives.

The four songs on the Guthrie Prestos—"(Them) Big City Ways," "Skid Row (Serenade)," "Do Re Mi," and "Ain't Got No Home"—give us a glimpse into what Woody's Los Angeles radio program might have been like.

Woody began broadcasting in Los Angeles in 1937 as a belated and minor addition to his cousin Leon "Oklahoma Jack" Guthrie's program on radio station KFVD, which featured Oklahoma Jack's renditions of cowboy ballads made popular by Gene Autry and Ken Maynard. *The Oklahoma and Woody Show*, as they called it, was short lived. Oklahoma Jack realized the demanding unpaid schedule made it impossible to support his family and sought work elsewhere, later scoring a hit with western-swing version of Woody's "Oklahoma Hills."[9]

Woody, who had often been relegated to back-up harmonica and percussion on his cousin's show, then took the helm and convinced Maxine "Lefty Lou" Crissman, a neighbor, to accompany him on the newly renamed *Woody and Lefty Lou* show in 1938. Woody and Crissman favored the more folksy noncowboy fare, especially the music of the Carter Family. According to Crissman's accounts, the duo was fond of a brother-sister duet vocal style that gave their act a sweetly-harmonious, almost androgynous sound, with Woody on the guitar, mandolin, and mouth harp, and Crissman adding an element of plaintiveness with what Woody called her "most saddest high tenor." Searching for a label decades later, Crissman called it "river, mountain and gospel music."[10]

The fact that Crissman's vocals do not appear at all on the Prestos and the fact that the discs remained in Los Angeles under Hay's care, however, suggests that Woody recorded them during a final solo year as host of the *Woody, the Lone Wolf* program on KFVD in 1939, after Crissman and her family had moved to northern California, and before he moved to New York City in 1940. Indeed, the first of these songs, "Big City Ways," is recorded in his personal songbook as being written in early 1939, so it would seem unlikely they had been recorded before that date. It remains similarly unlikely that they had been recorded after his move to the East Coast given the West Coast theme of the first two songs and that their ultimate resting place remained in South Central Los Angeles.

In the four tracks that appear on the Prestos, we see elements of both Woody's *Woody and Lefty Lou* era, when he concentrated on marketing himself to fellow Dust Bowlers who had settled in the Los Angeles region with largely nonpolitical fare, and his more political *Woody, the Lone Wolf*, when he began to more firmly embrace unions and left-wing politics, linking the plight of his fellow Dust Bowl migrants with the hardships of other refugees.

Woody's banter at the beginning of first song, "Big City Ways," offers a glimpse of what his personality might have been on the air. His spoken introduction to the song seems unrehearsed and allows him to take a jab at the intellectual classes. "Here's a song . . . that's got sorta thee ay uh college education in it," he deadpans. Woody then notes that he wrote the song while he was observing "the *ways* of the big city," overemphasizing the second word of the phrase in an exaggerated drawl. His emphasis on the word sounds as though he is almost inviting listeners to envision him as a hick or a rube. Woody's rube shtick and anti-intellectualism, however, seems to be part of a façade he created for his public personality, somewhat similar to the deliberate misspellings and folk grammar he used in his journalism of the era. Although Woody never finished high school, he had spent hours in the county library back in Oklahoma reading and educating himself.[11] In Los Angeles, he read a wide variety of newspapers and was fond of quoting the poetry of twelfth-century Persian thinker Omar Khayyam.[12]

"Big City Ways," the song that follows this spoken introduction—one of two Presto songs that do not appear to have been rerecorded in later sessions—is set to the tune of the Delmore Brothers' "Brown's Ferry Blues," a popular hillbilly song of the era that Woody may have heard over the air or on phonograph. Still popular among bluegrass fans today, the Delmores had put their unique string-band style to work crafting "Brown's Ferry Blues" into an infectious spry song with slightly irreverent lyrics. Featuring Alton and Rabon Delmore's expert nasal harmonizing and guitar work, "Brown's Ferry Blues" seems to poke fun at the courting activities of the residents of a small township near their hometown in northern Alabama, depicting among other things a cuckolded "hard luck poppa" and two "old maids" whom the song suggests may be lesbians. On "Big City Ways," Woody takes the tune and the basic chorus—Lord, Lord, I got them Brown's Ferry blues"—and slows it down into a warning about the humiliations that rural families face in the big city. The finance company seems to wait outside the door ready to repossess the family's belongings, while "Brother" and "Sister" are coaxed by the city into making poor selections in their choice of mates. Even "Mother" is reduced to scrubbing a wealthy man's floor. The song does not present solutions like Woody's later compositions would. Nor does it suggest that the poor transplants should join unions or try to fight the finance companies. Instead, it offers a salve of grief in common, recognizing a need to document the indignities of big city life. Misery among company, it seems to say, is more easily endured.

Although the name of the city goes unmentioned, "Big City Ways" appears to be part of a larger group of typed and handwritten songs from this era in which Woody explores "Lost Angeles," a city plagued by significant problems—downtown traffic congestion, a corrupt jail system, greedy finance companies, overpopulated Skid Rows, and disease-ridden flophouses. The 1939 song "Los Angeles New Year's

Flood," for instance, chronicled a potentially preventable 1934 deluge that killed more than forty people, many residing in a poorly developed exurb near Tujunga populated by the unemployed and the working class.[13] Likewise, "Fire in Los Feliz Hills," also penned in 1939, honored twenty-nine unemployed county conservation corps workers who were burned to death in 1933 trying to defend Griffith Park and the surrounding expensive homes from a brushfire.[14] Other songs included in this group are the 1938 ballad "Downtown Traffic Blues," which complains about traffic and reckless drivers and "Lincoln Heights Jail"—set to the tune of the folk song "Crydersville Jail" and containing a lyric fragment that may extend as far back as the Civil War—which warns drivers against speeding lest they end up in the "lousy" downtown L.A. jail.[15] In such other songs as "Fifth Street Blues" and "Hungry Hotel," Woody painted gritty portraits of homelessness, unsanitary conditions, and flophouse living, while making specific references to Los Angeles landmarks that his listeners would have known.[16]

In "Big City Ways," Woody does not complain about the authorities as he does in "Lincoln Heights Jail." He instead envisions the urban landscape as a place filled with uncontrolled materialism and distorted morals that seem to have their own logic and cruelty. Woody made similar critiques in his nonmusical writing. Turning the Southern California citrus orchard motif on its head, Woody argued in the side notes of one songbook that the "Big City" was "like a bunch of warts on yer hide, formin' and growin' like bacteria on an orange, and a spreadin' its racket and noise and greed and heartbreaks and selfishness in every direction."[17] Woody also seems to be tailoring the politics of the song to a wider and possibly more liberal audience. In two versions of "Big City Ways" (one hand-printed and another typed) from his personal songbooks from the era, he includes a line that seems to suggests that the song's working class protagonists are loafing while working for government relief with the Works Progress Administration— waking up only to eat.[18] On the Presto version of the song, however, the message is more in line with the New Deal ideology and the protagonist more industrious, tragically losing his job on the WPA perhaps because of a cut in federal funding.

There is also something eerily conventional about the gender politics of "Big City Ways," in that its women seem either predatory or in need of protection; it is not exactly the kind of verse one would find in later, more feminist songs such as "Union Maid." Yes, "the working man he gets run down," but the narrator also complains that Sister "married a gigolo honey" and that "Brother's a-payin' alimoney." It appears that his views of women's roles in the world, like his attitudes about race, were an evolving matter.

Neither the Dust Bowl migration, nor the Okies that came with it, are mentioned in "Big City Ways," but the song's theme of rural-to-urban migration appears to be just the sort of material that Woody and Crissman had sought out for the *Woody and Lefty Lou* program. The pair had tried to reach out to fellow migrants from Oklahoma, Texas, and surrounding states by talking wistfully offering romanticized portraits of the life in the Plains before the Depression and singing such songs as "Dust Bowl Blues," which joked about how "thousands" of feet of dust buried one farmer's tractor and, later, his sweetheart.[19] Although it is difficult to reconstruct the full details of the *Woody and Lefty Lou* audience, surviving evidence suggests that much of the duo's mail came from Dust Bowlers. Of some eighty-one names and addresses on a 1939 handwritten inventory of incoming fan mail, more than a quarter either resided in areas of heavy migrant settlement such as South Gate, Lynwood, and Downey, or used nicknames and pseudonyms such as "Tex" or "Oklahoma Cowgirl" that suggested they originated in the greater Dust Bowl region.[20] Other accounts seem to concur. *The Hollywood Tribune*, for instance, reported that Woody's fan mail came from mostly "Okies and Arkies," while fellow KFVD broadcaster Ed Robbin remembered that write-in listeners were mostly blue-collar workers and the unemployed: "The people who listened to him were the people he sang about, his own people, the Okies."[21]

The second song on the Prestos, "Skid Row (Serenade)," depicts a skid row on Hollywood Boulevard, a place that, along with Fifth and Main in downtown Los Angeles, was populated by hundreds if not thousands of homeless people in the late 1930s. The song is, in many ways, a novelty number that uses rhyme and wordplay to poke fun at how one might "skid around" on Skid Row. But it also has a serious side, drawing stark contrasts between the down-and-out residents of Hollywood Boulevard and the more well-heeled pedestrians of other parts of town. As the song continues, it begins formulating something akin to a political position. "My senator," Woody sings on the Presto, "sent me down on the Skid Row." We are not told exactly what policies were enacted or how the senator managed to leave the narrator homeless, nor are we necessarily told how to alleviate the poverty that creates conditions, but Woody, for the first time in recorded song, seems to be laying blame at the political structure.

Woody was well versed on the conditions on Hollywood Boulevard, having published columns in the *Hollywood Tribune* describing skid rows on both Fifth Street and Hollywood Boulevard in 1939. In these pieces, he took pains to depict the dirtiness and bleak grayness of Skid Row and to describe how police were out to pick up residents on trumped-up charges of vagrancy. In cartoon panels that Woody drew to illustrate the story, he included such captions as "Fast Cops and Slow Tranes Put me on the Skid Row!" and "Fast Wimmin & Slow Hosses Put Me on Skid Row!" suggesting that police and railroad security guards, unfaithful and promiscuous women, and gambling on horses races were major causes of the plight of the homeless.[22]

Woody later reused the tune to "Skid Row" for more solemn purposes in the 1940 song "Slipknot (Hangknot, Slipknot)," an anti-lynching song which Seth Archer eloquently argues may have been an attempt on Woody's part to document the 1911 lynchings of Laura Nelson and her teenaged son, L.D., in Woody's hometown of Okemah, Oklahoma. Archer postulates that Woody's father, a rabidly anti-socialist Southern Democrat who appears to have been involved in the local Klan, may have been involved in those killings of an African American mother and son.[23] Although not born yet, Woody later memorialized the lynching of the Nelsons in a note at the bottom of the "Slipknot" where he dedicated it to "negro mothers, fathers, and sons" who were hung under a bridge of the Canadian River near Okemah. "[T]his note," Archer argued, "jotted at the bottom of a mediocre folk song was a step, as I see it, toward his becoming the Woody Guthrie America knows and loves."[24]

Archer suggests that Woody may have picked up the tune among "the many 'hangman' blues songs" he heard along the road, but its earlier appearance as the tune of "Skid Row" complicates that. If indeed it was based on a blues, Woody appears to have first toyed with using it in "Skid Row" in a half-serious way to document homelessness, before slowing it down, spacing out his vocal delivery, and applying it ultimately to one of his more well-remembered numbers about racial violence. I can't help but be struck by the thought that rather than a blues, the "Slipknot"/"Skid Row" tune may simply be a variation of the well-known and often parodied "She'll Be Coming Around the Mountain"/"When the Chariot Comes" song family, which has its roots in black spirituals.

The third track on the Prestos, "Do Re Mi," is most likely the oldest of the four. Woody did not record the dates he penned "Skid Row" and "Ain't Got No Home," but attributes "Big City Ways" to dates in both January and February 1939 in separate notebooks. "Do Re Mi" however, was first printed on *Woody and Lefty Lou's Favorite Collection of Old Time Hill Country Songs,* the program's only professionally printed and commercially available songbook in 1937. The song would later be rerecorded on Woody's first commercial release in 1940, the *Dust Bowl Ballads* album.[25]

Much has been written about "Do Re Mi," and its appearance on *Dust Bowl Ballads* has guaranteed that it remains the most widely known of the four tracks, but it must be pointed out that the song focuses much more explicitly on the Dust Bowl migration than the first two tracks. Here Woody uses the tune of the 1908 Tin Pan Alley number "Hang Out Your Front Door Key" to reveal himself as the ferocious defender of his Okie kindred. Unlike the final song of the four, "Ain't Got No Home," which seems to focus on the most desperate of Dust Bowl migrants, this song focused on relatively more comfortable, land-owning migrants, warning them against selling off the farm. California was after all no "garden of Eden." "Do Re Mi" reserved its ire for its Californians: the LAPD officers who were sent unconstitutionally to the Arizona border in 1936 to bar Dust Bowl migrants such as Woody entry into California. In the song, the border guards bark out statistics—"You're number 14,000 for today!"—that reduce migrants to an impersonal number among the multitudes. Woody's experience with the LAPD's "foreign legion," however, was vicarious at best because he had not entered California until a year after the checkpoint was dismantled. Woody most likely read of the blockade in the press. His willingness to challenge authorities and the police, however, apparently put him on a track toward more politicized offerings.[26]

The ballad, which appeared in print more than a year before the appearance of Steinbeck's *The Grapes of Wrath* and several months before the novelist's political pamphlet on the Okies, proves overwhelmingly that Woody was not merely a clever musical emulator who drew from Steinbeck's literary depictions of migrants, as some have argued, but had developed an independent, humorous, and yet potent early critique of the injustice suffered by migrants when Los Angeles police attempted to blockade state borders.[27]

The final song, "Ain't Got No Home," depicts the same Dust Bowl migrant, but now at a much more desperate stage, that of a sharecropper reduced to an itinerant "wandering worker." Like "Do Re Mi," it too takes aim at the police for singling out the most desperate. The song may in fact reflect the real observations Woody made in late 1938 when he was asked by KFVD's liberal owner, J. Frank Burke Sr., to serve as "special hobo correspondent" for the Democratic-aligned newspaper *Light*. In one article, Woody argued that railroad guards and police harassed the "starvation armies of wandering workers" by callously ordering stowaway passengers to get off boxcars in the middle of the scorching Mojave desert in late summer. "I saw one bunch—two married couples, two soldiers, and two others—on the outskirts of Needles [California] head into the oven of the desert on their way home," he wrote. Other migrants feared being arrested for idleness or vagrancy because local authorities marched them "almost chain gang style to the bean patch to work without pay."[28] Changed by the experience, Woody not only talked about their plight on the radio but also began to write about them in his "Cornbread Philosophy" and "Woody Sez" columns in local liberal and radical newspapers, using humor and a not-too-transparent emulation of liberal Oklahoma humorist Will Rogers to counter negative stereotypes and publicize the bleakness of migrant life.[29]

This song suggests that Woody had come to terms with what demographers were noticing: The average agricultural migrant was not a farmer who had been booted from the land, but a family of itinerant farmworkers who had been unable to find work. This situation that may have been caused by the drought and drop in farm commodity prices, but was aggravated by the Agricultural Adjustment Agency's policy of trying to raise crop prices by paying farm owners to keep land fallow. "By 1940, the region's tenant population had been reduced by 24 percent, headed towards an even bigger reduction in the following decade," wrote historian James N. Gregory in his analysis of the situation.[30]

Although none of the final three Presto songs endorse specific policies or political movements, they criticize authorities in a way that "Big City Ways" does not. They certainly point toward a more substantial political activism that eschews simple documentation of indignities and injustices. They also point to the gradual, uneven way in which Woody's political outlook had transformed between the initial publication of "Do Re Mi" in a commercially published radio songbook in 1938 and the recording of the Presto, likely in mid-to-late 1939. By late 1939, Woody had extended a hand to the "people's politics" of organized labor, publicly pledging his support for striking Northern California dam workers while performing at fund-raisers for motion-picture unions, rallies for CIO farm and cannery locals, and a few marches for the unemployed Workers Alliance. Taking a cue from some of the more radical members of organized labor and the Los Angeles left, Woody also promoted an emergency nationalization of some types of industrial property.[31] By the time he signed off of his last broadcast of *Woody, the Lone Wolf*, most likely in late 1939, Woody was advocating "Production for Use," a program once espoused by the EPIC movement and the liberal Utopian lodges in which idle factories would be seized by the state and returned to production, thereby employing the jobless.[32] He had come full circle from simply being interested in documenting the plight of migrants to taking political stances that, if made policy, involved profound transformations of the economic system.

The existence of the Prestos themselves suggest that Woody harbored a complicated attitude about the role of commercialization in his music while in Los Angeles. Initially, Hay had described the Prestos as "radio air checks," which were made by recording Woody on the air. Michael Kieffer, a vintage recording expert who helped secure recordings of the discs for their release on the Grammy-nominated release *Woody at 100: Woody Guthrie Centennial Collection* (Smithsonian Folkways 2012), doubts that. He argues that the relatively high quality of the recordings suggests they were not recorded from a broadcast signal, but may have instead been recorded in a booth, producing a sort of a demo that Woody might have used to get the attention of broadcasters and record companies. Indeed, considering the technology at the time and the haphazard way these discs were preserved, there is relatively little pop and hiss on the tracks. Furthermore, Alan Graves, an expert on the Presto recording company, argues that these discs were likely cut by radio-studio staff using a heavy, professional-level Presto lathe because of the neat way the machine handled the lead outs. The tracks appear, however, he noted, on the Orange Seal Presto disc, discs that were primarily produced for home, rather than commercial, use. Blank Orange Seal discs were the less-expensive, second-choice option for Presto users—of lesser quality than the company's top-of-the-line Green Seal discs but of higher quality than its Blue Label and Monogram product lines.[33]

Graves also noted that many broadcasters made "line checks" rather than "air checks" by simply recording the Prestos directly through the radio station microphone while a performer was broadcasting rather than transcribing them as a signal off the air. Ultimately, this presents three possible scenarios, with each equally plausible:

a) Woody snuck into the KFVD studio and recorded his own demo with his own discs using KFVD's equipment. (Free spirit that he was, Woody was certainly not above such antics.)

b) Woody recorded them with permission from the station owner without broadcasting.

c) Woody recorded them from an internal line in the station while broadcasting.

The latter choice is perhaps the least compelling largely because only "Big City Ways" includes introductory chatter that one would expect on a live radio program, and all four tracks fit so nicely within the specified length of the ten-inch disc.

So what then about the purpose? Did Woody record these discs because he was trying to get the attention of broadcasters or record companies? In his biography of Woody, Ed Cray notes Woody's excitement in 1938 when the sponsors of the Chicago *National Barn Dance*, a prominent hillbilly program akin to Nashville's *Grand Ole Opry*, expressed interest in having Woody and Lefty Lou on that program. That performance never happened for reasons that have not been entirely explained.[34]

Perhaps Woody was hoping to make a second stab at a national commercial radio career by cutting the four songs on these discs? We may never know, but it is intriguing to consider whether he might have been pitching them around in an effort to launch a commercial hillbilly career.

This then presents a dilemma of a commercial Woody Guthrie cutting a demo and shopping it around while also remaining a fierce critic of the commercial recording industry in his journalism. In his newspaper columns, Woody vehemently chastised the recording industry as "the Monopoly on Music" and openly worried that "fonograft records" might replace live musicians at "saloons and radeo stations."[35] In fact, at the bottom of one song in *Woody and Lefty Lou's Favorite Collection* songbook, he penned a note that went so far as to swear off his own right to copyright as well:

> This song is copyrighted by us. And if we ketch you a-singin' it, we'll shake yore hand like never before.'Cause anybody we ketch a-stealin' our material, we figger they must like it, so that's what we want. We don't care who sings it, swings [it], yodels it, warbles it, or uses it to start a fire with. We wrote it, that's all we wanted to do.

Woody ended the note by paraphrasing Scottish patriot Andrew Fletcher: "They once was a feller that said: Let me write a nation's songs, I don't care who makes their laws."[36]

Indeed, taken at surface value, his arguments about the music industry in his columns and published songbook placed him in line with a group of fiercely conservative contemporaries, the Vanderbilt Agrarians, a group of Southern intellectuals who in many ways laid the groundwork for modern conservatism's criticisms of Hollywood and popular culture. In fact, Woody's worry that live performance was being steamrolled by recordings and his disregard for copyright law echoed those of the ultraconservative Agrarian professor and poet Donald Davidson, who argued that true regional performers "must let go, must set no copyright claim" and must instead let their works be carried on by "whoever would like it, for what it is worth."[37]

And yet despite the fierceness of his statements, Woody may indeed, through the 1939 Prestos, been courting the same industry he so ferociously lambasted. Was it desperation? A need to support his family? Was he caving in? Rather than straightforward hypocrisy, perhaps Woody was figuring out how one could be both a working, paycheck-receiving artist and a critic of commercial consolidation at the same time? Ultimately, I suppose, these are questions that all artists must face. Davidson had the luxury of not having to make his living by making music. Woody did not.

Perhaps more than anything, Woody's oldest-known recordings compel us to ask more nuanced questions about an intriguing figure who still looms large in American culture. What compelled Woody to take a political path to songwriting by 1939? Was it merely his experience of covering the plight of migrants in the desert or was there more? How can a supposedly committed partisan of the Left like Woody hold positions nearly identical to those on the Right? How does a performer balance a desire to make truthful art with the need to support a family? The Presto recordings don't provide us with tidy, concrete answers to any of these. The four songs, their messages, and the very existence of the Prestos, instead, capture a singular moment in time when a complicated figure was trying to cope with some pretty complicated issues.

Five

WOODY'S LOS ANGELES EDITORIAL CARTOONS

TIFFANY COLANNINO

Although best known for his songwriting, Woody Guthrie is also an accomplished visual artist whose interest in painting and illustration predates his career as a folk musician. In high school, Woody was the jokes editor for his Okemah, Oklahoma, high-school yearbook, where he drew animated cartoon figures, the earliest-known examples of his artwork. Woody then took up sign painting, earning a meager living painting bold signs for grocers, soda fountains, and local shops.

Only after he lost his brushes while hitchhiking to California did Woody turn to the guitar as a serious source of income. He reasoned that that he could sell a drawing once, but a song could be offered over and over again.

Woody's approach to artwork was constantly in flux. He created simple doodles and elaborate oil-on-canvas paintings, tender charcoal sketches and fantastical oversized watercolor works, as well as fun colorful drawings using his children's crayons and art supplies. Woody left behind over one thousand pieces of artwork, which provide a visual record of his life. He illustrated his autobiographical novel *Bound for Glory* with drawings capturing his childhood in Oklahoma and his journey to California. He drew portraits of his Almanac Singers bandmates in New York City, and of his children growing up in Coney Island. Woody's *At-Sea* illustrations, from his days as a merchant marine, provide a unique glimpse into life on a World War II cargo ship. And his later sketches show the deteriorating effects of Huntington's disease on his ability to write and draw.

Dating to 1938, the *Los Angeles Editorial Cartoons* are Woody's earliest known series of artwork, a collection that has quite surprisingly survived in pristine condition. The bulk of Woody's known archival materials were collected during his time in New York City; however, the two blue, spiral-bound composition notebooks containing the editorial cartoons drawn in Southern California were created several years before Woody arrived in New York. No one knows if the notebooks traveled with him as he hitchhiked his way cross-country, or if they were forwarded by family, friends, or even a proactive Woody, himself. Except for a handful of pieces that predate this New York period, these rare cartoons are the earliest examples of his original style as a visual artist and provide insights into his use of artwork to share information.

The strong, bold fonts; clean, crisp lines; and simple, clear graphics he chose for these editorial cartoons reflect Woody's experience as a sign painter. The form and style of the cartoons vary dramatically throughout the notebooks. Some contain elaborate coloring, while others are composed solely with pen and ink. It is unclear whether there was an intended audience for these pieces. Through research, it appears that none of the pieces were contemporarily published. However, after their creation, Woody went on to compose editorial cartoons in a similar style for several newspapers, including the *Hollywood Tribune*, the *Daily Worker*, and the *People's World*.

The survival of these notebooks shows us that they were personally important to Woody, and may have acted as his portfolio, showing a variety of examples of editorial cartooning styles.

Visually appealing, Woody's L.A. works show the impact of editorial cartoonists. These cartoons are of multilayered importance to researchers today. Through his remarkable ability to succinctly describe a situation, express his opinions, and encourage others to do so, these cartoons provide insight into his view of Los Angeles of his day. At a broader level, they also provide unique primary-source material that chronicles localized Los Angeles politics in the 1930s.

However local by inspiration, these topical cartoons focus on subject matter that is of national importance, topics that editorial artists still confront at the top of every news cycle, as well as problems their readers still face daily as unfortunate facts of life: mortgage foreclosures, inadequate family housing, unsatisfactory old-age pensions, corrupt politics, and denied civil liberties. Although this selection of cartoons captures Woody's view of his world in the late 1930s, he speaks out on topics Americans battled then and still battle in a century he never knew.

Opposite: Woody endorses reformer Fletcher Bowron, who was elected mayor of Los Angeles in 1938 in the aftermath of City Hall scandals that forced the recall of Mayor Frank Shaw.

Woody is radicalizing before our eyes. Drawn without mouths, Civil Rights is mute behind bars, guarded by a gun-toting thug answering to the government.

Elected governor of California in 1939, Culbert Olson stood atop a reform ticket
that Woody wondered might be longer on rhetoric than action.

THE OLD MAN OF THE MOUNTAINS

With Los Angeles City Hall in the background, Woody draws a classical Diogenes-like figure to usher reform Mayor Fletcher Bowron to his new task.

Woody knew that many a farmer did not own his land. As he sang in protest, heavily mortgaged land rendered farmers more vulnerable to banks and politicians unlikely to sympathize with their Depression plight.

OLD POLITICAL MACHINERY

"ALL THINGS ARE
TRANSIENT, FLEETING,
AND DESTINED TO PASS
AWAY"———————"BUDDHA".

Quoting Buddha, Woody suggests an inevitable and evolutionary transition in politics,
wherein "old political machinery" would fall to rust and disuse.

Woody wonders how long Los Angeles Mayor Fletcher Bowron will stay in office, given the challenges he'll face after being elected.
A long time, it turned out; Bowron served four terms. He reformed City Hall and the LAPD,
but he also pushed for the internment of Japanese and Japanese Americans following the bombing of Pearl Harbor.

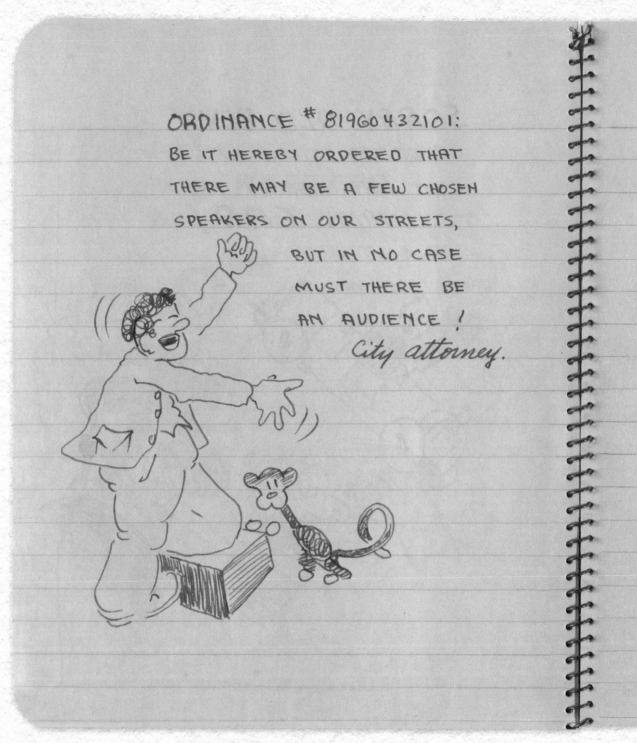

Woody lampoons Los Angeles laws restricting rights of assembly and free speech.

In one of Woody's most interesting cartoons from the California years,
he is angry about environmental degradation, and he blames politicians and their politics.

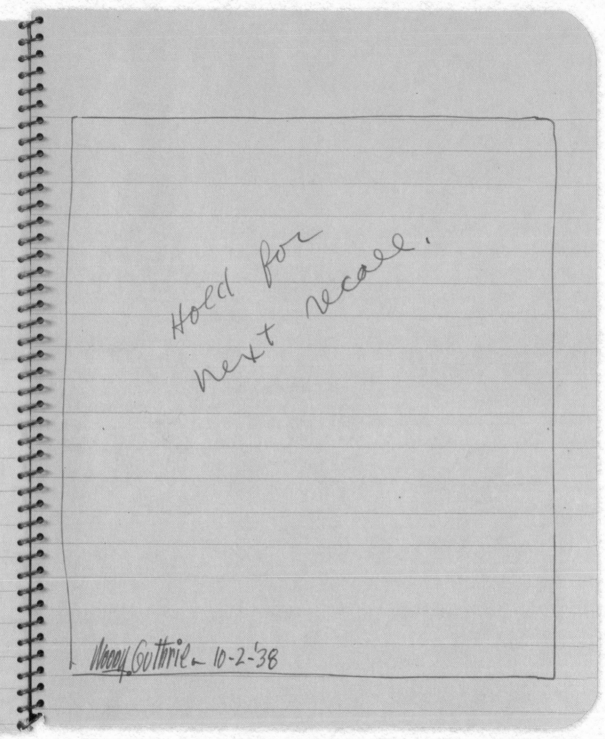

Hold for
next recall.

Woody Guthrie — 10-2-'38

This is what Woody wrote on the back of his ledger book on October 2, 1938, only two weeks after
Los Angeles Mayor Frank Shaw had been recalled. Other political figures would descend into corruption or ineffectiveness,
Woody assumed. But using their recall tool, the people could act.

Captioned in Okie vernacular, the cartoon shows a farm couple looking quizzically
at the fight that's broken out over "the interests" battling for their land and livelihood.

LITTLE COUNTRY CHURCH OF HOLLYWOOD, CAL.

Six

IN THE SHADOW OF THE STEEPLE
I SAW MY PEOPLE

PHILIP GOFF

In his most famous song, Woody Guthrie claimed that it was in the shadow of the steeple that he saw his people. At no moment was that truer than when he arrived in Los Angeles in May 1937. There he joined a migration from the western South—Oklahoma, Arkansas, Texas, and parts of Missouri and Louisiana—hit hard by the double fists of Depression and Dust Bowl. Wonderfully documented in Darren Dochuk's award-winning book, *From Bible Belt to Sunbelt*, these "plain folk" began arriving in Southern California in the 1920s, when more than 250,000 moved to the Golden State. That number escalated sharply during the troubled 1930s. According to Dochuk, when it came to faith, "The relative absence of . . . top-down authority permitted a purer populist doctrine that combined radical individualism, experimentation, and egalitarianism with a willingness to unite in protection of their interests."[171] It would prove to be a migration that changed the very nature of religion and politics in Southern California.

Woody arrived and settled in with relatives and old family friends, taking odd jobs and picking up evening nickel-and-dime gigs in smoky bars when he could. Oddly, he found himself not just in competition with singing cowboys and troubadours of the developing country and western sound, he also had religious competition. In fact, religious programming in 1930s Los Angeles, before it was segregated to its own stations, played an immense role in shaping the popular radio market, a market Woody hoped to break into with his folk sound of ballads and old gospel songs. His interaction with religious radio in Los

Angeles in 1937 and 1938 helped to radicalize his message and music during the explosive period when lyrics dripped unimpeded from his revolutionary mind to the typewriter keys.

Woody came by his religious interests honestly. Raised in the fluid world of populist Protestantism that effortlessly mixed homespun music and Democratic religious experience, Woody had plenty of Dust Bowl religion to draw from. Jesus was ubiquitous in the culture and appeared in many ways—not just in church sermons but also in popular songs, on funeral parlor hand fans, needlepoints hanging in the living room, and in the large portraits Woody painted of him (and Abraham Lincoln) out in the garage. Jesus as the Good Shepherd, the Suffering Servant, the Healer, and the Coming King greeted Okies at every turn. And with the radically individualized religious expression of the region, people mixed and matched their Jesus with various clusters of other practices and currents of thought.

For instance, Jeffrey Guthrie, Woody's uncle who fancied himself a faith healer, combined Protestant revivalist tradition with New Thought philosophy first popularized by Viennese physician Franz Mesmer and then introduced it to the rest of the family. Many nineteenth-century American religious leaders— Phineas Quimby, Mary Baker Eddy, Charles and Myrtle Fillmore—followed in Mesmer's train, creating a long line of what historians refer to as the harmonial tradition, a cluster of principles that, when applied to one's life, would result in this-worldly benefits, including physical healing, psychological well-being, and perhaps even financial success.[1] There were many religious iterations of this broad philosophy. What caught Uncle Jeff's fancy was Robert Collier's *The Secret of the Ages*. Initially published as seven booklets, Collier's writings appeared as one volume in 1926. Emphasizing a "Universal Mind" shared by all things, it wrapped many familiar characters and stories from the Bible with other religions of the world and various "scientific" claims about the nature of reality. Eventually Woody's stepmother, Betty Jean, also bought into this mingling of Christianity and harmonial positive thought, opening her own clinic for sick souls. Soon thereafter, Woody painted a placard outside his place announcing "Faith Healing, Mind Reading, No Charge" and jokingly referred to himself as "Alonzo M. Zilch." With shoulder-length hair, he spent seven months in 1935 healing people with a mixture of Bible beliefs and positive thinking. It was, as he later recalled, "the superstitious business."[2]

This public performance of religion—or superstition—that Guthrie played with shortly before his westward migration to California was not without a more traditional grounding. He had previously befriended the Reverend Eulys McKenzie, pastor in the Church of Christ denomination, who loved country music. On a continuum of strict Protestant fundamentalist sects in the western South, the Church of Christ was near the furthest reaches of severity. So literal was their reading of scripture that they banned musical instruments as modernist additions that watered down the pure gospel: musical instruments are not mentioned in the New Testament. But Reverend McKenzie loved country music, and he loved the Guthries, even acting as their announcer when Jeff and Allene Guthrie pulled radio time in Amarillo, Texas. McKenzie kept watch on Woody's soul, eventually persuading him to be baptized into the Church of Christ and to begin studying the Bible closely for himself. While Woody's membership eventually lapsed, his love for the Bible—its stories, proverbs, images, and most importantly, its Savior—never did.[3]

Soon after Woody arrived in California, he connected with his cousin Jack and moved to Los Angeles so they could try their luck at breaking into the singing-cowboy acts that deluged the city. With the recent success of Gene Autry and Roy Rogers, Jack believed there was money to be made in playing the part of a western troubadour and Woody acting as the "Okie" country singer. With so little money to be made in a highly competitive radio market, Jack figured they could simply use the medium to land paying gigs singing in venues that aligned with their music. "You see," he reportedly told his partner, "you can get more jobs at saloons, churches and markets if you've got a radio program every day."[4] His plan was sound. All three of those settings rarely competed with each other's schedules: markets did most of their business during the day, saloons in the evening, and churches on Sunday mornings, when neither markets or saloons were allowed to open their doors.

Despite the unevenness of the duo—Woody never cared for the singing or playing style of his fancy-dressed cowboy cousin—by July, they won fifteen-minute time slots on KFVD at 8:00 a.m. and 11:00 p.m. In order to play more of the old gospel and "heart songs" of the Dust Bowl alongside the ballads Jack preferred, Woody invited Maxine Crissman to join the act, at least on a limited basis. The Crissmans, old Guthrie family friends, had enjoyed Woody and Jack singing for fun at their home in Glendale since they arrived in Los Angeles. Once Woody discovered how well his sound meshed with Crissman's, he longed to sing the old songs with her rather than continue backing up Jack. He got his wish in September when Jack quit and moved back north. The station, meanwhile, so pleased with the number of letters gushing over Woody and Crissman (called "Lefty Lou from Old Mizzou" on the program), offered the two a contract for the morning and evening shows.

Gone were the cowboy songs, replaced by hymns and gospel tunes, hillbilly songs, and old-time ballads. Listener letters extolled the songs long-lost since youth, songs that "reminded them of distant homes, of Saturday-night church socials, and Sunday-morning church services."[5] The show attracted a loyal audience, removed from all they had known and loved back in the South and Midwest. "It floats me away from these hectic days of rush and heartache and jazz into a green valley of rest and peace," wrote one person. "I have never heard any program like it—two perfectly blended voices, quiet, restful, unpretentious, singing sweet old melodies of the past, to me, alone." Beyond the songs, listeners appreciated the down-home conversation on the program. "Would love to have both of you out to a chicken dinner. We are just plain Texas people—your talk gives us a thrill, and those beautiful songs." Or, as another put it, "We sure love to hear Lefty Lou laugh—it sounds just like I think people laugh in heaven."[6] It didn't hurt matters that the station-owner's wife was particularly fond of the old hymns and gospel songs the duo sang.[7]

Mixing such genres as country humor, lines from joke books, religious language, superstitious assumptions, and biting observation of recent events, Woody played to an audience well versed in the practice of populist syncretism. The show included a recurring segment called "Cornpone Philosophy" in which he asked listeners to send in the biggest lies they'd heard, their favorite tornado stories, or the best miracle stories. Once he read off a list of thirty-five sorts of miracle stories they might consider—messages that came to them, how faith got them a job or out of trouble, how God causes strange things to happen.[8] Many on the list are reminiscent of the Christian positive thought that Woody had practiced on others back in Texas shortly before moving to California.

In all, Woody situated his show at the heart of "his people"—not in the pew, but in the shadow of the steeple. He played with religion much the way he had as Alonzo M. Zilch two years earlier, but radio gave him the medium to do much more. Mixing and matching genres, styles, and messages as needed for the moment, he turned on and off his rural accent to attract audiences and speak to them about the troubles that surrounded and, too often, defined their lives.

But Woody was not alone in this type of performance, part religious and part entertainment. Two religious radio programs are of interest here, for they held local and eventually national attention because of the style and sentiment they put forward in their music, homespun humor, and nostalgic religious messages. Most importantly, both of these shows shared the same quartet, a group that reworked and repopularized a song that both infuriated and inspired Woody to sharpen his message through music.

The first program, the *Little Country Church,* had its roots, as one might expect, in the country. Its founder, William B. Hogg, was a rural Arkansas minister who, as a chaplain in France during World War I, entertained wounded soldiers with the sound of hoofbeats from his hollow hands and down-home tales that comforted the young men far from home. After a stint in late-1920s Chicago with religious-radio pioneer Paul Rader, during which Hogg developed the radio character of a simple, rural preacher interested in common-sense religious values, Hogg moved to Los Angeles. There he was coupled with a city filling with rural folk seeking work and at the cutting edge of radio, the new technology that could reach both the literate and the illiterate.

In 1933, Hogg sold an idea for a show to station KFAC. It would be an entertaining and uplifting program that would evoke happy memories, feelings of bygone days for those rural folk who now struggled to fit in and find acceptance in Los Angeles. The music would be fun, soothing, and optimistic, not dull and dreary-sounding "church music." Likewise, the skits would be humorous as well as moralistic.

But Hogg did not rely merely on his own abilities. He wisely employed several talented musicians who collectively became the Goose Creek Quartet, one of the top groups in a city increasingly built on entertainment. With Rudy Atwood at piano and bassist Thurl Ravenscroft (later the voice of Tony the Tiger and the resonant bass who sang the theme song for *The Grinch Who Stole Christmas*), Hogg led a fifteen-minute broadcast each morning full of uplifting gospel music, funny stories, and homespun religious messages. Set in an imaginary rural town where neighbors knew one another, cared for one another, and helped each other through crises, Hogg posed as Parson Josiah Hopkins, his wife played Sarah Hopkins, and Atwood and the quartet sang, played the parts of town folk, and created sound effects of horses, buggies, and various farm animals. The program was such a huge success throughout the city that the program went national through syndication on the CBS network in April 1934.[9]

Each program ran according to a set script. The quartet sang the first verse of "Come to the Church in the Wildwood," a favorite among displaced conservative Protestants who pined for the old days. Then, Strollin' Tom, played by Ravenscroft, welcomed the listeners by describing the rural town and the church's central position. He then directed the audience to listen in on the conversation of Josiah and Sarah Hopkins in their buggy as the couple talked about recent problems in the village on their way to church. They might stop to talk with others about topics that would then show up in the Parson's short message, followed by a few songs by the Goose Creek Quartet.

It was a combination that resonated with Okies and other rural southerners now living in Los Angeles. In one example, replicated many times over, Parson Josiah Hopkins and his wife ("Sister Sarah") discussed country-related topics in a confused fashion that coyly overlapped with social and political issues.

> Sarah: Josiah, what is your favorite preserve?
> Josiah: Mine?
> Sarah: Um-hum.
> Josiah: Oh, well, raspberry jam is mighty good.
> Sarah: Heh-heh!
> Josiah: And you know plums ain't bad.
> Sarah: No—
> Josiah: Watermelon rind, too, that's another one of my favorites.

Sarah: Yes, that's good.

Josiah: But, honey, you know the gov'nment is getting out a new kind?

Sarah: The government?!

Josiah: Yes sir! I reckon they give 'em away sorta like they do garden feed.

Sarah: Well, what kind of preserves is the government givin' away? I hadn't heard about 'em.

Josiah: Forest Preserves!

Sarah: Oh! Ha ha ha! Where did you get that idea, Josiah?

Josiah: Well, when we was all talkin' about it there in Lige Guyton's shoe shop.

Sarah: They was?

Josiah: Yes, they was! And I see they put up a thing over there at the post office, some sort of a showin' about the gov'ment furnishing forest preserves.

Sarah: Hmm-hmm?

Josiah: Yeh, and Bill Evans says that he thinks that the forest preserves is a mixture of all the sorts of wild berries that grow in the woods.

Sarah: You know it might be that!

Josiah: Yeah, it might be. But [unintelligible], he thinks that—akerns! You know, oak tree akerns? Put up some sort of way. But, law me, I says, you never could make no preserves that suit my tastes out of akerns.

Sarah: Nah.[10]

Although the program remained on a national CBS hookup only briefly, its ability to speak to Southern and Midwestern migrants in Southern California kept it on the air locally for years. In fact, the show played so well locally that many listeners began to clamor for a real "Little Country Church" to attend—one that replicated the imaginary rural oasis they escaped to each morning with Josiah and Sarah Hopkins, and the Goose Creek Quartet. Soon they procured property on Argyle Street and created the "Little Country Church of Hollywood," replete with meandering sidewalks and climbing rose vines and a full-service radio studio inside the building. What had been merely a broadcast that appealed to distant memories became in fact a church congregation, seeking to recreate an imagined, or at least, a highly-sentimentalized past.[11]

Meanwhile, although he'd been toiling away in Los Angeles radio longer than Hogg, businessman-turned-radio preacher Charles E. Fuller would eventually reach a much larger audience. He accomplished this by assuming some of the approaches of the *Little Country Church* into his own show's rise to success in the mid-1930s. After experimenting with various programs since his initial broadcast in 1925—including Bible studies, prophecy studies, and children's programming—Fuller settled on a format that sounded like an old-fashioned revival though it was beamed from Hollywood's KNX studio. With a look and sound similar to Will Rogers and a more comforting form of evangelization than his revivalist competitors, Fuller and his quartet were a huge hit in California and across the western states. Hundreds of thousands of letters arrived, many from rural migrants. In 1937, just as Woody Guthrie began his radio work in Los Angeles, Fuller parlayed his radio and live service success into a deal with the fledgling Mutual Broadcasting System on fourteen stations from Los Angeles and San Francisco to Chicago. The *Old Fashioned Revival Hour* then made the jump to a skeleton coast-to-coast network of thirty Mutual stations that October, a month after Guthrie brought in Crissman to his station-KFVD program.[12]

Country and folk music, old-fashioned gospel songs, and nostalgia were the rage on L.A. radio in the Fall of 1937. Fuller pushed to dominate the local market and position his program at the center of the Venn Diagram of evangelicalism—where hardcore Biblicist fundamentalists, experience-based Pentecostals, and populist traditional Protestants who sinned on Saturday night but repented on Sunday morning overlapped. To do this, he needed the right music, so he raided the Goose Creek Quartet of the *Little Country Church* program. By putting together a more professional set of musicians to appeal to a broader audience, the newly fashioned *Old Fashioned Revival Hour* made its schedule on Mutual, paying one week at a time. By 1944, the show ran on 575 stations and short-wave bands around the world and boasted twenty million domestic listeners.[13]

Guthrie's arrival in Los Angeles and his foray into radio corresponded to the popularity of the *Little Country Church* and the rise of the *Old Fashioned Revival Hour*. They were not just two popular programs in Los Angeles during Guthrie's time there, they were also direct competitors for the religious audience he sought to attract to his program through gospel songs and hymns in the hope of getting invitations to sing in their churches and at their church functions. Saloons were not open on Sunday mornings—and this was his chance to pick up much-needed cash at an hour when other venues were closed. The letters to Woody and Lefty Lou clearly indicate they appealed to the very same audiences as the *Old Fashioned Revival Hour* and the *Little Country Church*. They shared songs, good-natured stories, and nostalgia.

To some, it might seem odd to see Guthrie in this light. That is largely due to our inclination to view his radicalized politics developing during these days as reflecting a Marxist interpretation of religion. But Guthrie's beef with religion was on its institutional level, not its lived, everyday level. He came by these opinions honestly. As a migrant of the Western South, he mistrusted religious institutions, but loved the

Bible and its lessons for the individual. While in time Guthrie moved on from any strict religious notions he might once have accepted in the Church of Christ, he continued years later to amaze others with his knowledge of the Bible, made apparent by his ability to aptly quote it to fit virtually any situation. Toward the end of his life, he returned to a more traditional view of Jesus, particularly as the divine healer. But by the late-1930s and early-1940s, he clearly viewed Jesus as an itinerant working class preacher whose message of loving the poor infuriated the rich man and elite-class preachers who "laid Jesus Christ in the grave"—all sung to the tune of "Jesse James" in Guthrie's 1940 song "Jesus Christ."

This is where his intersection with Los Angeles religious radio from 1937 to 1939 becomes so important. His various biographers tell us how his hearing in a California migrant camp the old Baptist song "This World Is Not My Home," re-popularized by the Carter Family with their 1928 recording, angered Guthrie. In fact, we're told, it angered him second only to hearing Kate Smith's "God Bless America." That song, of course, inspired his classic, "This Land is Your Land."

The ideas presented in the song "This World Is Not My Home" infuriated Guthrie. When he heard it in 1938, there was more than one popular recorded version of it. Initially a hymn in the Primitive Baptist folk tradition—a tradition that was vehemently world denying, preferring to see believers as pilgrims in an unwelcoming world that would never accept them—the Carter family had personalized the song with names of people they would see in heaven. But by 1938, the Goose Creek Quartet, now called the Old Fashioned Revival Hour Quartet, was singing it as well to a saturated western radio market and taking it on the road through concerts and open-air services, at times attracting more than ten thousand people.

The Old Fashioned Revival Hour Quartet version had traditional elements to it, yet added a synthetic revivalist sound that even incorporated black church phrasings. The result was one of their most popular hits—a song that would be requested by listeners many times over the next twenty years of the program. Their version was de-personalized in comparison to the Carter Family's recording, yet their "hitting the middle" of the evangelical Venn Diagram allowed their version to attract a larger audience than the twangy version.

> This world is not my home, I'm just a-passing through
> My treasures are laid up somewhere beyond the blue
> The angels beckon me from heaven's open door
> And I can't feel at home in this world anymore
>
> Chorus:

O Lord, you know I have no friend like you
If heaven's not my home, then Lord what will I do?
The angels beckon me from heaven's open door
And I can't feel at home in this world anymore
They're all expecting me and that's one thing I know
I worked it out with Jesus many years ago
I know he'll take me through though I am weak and poor
And I can't feel at home in this world anymore
Just over in glory land we'll eternally
The saints on every hand are shouting victory
Their songs of sweetest praise drift back from heaven's shore
And I can't feel at home in this world anymore[14]

Guthrie, increasingly radicalized by the plight of migrants, became angry. According to biographer Joe Klein:

> He was hearing the words in a different way than he'd ever heard them before. He was beginning to understand that the effect of the song was to tell the migrants to wait, and be meek, and be rewarded in the next life.

The song by the Goose Creek/Old Fashioned Revival Hour Quartet ran against both Guthrie's understanding of this-world Christianity and the positive-thought philosophy he espoused earlier.

> It was telling them to accept the hovels and the hunger and the disease. It was telling them not to strike, and not to fight back. He was outraged by the idea that such an innocent-sounding song could be so insidious. An alternative set of words exploded out of him, and stood the song on its head.

Indeed, the song Guthrie wrote in an "elegant rage" converted the old Baptist hymn of delayed reward, sung almost joyfully by the quartet, to a "furious anthem of homelessness."[15] It was not just a rejection of the notion that God's forlorn children will be rewarded after death; Guthrie's lyrics also showed his dissatisfaction with the "secrets" of harmonial thought in such dire circumstances. No amount of positive thought or hard work could overcome the odds of a system set against the little man. Eschewing

RADIO REVIVAL HOUR
KNX HOLLYWOOD CALIF.
SUNDAY 6:30 = 7:30 P.M. P.S.T.

First national radio broadcast of the Old Fashioned Revival Hour on the Mutual Broadcasting System, 1937.

a chorus that would break up the verses, Guthrie's "I Ain't Got No Home" built up steam from one verse to the next.

> I ain't got no home, I'm just a-ramblin' 'round,
> I'm just a wandrin' working man, I go from town to town.
> Police make it hard wherever I may go
> And I ain't got no home in this world anymore.
> My brothers and my sisters are stranded on this road,
> It's a hot and dusty road that a million feet have trod;
> Rich man took my home and drove me from my door
> And I ain't got no home in this world anymore.
> I was farmin' on the shares, and always I was poor;
> My crops I lay into the banker's store.
> My wife took down and died upon the cabin floor,
> And I ain't got no home in this world anymore.
> Now I look around, it's might plain to see
> This wide and wicked world is a funny place to be;
> The gamblin' man is rich an' the working man is poor,
> And I ain't got no home in this world anymore.[16]

In the liner notes taken from one of the song's four manuscript copies, Guthrie reflected on the initial gospel song: "The reason why you can't feel at home in this world any more is mostly because you ain't got no home to feel at."[17] His own song seems to vacillate between a rejection by the system of this world and a rejecting of that world. It must be understood in its context as an answer to a gospel song being whistled by migrant workers. Guthrie's "I Ain't Got No Home in This World Anymore" played with imagery that would come to fruition two years later in his song "Jesus Christ," who, according to the gospels had no place to lay his head—a life the rail-riding Guthrie knew well. Rather than accept a corporate-friendly version of Jesus welcoming his pilgrim, beaten-down children to heaven at the end of their difficult lives, Guthrie challenged Christians using the same tune with a different worldview, one in which people are homeless because of the same bankers, moneychangers, and elite who earlier put Jesus to death.

It is worth remembering that in 1938, when Ed Robbin, Guthrie's booking agent, asked him whom he most wanted to be like, Guthrie responded, "Will Rogers and Jesus Christ."[18] He meant it. Indeed, he meant it a few years later when he gave the same answer to Will Geer, his longtime friend who was black-listed from acting during the McCarthy Era. But the Jesus that Guthrie emulated was the one he found in the Scriptures—the carpenter who was rejected, the itinerant preacher, the lover of the poor and the downtrodden, the outlaw who threatened the money changers in the temple—not the Christ, the savior of individual souls.

One might argue that the devotion of Guthrie's ardent fans one hundred years after his birth has something to do with his echoing in his life the revolutionary Jesus he sang about. Homeless itinerants (Jesus: "Foxes have holes, and birds of the air have nests; but the Son of Man has nowhere to lay his head.") and ascetics renouncing the present world (Jesus: "No man can serve two masters: for either he will hate the one, and love the other; or else he will hold to the one, and despise the other. Ye cannot serve God and mammon."), Jesus and Guthrie, in the words of New Testament scholar James Knight, "serve as superglue for larger social movements by embodying a set of abstract principles around which diverse individuals have assembled."[19] Himself something of an itinerant prophet, often living as an ascetic who rejected the world that had rejected his kind, and yet the crusader whose instrument killed Fascists—Guthrie provided the hope of another world not based on the rules that dominate this one. Not a world where the "gamblin' man is rich and the workin' man is poor," but where the first shall be last and the last shall be first.

It has been argued that Woody Guthrie "went so far as to proletarianize Christ."[20] Joe Klein chalks up Guthrie's vision of Jesus as a revolutionary as another of his "ideological flights of fancy."[21] The first point is half correct; the second misses the mark altogether. Guthrie's Jesus was an ever-present inspiration and foil for not only art, but his life from his youth until his final days, when he rejected any secret teachings in scripture and looked simply to Jesus as his savior and healer. And, clearly, Guthrie did baptize Jesus in the politics of the day in his music. But that obscures the point that he also sought to Christianize the proletariat—that is, he brought the masses to the revolutionary Jesus with the hope of inspiring those who already believed in their Savior to also follow his more radical teachings.

Ever willing to combine, mix, match, and stir together populist notions of the day, Guthrie used the character of the bespectacled young socialist to make his Jesus argument in *Bound for Glory*. As the book nears its end, Guthrie takes the reader into a meeting of migrant workers (likely populist Protestants), Marxists, and social movement leaders. After several have had their say about the present troubles, the young man speaks.

> That's what "social" means, me and you and you working on something together and owning it together. What the hell's wrong with this, anybody—speak up! If Jesus Christ

was sitting right here, right now, he'd say this very same dam [sic] thing. You just ask Jesus how the hell come a couple of thousand of us living out here in this jungle camp like a bunch of wild animals. You just ask Jesus how many millions of other folks are living the same way? Sharecroppers down South, big city people that work in factories and live like rats in the slimy slums. You know what Jesus'll say back to you? He'll tell you we all just mortally got to work together, build things together, fix up old things together, clean out old filth together, put up new buildings, schools, and churches, banks and factories together, and own everything together. Sure, they'll call it a bad ism. Jesus don't care if you call it socialism or communism, or just me and you.[22]

Guthrie had learned plenty during his California days, not just about the plight of once-hopeful migrants, but about how religion could both inspire folks personally and hold them back from changing the world that took advantage of them. Guthrie's time in Los Angeles singing to the same believers who listened to the *Little Country Church* and the *Old Fashioned Revival Hour* helped him sharpen his message and make clearer his vision of a world to come—on this earth, not later heaven. Robert Collier advised his readers in *The Secret* to "see things as you would have them be instead of as they are." From 1938 on, Woody Guthrie used in his music the image of Jesus to do just that.

Seven

WOODY AND WILL

ED ROBBIN

As I look back to the day I brought Woody over to Topanga Canyon near the Santa Monica coast to meet Will, I ask myself how it was that there was such immediate contact between these men, contact that became a long and deep friendship. That friendship lasted through Woody's life and long after, because Geer made a second career of singing and talking about and promoting the life and legend of Guthrie.

Now I can see that the two were very much alike in many ways. Take politics. Neither was a political theorist. Neither bothered about what was the correct line to follow. Both Guthrie and Geer had always known which side they were on. Woody often sang the song, written by the wife of a Harlan County, Kentucky, miner, with the refrain, "Which side are you on, Which side are you on?" But that never was a problem for him. He and Geer both had always been on the side of working people, of the poor and the oppressed. They both had a passionate need to search for a way to a better world.

For many years Will was blacklisted, both in Hollywood and on the Broadway stage, because he lived out that need. Even when he was at the height of his success in movies and television, he traveled the country, speaking for any progressive candidate who needed help in his campaign.

And both had a creative need to bring their talents to people everywhere, to entertain and teach and plead for an end to war and exploitation. Together they traveled the country, to towns and villages, union halls, money-raising gatherings, to homes and halls, singing, playing, acting, and always trying to get people to organize on their own behalf.

When I first wrote this chapter, it was mostly about the friendship that grew between Will Geer and Woody Guthrie. I had just been working over the introduction to this chapter and recalling how I brought Woody to meet Will in 1939, when I heard that Will had died in Los Angeles.

On the evening of the Sunday when I heard of Will's death, I was scheduled to be part of a program on Woody Guthrie at La Pena, a Berkeley cabaret frequented mainly by Chilean and other South American supporters of guerilla and revolutionary movements of the Latin countries. This was a program that Lennie Anderson, Bruce Greene, and I had done many times. Usually Lennie sang Woody's songs, Bruce read from Woody's writings, and I told of my friendship with Woody and of the political and social background of the Thirties that shaped his songs and his writings.

However, that night I dwelt on my long friendship, and Woody's, with Will. I realized as I spoke that Will's passion for his gardening was closely related to his relationship with people, particularly young people. For just as he planted and nurtured growing things wherever he was, Will was always surrounded with young people whom he helped, loved, and involved in both theater and politics.

Will Geer, known and loved by so many people as the grandfather in the TV show *The Waltons*, was part of the fabric of the American theater.

Years ago, he played Jeeter in *Tobacco Road* on Broadway.

He was a Shakespearean actor and spent a long period on the East Coast with the Stratford Theater. He had been a political radical since the early Thirties and was one of the first to feel the heavy hand of the blacklist in Hollywood and on Broadway.

At the time I got to know Woody, Will was living in a canyon in Santa Monica. He got occasional movie work. But he spent much of his time doing political skits or with his own group of people, singing madrigals and Elizabethan songs in colleges or at parties. Mostly, however, he was busy developing his garden.

For his great love, next to the theater, was gardening. He had graduated from the University of Chicago in horticulture, and ever after, whenever he had the chance, his fingers were in the earth planting, pulling weeds, and cultivating whatever little patch of ground he occupied. He became an expert; the plants and flowers referred to in Shakespeare. When I went to see him play "Coriolanus" at Stratford in Connecticut, he took me to look at the Shakespeare garden he had developed.

Sometime in the Thirties, when he was with some company in Chicago and I was living in the close-by city of Gary, Indiana, he came to visit and stayed a couple of days with us. Early in the morning after his arrival, I peeked in the attic, where he was supposed to be asleep, and found the bed was empty. I stepped out to the porch and looked out over the big, straggly, neglected yard with some fruit trees, lots of weeds, and wild flowers. And there was Will, in his shorts, digging around the trees so they could be properly irrigated.

"Ed, you're a disgrace to the human race, letting this garden go like this. These trees tell me they haven't had a drink for weeks. You could have a fine vegetable patch and some real good flowers. Shame on you."

"Clara is the gardener, not me. We haven't been in this house that long, but she'll get to it. She loves flowers. The only thing I can raise is radishes. I'm really good with radishes."

In the afternoon, Will said he wanted me to take him to the adjoining town of Hammond, Indiana, to see a nursery he said was famous for its development of all kinds of herbs. At that time I was in the house-remodeling business and had an office right there in Hammond, but I had never heard of this plant nursery.

We drove out, and for a couple of hours Will talked to the robust owner and picked seeds for his Shakespeare garden. I learned later that that nursery was famous among gardeners all over the country.

I speak of this because I think there is a key to the kind of person Will was in his love of trees and plants. Through all the years I knew him, he loved and nurtured not only things of the soil, but also people, particularly young people.

I'm sure that dozens of youngsters got their start in the theater through the various theater groups he put together in different parts of the country. Wherever Will lived, wherever he stopped, there were theatricals and performances and young people clustered around him to work with him.

When he was blacklisted on Broadway, he started a coffee cabaret on the east side of New York. I believe that was in the late Forties. It was called Folksay. Anyone with any talent for singing, dancing, or acting could perform there. I remember that my daughter Tamara, who was attending dancing school at Julliard, danced there one evening.

I met Will in 1926 through my friend Meyer Levin, the novelist. That was fifty years ago. Meyer and Will had just graduated from the University of Chicago and invited me to travel with them to Europe. We hitchhiked from Chicago to New York and then to Montreal. Hitchhikers were not as common then as they are now, nor were there as many cars on the road. So we spent many a day walking. And as we walked, tall, lanky Will, with a stick in hand, pointed to trees and plants and named them for us. And he stopped to talk to farmers and discuss the crops, while Meyer gloomily trudged on ahead of us, impatient with our dawdling.

When we got a ride, Will was always the one to sit with the driver, and before long, whoever was driving the car would be on close terms with him. One fellow who picked us up was coming from his fiancée's funeral. Soon, with tears running down his cheeks, he was telling Will all about his troubles. Will nodded and softly consoled him. The fellow was on his way to Washington, D.C., and that was quite a jump for us. We had been sleeping out in the fields at night. The first night, that man insisted that if we were going to sleep out, he would, too. The poor fellow got very little sleep because the ground was hard, and the mist was heavy. The next night, he begged us to take a room in a hotel, and he would pay for it. When we got to Washington, there was an emotional parting from Will, and we had to promise that man we would look him up on our way back.

Eventually we got to Montreal and down to the docks there. After a few days we signed on to a cattle boat for Liverpool. The day we arrived in Montreal, we decided to celebrate by stopping at a fancy tea and pastry shop. It was all so foreign and English and exciting, as though we were already on the continent.

The menu said tea and pastry for a set price of a shilling. The friendly, blond waitress brought us a large pot of tea and then set a platter of lovely French pastry on the table. We looked at each other in some amazement. All this for a shilling a piece? So we ate the whole platter of pastry. When the bill came, we were flabbergasted to find that we owed several pounds, quite a dent in our meager finances. We acted, though, as if we were quite aware of what we were doing, paid the bill and then laughed it off somewhat ruefully when we were outside.

The work on the cattle boat was rough, particularly for a tenderfoot like me who had never done any heavy work. You'd carry full buckets of water down to the cattle stalls, two buckets at a time through the long passageways, and then the damned cows would knock the buckets over in their eagerness to drink. During that trip, Will often found ways to help me with my end of the work when he saw me wearing out.

Since that adventurous trip, Will's path and mine have crossed many times. We met at the Goodman Theater in Chicago, soon after I got back from Europe. I was a student actor, and one day while sitting in the green room studying my lines, I saw an elegant gentleman come in with spats, a cane, and a monocle around his neck. I looked real hard. Sure enough, it was Will Geer. He'd come to see about directing a play. And a couple of years later, he did direct a play for the Goodman.

Sometime in the middle Thirties, I was asked to direct a play at a settlement house. The cast was mostly black working people from South Los Angeles. The play was *Stevedore*, written by Paul Peters and George Sklar, and had been very successful in New York with Rex Ingram playing the leading role. The play was about longshoremen on the New York waterfront. I needed a white sheriff and asked Will to do the part. Although he was an old pro and I was not, he never hesitated, attended all rehearsals, and never interfered with my direction.

I still remember one incident on opening night. The first scene is played in a tiny beat-up waterfront coffeehouse. The sheriff comes in to roust some of the lads around who are sitting on the stools. One of the lads had hidden himself behind the counter because he figured the sheriff was looking for him. After the sheriff leaves, the fellow who was hiding had a cue he failed to pick up. But the man who played the lead wandered back of the counter and found him fast asleep. He had to shake him awake. The fellow had worked hard all day and simply fell asleep back of the counter.

The play was a big success. These working men were amazingly good actors, although none—except for Will and Clarence Muse, who played a preacher—had ever been on stage before.

In 1976 I was doing an article about Woody and the making of the film *Bound for Glory*. I thought it might be useful to talk to Will so I called him in Los Angeles and asked if he could spare me some time.

Will said, "I'm having a birthday party in a couple of weeks. It's my seventy-fifth birthday, and some people want to celebrate. So why don't you come down for the party, and then afterwards, we can talk."

So a couple of weeks, later I piled Clara into the car, and we beat our way down to Los Angeles. It turned out that the little birthday party was at the Santa Monica Civic Auditorium, which was packed with thousands of people, and hundreds were turned away. Will was using the occasion to stage a folk song and drama festival to raise money for a Woody Guthrie fund. The money would be used to find a cure for Huntington's chorea, the disease that killed Woody.

There were streamers all over the auditorium congratulating Will, and he sat in center of the stage rambling and directing the proceedings in an easy, informal way. But the whole performance centered on Woody. It was a loosely knit program that included Pete Seeger, Arlo Guthrie, Will's number-one wife (he always referred to her that way) Herta Geer, his daughters Ellen and Katie, and his son Thad. There were other singers and actors. The performance included dozens of Woody's songs and anecdotes, and I was surprised when Will told about how I had brought Woody to see him not too long after I met him at KFVD.

The meeting was a great success. The wildly enthusiastic audience was made up mostly of young people, lots of girls with their hair loose over their shoulders, men with beards and moustaches, and young children running up and down the aisles or sitting close to the stages.

The next day, I went to Will's house. He lived in one of those Spanish cottages in a courtyard. He had the rear cottage and apparently owned and rented five or six other flats. A big sign at the gateway read, "No actors allowed on these premises," which I took to be a joke because the young people I saw lounging around the courtyard were obviously reading or studying lines, and others, who wandered in and out of the living room while Will and I talked, came to take up various problems they were having with the agents or studios.

On the way to Will's cottage, I had noticed that the courtyard was thick with plants, flowers and trees, all carefully nurtured, and I remembered again that plants and trees had been the love of his life and that he had been trained as a horticulturist.

Will, when I met him some five decades ago, was a tall, slender, Lincolnesque figure. He had now grown considerably in bulk and had a flowing mane of gray hair. He wore flowing garments and sat like a great, calm Buddha, waving people in and out of the crowded little living room, which was cluttered with comfortable old furniture that looked as if the pieces were early vintage Goodwill and Salvation Army. On the walls were pictures of Will in some of the many movie and theater productions he had been in—pictures with Katharine Hepburn, Katherine Cornell, Claude Rains and dozens of other movie greats. There were pictures of the scenes with the people in *The Waltons* of whom Will spoke as though they were really his own family. Will was a warm, affectionate man who genuinely loved people and surrounded himself with them.

Will sat on the couch next to me, and I taped our talk. Here is the transcription of that conversation:

ROBBIN: You must be worn out after that great shindig last night.

GEER: No, no. I've had a fine rest, and I'm ready to go. You want to talk some more about Woody? You brought him out to the canyon, and Herta and Woody got together and played duets and sang together right away. Herta said, "What a marvelous man—too bad he can't sing." You remember Woody had a kind of monotonous way of singing. All those wonderful words and sometimes he sang them so poorly. You really had to listen to the words to appreciate him.

ROBBIN: You really took him under your wing, didn't you?

GEER: Well, Woody felt at home with us. I took him up to the studio and introduced him to David Ward Griffith and to Louie Milestone, but I could tell they were thinking what's Will doing with that hillbilly singer. I was testing along with Burl Ives for the part of Slim in *Of Mice and Men* because I'd been in the play on Broadway—you know that Steinbeck thing. I met Steinbeck there at the studio.

ROBBIN: I guess you met Steinbeck later, too, didn't you?

GEER: Yes, quite a bit later, don't remember just when, but after Woody's songs had begun to be sung around. I introduced Woody to Steinbeck, and he said, "Took me years to do *Grapes of Wrath*, and that little squirt tells the whole story in just a few stanzas." We all had a good laugh over that.

ROBBIN: He was talking about "The Ballad of Tom Joad."

GEER: At that time we were making that film *Fight for Life*, and I got Woody into that picture, I suppose because his wife Mary was pregnant—fragrant, he always said—and I played the doctor. And Herta was pregnant, too, and my daughter Katie was the one who was born during that picture. At that time, too, I met two young boys sunning themselves somewhere out on Eagle Rock, and they turned out to be Cisco and Slim Houston. You remember how close Woody and Cisco became. Cisco was a fine musician. He and Woody worked together a lot and later shipped out together and were torpedoed several times in the same ships. Slim lost his life when one of his ships sank.

Anyway, while this picture was being made as a side thing on a very short budget, we'd get together every weekend. John Steinbeck and Paul de Kruif supervised and directed. John lived just a couple of blocks away, at the Garden of Allah apartments. I remember walking over to John's with Woody one time. We picked up John, and we walked right up to the drugstore just about a block away. John stopped on the corner and picked up a copy of the *People's World* at the newsstand and a copy of Hearst's *Examiner*. Glen Gordon, one of the actors in the picture had joined us. He said, "How in the hell can you read that paper knowing the things you know?" And Steinbeck said, "Well a writer has to know all sides of a question. I have to know what that old buzzard Hearst is thinking and writing." And Woody was impressed with that. It really made a great impression on him, about learning everything.

So later on in New York when I'd take him to whorehouses, he'd say, "Well, Walt Whitman used to go to whorehouses to study." And he'd say, "John Steinbeck said you gotta study all sides of a thing." Woody was a great student and lover of Will Rogers, who came from his own home state. Like Rogers, Woody took his columns right from what he read in the daily papers. Woody saw a song in every headline. And he practically wrote a song every day. Just as in those days, my hobby has been, and I guess it always was, to learn a poem every day.

ROBBIN: And what did you see in Woody in those early days?

GEER: I saw this wonderful combination of a fellow who wrote his own poem every day and sang it every day. And I said to myself, what a sorry fish I am. All I do is take words from someone else and say them over and over again. Here was a guy who was creating, even though his things seemed kind of monotonous to me in those days—a lot of people felt they were. He wrote songs about the Ladies Auxiliary of the Union or about, L.A. traffic jams, or about the Lincoln Street jail. And now I can see that all these songs touched the lives of the people he was singing to, and each had a germ of an idea. He was talking about changing things, making them better. And there was so much sly humor in a lot of his songs. He came over to our house often during that period, when Mary was pregnant and we were all waiting for the picture to start. That was the first real money he ever made—in this picture.

He'd come over to the house, and frequently we wouldn't be there. He'd go into the icebox and help himself to something and in return payment, he'd scrawl a song on an old grocery bag. And we couldn't wait to find out what tune to sing it to. Too bad I've lost songs Woody just tossed off. None of us knew his songs would last the way they have. I think one thing we missed in the beginning about Woody was not seeing that he was a genuine radical. Since Woody loved Will Rogers and tried to emulate him so much, I guess at first we saw him as a kind of Will Rogers. He didn't seem interested in politics—just in people.

ROBBIN: People were his politics. His radicalism consisted in the fact that he always knew which side he was on. In his songs and in his talk you could see that he always knew who the enemy was—the bankers, the big-moneyed people, the men who ran the munitions factories and helped make wars. It was that simple, like in the western movies where the enemy almost always was the banker and the big railroad tycoon against the small rancher or farmer.

GEER: Yes, and in his outlaw songs the outlaw is a kind of Robin Hood, a good guy compared with the banker who robbed the poor, not with gun, but with a pen.

ROBBIN: As you say, the songs, the way he wrote the songs. Anywhere—on any scrap of paper, picking them out on the guitar as he wrote. He'd be sitting in the backyard, picking on the guitar and then all of a sudden he'd begin singing a brand new song.

GEER: The interesting thing to me about one time like that—speaking about this facility—we had a contest up there at my place in Topanga Canyon. This was a good deal later on, after the war and all. He already showed signs of that Huntington's chorea and his mind was a little wobbly and his pen was scratchy. He was even having trouble with the guitar. We set this up one day, this contest, I mean, and I was emcee. I don't remember who all was there but Peter Seeger and Vern Partlow, a newspaper man and songwriter, and a lot of other singers and writers and, of course, an audience from around the neighborhood. And I said, "Let's see who can sing the best love ballad." Everyone else sang fairly well known ballads. But when Woody's turn came, he wrote a new one right there and sang it right off. I wish I could remember it because it was a good song, and I don't believe he ever recorded it.

ROBBIN: When did you first notice his sickness—this Huntington's chorea that killed him?

GEER: Well, it began first in New York. I didn't notice it much until then. When he got to town he came to live with us on 7th Street. He asked me, so I told him we were paying $250 a month for this apartment. At first he thought it was $250 for the rest of the year. He was so upset when he found out that he went down to the Bowery to sleep around and said he wanted to find out the difference between the rich and the poor. At that time, I was working in *Tobacco Road* playing

Jeeter, so I could afford a place like that. Anyway, I remember I started taking Woody to bookings. I think the first time was something being given by the League Against War and Fascism, somewhere out in Queens among the aristocrats. It was a big fancy house and he didn't like the setup too much, but we were getting ten or twenty dollars for the night. We didn't have a drink, although they had a big punch bowl there. And as he got up to sing, he started to jerk like this. Sometimes you've seen drunks with that kind of jerk. So the hostess accused me of bringing him drunk. I said, "Woody, you haven't been drinking at all, have you?" And he said, "No, no, I haven't been drinking." He had this twitch, and she thought it was a drunken thing. Actually, I thought he was acting like some of the Bowery drunks as a kind of joke because he didn't like the swells. But then, over and over again, he was doing it more.

ROBBIN: Was there pain attached to the disease?

GEER: There didn't seem to be any, but he would feel confused, as though he were taking something. He once described to me—we had tried smoking marijuana together, and he said you think two or three things at the same time. He said "I sometimes get the same feeling as with the drug when the sickness comes on me. I think several things at the same time." The same thing happened to me. Once my kids slipped some marijuana in brownie cookies. I ate a couple of these brownies on this trip back in the car when we were coming from a performance, and I thought I was going out of my mind with my head spinning off all these strange mingled thoughts. Then the kids laughed and told me what they had done. And then I remembered that that was exactly how Woody had spoken about feeling when he was first beginning to feel the disease.

ROBBIN: I was wondering whether—it had occurred to me, the last I saw of him in California when he had come back from New York for a second time—he was drinking very heavily.

GEER: After he had the chorea.

ROBBIN: Well, I didn't know that he had Huntington's chorea or that anything else was wrong with him. He always drank a good deal at parties, but he was in control. I believe this was the time when he was traveling with the Almanac Singers. There was a big party at our house. and Woody came over with Pete Seeger and a couple of other people. Maybe Cisco Houston was with him. He drank everything in sight. He got very angry with me—the only time he'd ever gotten angry with me—because I ran out of liquor, and I didn't want to see him drink anymore. He said, "Ed, get some more liquor," and I said, "No, I'm not going to get any more liquor, Woody, not tonight." He got so angry he just left the party. And I wondered when I heard about the illness, whether ....

GEER: The liquor diverted his mind from it. I remembered he brought Cisco Houston to a party in

Topanga Canyon—it was after the second World War. You remember Cisco and Woody and Cisco's brother Slim were all in the merchant marine together and had two ships shot from under them. Slim was due in the engine room, and Cisco and Woody were topside, and Slim never got out. But Cisco, who was very close to his brother, never believed he was dead, figured he had somehow gotten out and been picked up by some other ship. So he kept searching for him. So he had this peculiar obsession, and Woody talked to me about it and said we've got to make Cisco realize that his brother is dead. Well, this went on for about a year, with Cisco searching the ships for some sign of his brother. In the spring of the following year, we were all in New York. I was up planting dogwood trees at my place in the country, and I remember it was the day Irwin Cobb died. Woody was with me. I was working on *Tobacco Road* at the time and someone had given me a jug of white lightning. So I went to the woods and Cisco and Woody came along and helped me dig up a couple of dogwood trees. And Woody and I talked it over and decided to dedicate these trees, one to Irwin Cobb and the other to Slim Houston. So we got back to the house and planted one tree and dedicated it to Cobb, this wonderful fellow who'd gone from our midst. And we were all drinking from the jug, and we poured a little on the tree we'd planted, and then we took the other tree to the other side of the house and planted it and took another swig from the jug all the way around, and I made a short speech dedicating this tree to Slim Houston who was killed in the engine room of such and such a ship—the ship Woody and Cisco were on. Well, the next thing I knew, I was out like a light. Cisco hit me right on the jaw, and I was out. I woke up with Woody bathing my head, and Cisco was just sitting on a log looking mad and drinking out of the jug. Woody took the jug and poured some down my throat and then bathed my head with this damned liquor. And pretty soon, we began to sing songs, and I can remember the girls coming out of the house—that time they were about four and five years old—and they saw me lying on the ground and they ran in the house yelling, "Mama, Papa's dead out in the yard and they're burying him." So the women all came running out, and by that time, we were all so drunk they had to carry us into the house.

ROBBIN: Did you ever make the rounds with him, to the bars and skid row?

GEER: Yes, lots of times. Where he liked to go with me a lot was up where the Queen Mary and all those ships docked. There were a couple, three bars there where the French sailors would come in. This was in New York. He'd come up to see me after the show, *Tobacco Road*. He must have seen that show forty times. And he'd come up and pick me up after the last act, and we'd walk over about three or four blocks down to the docks, and there'd be one bar where nothing but the British sailors hung out, another bar where the French sailors were, all during the war years, back and forth, you know. And he liked to drink with me there. I never saw him seriously drunk except on one occasion, like I said, and also at a party or two, which was when he was jerking at the same time, and it made a peculiar sort of thing, you know. At that time, none of us realized what it was. In fact, Woody himself turned himself in. He saw he was beginning to jerk like his mother.

ROBBIN: There was a period when he stayed with you in Topanga.

GEER: That was later on. He came down saying he had chorea. He'd just come back from a hospital, and they told him about it, and he decided to take another trip West, and he came out and stayed with us for a time. He lived there at the house in Topanga Canyon for about almost a year, in that little shack there. Woody stayed long enough, he got interested in a piece of land down the road from us. It was mostly straight up, called Pretty Polly Canyon. An old fellow down there sold him a piece of land. We were going to homestead it. In the first place, the fire department threw him off because he was always building fires to cook himself coffee and things, and he couldn't do that. So he came back to the shack and stayed with us, and a little later he was going to develop it. In fact, he was still paying on it when he ran off from our place with a girl.

ROBBIN: She was the wife of this friend of yours, wasn't she?

GEER: Yes, she was the wife of the man I'd taken off to do *Salt of the Earth* with. Marshall, his name was. He played one of the deputies, and I'd driven out with him.

ROBBIN: You were building a house? Was it on Woody's land you were building a house?

GEER: Yeah.

ROBBIN: You building a house for Woody at that time?

GEER: Yeah, it was out of sod.

ROBBIN: He was sick. I remember you telling the story that he was sick, sitting on the hillside, singing songs.

GEER: She fell in love with him. Off she marched; off she went with him. Of course, I moved this fellow Marshall into my house; I was so sorry for him. Here was my best friend running off with his wife, and I gave him the lead in the show. And we'd been playing for about six months. I was blacklisted so I couldn't play at the colleges and universities; they wouldn't let me go. So I cast him opposite Herta. And old Mary Virginia Farmer one day says, "You notice what I notice, Will?" And I said, "What?"

"Well, they're playing those love scenes real!" And they really were.

ROBBIN: This was *Salt of the Earth*?

GEER: Oh, no, these were just bookings we went out on, our folklore and bookings. We'd come back from *Salt of the Earth* with this fellow, Marshall, and while we were away doing the picture, Woody had absconded with his wife. And Mary Virginia says, "That's just too bohemian. I thought you were just good solid working-class people. That's just too bohemian."

    The summer about a year later he came to visit us in New York. He was living with Anya then, the girl he'd run off with Marshall's wife, and Woody and Anya had had this baby, a little girl. I was living in this house in the village which we had converted into a Folksay cabaret, because I was still blacklisted and couldn't get any work.

ROBBIN: Why were you blacklisted, Will?

GEER: Well, that was the time when we were doing everything we could in the anti-fascist and anti-Nazi fight—singing and talking and trying every way we could to show people the meaning of Nazism, and so a lot of writers and actors were being blacklisted. That was a long time before McCarthyism which came after the war. Anyway, Woody would lay the baby on the kitchen table and it would be yelling and screaming there while he wrote skits for us to do or new songs, and Anya—I think that was her name—would be trying to quiet the baby. But her crying didn't seem to bother Woody. He'd just keep right on writing. Anyway, I should mention that the baby was adopted out because Anya didn't want to keep her. And that girl grew up and then ran away from her adopted parents—she took dope and lord knows what else—and she was finally killed in an auto accident. I only heard about that recently, when the family that had raised her wrote me about it.

ROBBIN: How old was she?

GEER: Oh, she was eighteen or nineteen years old and was killed in an auto accident about a year ago.

ROBBIN: I don't think I've ever known anyone who was so pursued by tragedy, disease, fire, and death.

GEER: Yes, that's true. Reminds me of Edgar Allen Poe with his child-bride and his constant failure in life—his addiction to drugs and alcohol. Arlo Guthrie, Woody's son, makes more money on one recording than Woody did in his entire life.

ROBBIN: But what was so extraordinary was that in spite of all the terrible things that happened to him and his family, his attitude was always so up. Look at his pictures and you'll see that he even held his head up high.

GEER: No matter what happened in the world or to him personally, he faced it cheerfully and confidently and tried to put it into a song that would make people think and feel.

ROBBIN: When he lived next door he'd sit out in the backyard with the kids, watching them play and picking out songs. I think that was when he started those children's songs. To my mind he created a new kind of children's song. They are all as though he was able to get inside children and see the world through their eyes—like

Why, oh why, oh why

Because, because, because, because

A hammer's a hard head

Why can't a dish break a hammer

Why, oh why, oh why

Goodbye, goodbye, goodbye

And then half a dozen verses that follow that are full of a child's questions and fantasies.

GEER: Or that song—"Put Your Finger on Your Nose, on your Nose." I've seen kids singing and doing that song all over the country. I think he must have written several hundred songs for children. Remember—"Wrap Yourself in Paper and Mail Yourself to Me" —and that marvelous patriotic children's song—"My Daddy Flies a Plane Ship in the Sky."

ROBBIN: Can you think of any of the other bookings you went out to?

GEER: Well, there were so many but, yes, I remember one of the first ones in New York was in a rich house up at Stevens Landing. Actually, it was at Katherine Cornell's house, you know, the actress. She was a friend of mine, and there were a whole group of people assembled on New Year's Eve. And I said, "Woody, we can make some dough here. They asked for a ballad singer, and I said we'd come over. They wanted somebody like Burl Ives, but he wasn't available, so I told them I had a fine new ballad singer." I had told Katherine that Woody's fee would be fifty dollars. So I took him along to this party with all this fancy food and bar and everything under the sun. All the women were dressed formal. I remember Woody noticed they were all shaved under the armpits, and that made a big impression on him. And the men had on white shirt fronts, dressed to kill. Well, I got Woody there to sing, and he was just impossible. He kept his eyes shut while he was singing and looked away from the people and just kind of yawled his outlaw songs. I went up to him and said, "Woody, sing your Dust Bowl ballads. This is a social-minded group. And why do you keep your eyes closed?" Woody said, "Their white shirts dazzle me. Get me outta here, Will." It's the same kind of thing that made him walk out of a job at Radio City when they called him a hillbilly singer. Money never meant anything to Woody.

ROBBIN: Along that line, I remember I read an account by Alan Lomax—who admired Woody greatly and did several hours of interviewing Woody for the Library of Congress—of how Woody walked out on a big radio contract during his first trip to New York. Apparently the Target Tobacco

Company had signed him up for a series in which he would be backed up by an orchestra of fifty musicians. Woody lasted just a few performances. That was all he could take. It was just too rich for his blood. He took that money he made and bought a brand new car and started back to Oklahoma.

GEER: I remember that very well.

ROBBIN: According to Lomax, he got rid of the car in Oklahoma City. But I know different. He picked up his wife Mary and the kids and drove the car back to Los Angeles to my house.

GEER: Yes, Woody loved a fast car, and he would drive it like hell on wheels, and he loved women, and they loved him and clustered around him like bees around a honey pot. I frequently quote that passage out of his book *Born to Win*—some of it goes like this—"I was torpedoed two times in the merchant marines during the war, and I figure that whatever guilty feelings I owed to the race I paid off by these two torpedoes, and I paid off some more by laying out eight in the army with a uniform on. So, my woman came to me so strong and so plain while I was at sea and in the camps that I swore and vowed that I was going to have to find love at its fullest and highest in order to make up for the wet dreams in my ship and army bunk. Every other man felt this same way. Several hundred thousand that I spoke to felt this same way. I went about with naked visions of naked, naked, naked you in front of my eyes for so many months that I vowed and swore that I would eat you up from your head down to your toes if you would so freely allow me to do it. I smelled your skin and your hairs just as plain, plainer, those days and nights on those troopships and in those army cots. I made you such a thing of glory in my mind that I wanted to lick you down like a big pile of dark brown sugar.

    "If there is a prettier sight on earth than those patched hairs between your legs, I've never seen or heard about it. If there's a prettier sight than this long and viney root that stands up here between my legs, I've certainly never seen that. My pecker hard, my pecker soft and limber, my balls, my sack and my bag, my crotch, my legs, my root, my rod, this climbing long and jumping pole, this thing that is my gate of life, this door of mine through which we flow, this chord, this rope, this prong that I pass my finest creation through, I pass my own self through, I pass you down and out and in and through, this planting tool, this hose, this dong, dick, this stick and rod and staff of birth."

ROBBIN: There's a big difference between the Woody who wrote that poetic passage and some of the other poems and prose in *Born to Win* and the Woody I knew in those early days in Los Angeles.

GEER: Yes, some of the folk quality, the naiveté is gone.

ROBBIN: I've tried to trace that—I think what happened was—sailors do a lot of reading, and Woody spent a couple of years in the maritime service. Between getting torpedoed, he evidently read a good many books. Then, after the war, those years in New York with his wife Margie were years of cultural growth. In one of his pieces, he speaks of Sandburg, Whitman, and Pushkin. A whole new world of literature and theater opened up for him in New York.

GEER: Yes. Years before, when he made the records for the Library of Congress, Woody said that the two greatest men who ever lived were Jesus Christ and Will Rogers. That sounds kind of simple, but Woody really loved Will Rogers and hoped to emulate him. But to get back to Woody's erotic or sensual writing—I know he was acquainted with Whitman way back, because I caught him reading a copy of Walt's *Leaves of Grass* right in my house, and we had a long talk about Whitman. And I think his song "So Long It's Been Good to Know You," which is sung everywhere now, comes right out of Whitman. Woody was very impressed with the fact that my number one wife Herta and I were married to the verses of Walt Whitman all those years ago. Herta was the granddaughter of Mother Bloor, the grand old lady labor fighter and organizer and one of the founders of the American Communist party. Woody loved the sensuality in Whitman. He had the same wide, democratic feeling for his fellow men—liked to move among them, live and touch all their lives. Like Whitman, he loved to catalog the names of places as well as the bodies of men and women and all their parts.

ROBBIN: Yes, he fingered people and places and names of places like a professional card dealer lovingly riffles a deck of cards. In his sensuality, he reminds me of D.H. Lawrence. That's why I feel he must have read him. The sexual lyricism in the piece you quoted a bit ago. . . .

GEER: Oh, he was full of that. People used to say that was part of his disease. That's nonsense. Like most poets, Woody was deeply, passionately sexual in his life and in his work. That reminds me—because I used to use those quotations in my folklore shows that I did traveling around the colleges. In fact, five or six years ago, at the University of Michigan, students said when I quoted that piece—you know I was doing a thing mainly on Whitman, and I quoted that piece, and they said, "Where is that in Walt Whitman? I've never read that in Walt Whitman." And I'd say, "That was Woodrow Wilson Guthrie." "Well," they'd say, "it sounds just like Whitman."

ROBBIN: Will, you had that period in New York—I guess it must have been in the early Fifties—when you were blacklisted, and you were doing a lot of the Folksay-type of things in the Village on the weekends.

GEER: Yes. Woody was living with me on Bank Street at Auntie Marne's and about that time he took to writing plays for us. We kept having to move from one place to another because the fire department or the city would kick us out. We played on the east side and on the west side. Harold Leventhal was one of our first managers. [Leventhal, in addition to being an agent for Woody, Pete Seeger, and Judy Collins through the years, was co-producer of *Bound for Glory*.] Harold was a young clothing manufacturer then. Rex Ingram and Fred Hellerman and lots of other actor friends joined us to put on these plays. We'd collect money and then split the take because we were all unemployed. I remember Woody had just come back from the south, just knocking around and playing and singing, and he fell into a fire and hurt his hand. Somehow the Guthries were always getting burned in fires. He made a little violin while he was laid up. And he left that violin at Auntie Marne's. Woody liked to sleep in the basement on a window ledge. He liked the air, and he liked to watch and hear the people in the street. There were some drunks living upstairs on the third floor, and one day they threw some water down just as Woody was sticking his head out the window, and he got soaked.

ROBBIN: You were saying something about the plays he was writing.

GEER: Yes, he started to write these crazy plays with casts of hundreds. He had a whole German army corps in one, and it was about some sisters who had a hotel that became a whorehouse. It was in a Soviet city occupied by the Germans. The sisters would invite the German soldiers in one at a time, and when the soldier would get excited, the sister would cut his dong off and shove him through a collapsible bed into the basement to bleed to death. And when they finally got to the general who was too old to get an erection, they had to poison him. The show ended with a new regiment marching in. The sisters got all worn out with cutting off and dropping penises through the floor.

Well, that was in the beginning when he was just feeling his way into playwriting. But he wrote many plays about strikes and the labor movement, and some we did. I had a pile of them, and they all disappeared or were stolen. I think it was about this time the chorea was sneaking up on him, and his writing began to get wild and uncoordinated. And then soon, he was in and out of hospitals as the disease progressed.

ROBBIN: Sometime in the late Fifties, I came to New York and visited the Folksay performance. There was Woody backstage. He was pretty sick by then and shaking all over. Apparently they'd let him out of the hospital for a while. He took me to a cold-water flat where he was living, and he showed me a thick manuscript he was working on. It must have been about a thousand pages. I thought it was a sequel to *Bound for Glory*. His wife, Margie told me recently that she has someone going through that and editing it. [This became the book *Seeds of Man*—a raucous, Rabelaisian account of a trip to Mexico to hunt for gold.]

GEER: Yes, we had a place out in the country, and Woody used to come out there and write on that book.

ROBBIN: You said something about his having been in a fire. Was he burned in a fire?

GEER: Well, Woody and Anya went down south somewhere—first to Florida and then to some town in Georgia where there was some struggle Woody wanted to be part of. And they were camping out along the way, and Woody had one of his spells of sickness and got to shaking so bad he fell into the campfire, and his arm was burned so bad he couldn't play his guitar. He seldom played after that.

ROBBIN: Fire just pursued that Guthrie family. Wasn't it his daughter Cathy who died in a fire?

GEER: Poor thing. Yes, that was later. He was living with Margie in New York, down in the Village. The little girl was only four years old, and how Woody loved that child. He wrote many of his children's songs at that time. They were for Cathy. No one really knows how it happened. The child was left alone for just a few minutes, and a fire started, caught her clothes, and she died in the hospital.

ROBBIN: I remember reading Woody's story about it. He told it as though he had to get it out of his system, the whole story in every small detail, with all the agony of the child's death in the hospital. She lived a few days after the burning. Fire pursued the family from way back. In Okemah, his father built a big house, and before they had hardly moved in, the house burned to the ground. Later, his mother was blinded, and his sister Claire died of burning from a coal fire. It's just incredible.

GEER: The Guthries were pursued by tragedy. The boy William, the one who was born in the movie we made, *Fight for Life*, that boy died in an auto accident when he was twenty years old. And Mary's two daughters have both been stricken with Huntington's chorea. One is already hospitalized. [That daughter, Gwen, has since died.]

[I turned off the tape recorder and suggested to Will that we go out for some lunch. We drove over to the Farmers Market on Fairfax. On the way, Will recalled early days with Woody. Back in the early Forties, soon after Will met Woody, they used to sing and play together on street comers or at meetings, or out at the camps of migrant workers, and at lots of parties for different causes. But at that time, neither of them was making any money. So they would get paid a small fee and take the rest out in eating—things like knishes or chopped liver and gefilte fish at the Jewish gatherings. Will figured that's where he learned about Jewish cooking.]

ROBBIN: Woody had four children with Margie. . . .Isn't that right?

GEER: Yes, Cathy, who we talked about and who died by fire—then Arlo, and a girl Nora, who's a very fine modern dancer in New York City, and Joady, who lives in San Francisco and teaches guitar there. Woody named him Joady after Steinbeck's character Tom Joad.

ROBBIN: Some months ago we were invited to Joady's wedding. He was marrying a lovely blond woman named Aileen, with whom he had been living for several years. I mention that because this seems to have become the new pattern for young people around our area. They live together, and then after a time, if the relationship survives, they get married.

GEER: Not a bad pattern . . . .

ROBBIN: They were married in a charming, vine-covered Lutheran church on the south side of San Francisco. It was all very traditional. Margie was there with her new husband, and Arlo dressed in an elegant white suit with a lacey shirt, and Nora, whom I hadn't met before, and her dance partner. The small church was filled with friends of Joady's and Aileen's—almost all young people in their late twenties or early thirties.

Will and I had spent the whole day together. It was almost evening and the room was darkening. Will was wrapped in his Mexican blanket. His head had dropped, and I think he was beginning to doze off. Time to leave. I sat opposite him, just staring and remembering all the years we had known each other, all the times our paths had crossed. Did I, perhaps, have a premonition that this was the last time we were to meet?

Soon I waked Will from his sleep.

"Will," I said, "you should write it all down. Tell the story of your life, if only for your grandchildren and your friends."

"I'm going to do it. I really will."

We embraced warmly.

"Come back soon. Lots more to talk about," Will said as I left.

Meet Woody & His Geetar

Bay Area readers of The People's World can meet **WOODY**, hear him play his guitar and sing his own ballads, this Sunday evening at 350 Battery street (corner of Clay), San Francisco.

It is a rare opportunity as the popular World columnist has a regular radio program in Los Angeles and can get up North very seldom.

Accompanying Woody will be Will Geer, singer, character actor and entertainer, beloved by labor audiences from coast to coast.

The People's World invites all its readers to meet, hear and see these two excellent entertainers.

Don't forget. This Sunday evening at 350 Battery street (corner of Clay)!

Eight

WOODY SEZ
THE PEOPLE'S DAILY WORLD AND INDIGENOUS RADICALISM

RONALD BRILEY

ound for Glory, director Hal Ashby's 1976 cinematic tribute to Woody Guthrie, concludes with the folksinger departing California for New York City in early 1940. As he rides a freight train, Woody, portrayed by David Carradine, sings "This Land Is Your Land," which he wrote in February 1940. Under the direction of Ashby and the cinematography of Haskell Wexler, the film's conclusion becomes a bicentennial tribute to the resilient spirit of the American people. Film viewers, however, would certainly not surmise that Woody had penned his anthem in angry response to what the folksinger considered the narrow nationalism of Irving Berlin's "God Bless America." In fact, the film ignores Woody's association with the Communist Party and radical politics during his sojourn in California from 1936 to 1940.[1]

In 1939, Woody wrote a column entitled Woody Sez for the *People's Daily World*, the West Coast Communist newspaper published in San Francisco. The Woody Sez columns provide evidence that the time Woody spent in California during the late 1930s, observing firsthand the harsh conditions experienced by the migrants from the Dust Bowl, contributed to radicalizing the folksinger. The myth promulgated by Ashby's *Bound for Glory* that Woody was simply a populist celebrating the American spirit before heading to New York City is negated by the folksinger's pieces in the *People's Daily World*. The Woody Guthrie who penned "This Land Is Your Land" in 1940 was an American radical who raised serious questions as to

Opposite: **Woody is featured in *People's World* newspaper, September 1, 1939.**

whether the American capitalist system was serving the interests of working people.

Woody's politics are often ambiguous, paradoxical, and confusing. There is considerable disagreement as to whether Woody actually joined the Communist Party during the late 1930s. Biographer Ed Cray accepts the view of many Guthrie family members and associates that the folksinger lacked the discipline and ideological commitment to be a party member. Communist Party organizer Dorothy Healey, however, described Woody as active in California party affairs during the late 1930s, and biographer Joe Klein accepts Woody's assertion that he joined the party sometime in 1936. Supporting evidence for Woody's association with the Communist Party may be found in the folksinger's Woody Sez columns.

Woody appeared faithfully to follow the shifting and often confusing Communist Party line in the late 1930s. With the rise of Nazi Germany, the Communist Party pursued the Popular Front policy from 1935 to 1939, emphasizing collective security and cooperation with anti-Fascist bourgeois democracies. The Popular Front was abandoned with the signing of the Molotov-Ribbentrop Pact, the Nazi-Soviet nonaggression agreement, in August 1939. While the Soviet Union cooperated with the Nazis and pursued a policy of aggression against their neighbors in Finland and Poland, American Communists denounced Western democracies for pursuing militaristic solutions to the international situation. This line, however, changed with the invasion of the Soviet Union by Nazi Germany on June 22, 1941. For the duration of World War II, the Communist Party in the United States dropped its oppositional policies, supporting the war effort and celebrating communism as twentieth-century Americanism.[2]

But Woody's political ideas were hardly limited to the Communist Party line. In *A Race of Singers*, Bryan K. Garman suggests that Woody fits within the democratic legacy of Walt Whitman championing the working people of the nation. Woody's political rhetoric expressed in his journals, music, and columns does indicate Whitman-like qualities—in addition to such traditional American ideas as populist denunciation of concentrated wealth, the democratic promise contained in the Declaration of Independence, debtor rebellion going back to Daniel Shays, and a Jeffersonian celebration of the pursuit of happiness.

In his 1943 autobiography *Bound for Glory*, Woody plays down his radical politics at a time when the United States and Soviet Union were engaged in a patriotic crusade against fascism. The book's title, according to Woody, was meant to convey that the common people were bound for glory and not simply to glorify a wandering minstrel who epitomized the struggles of working people.[3] In his examination of Woody and the Communist Party, however, Ronald Cohen finds no contradiction in Woody's admiration for the party and celebration of the American experience. Like many in the 1930s, the folksinger was attracted to the party's basic domestic goals, "while resisting any slavish obedience to Party doctrines or dictates." He was more a follower of Debs and Lincoln than Lenin and Stalin, but he perceived communism as offering a vision of equality, democracy, and peace. Cohen concludes that Woody was "a Red, but of his own stripe—no contradiction in a political climate where anything was possible, as Woody demonstrated."[4]

Thus, the political ideas of Woody were unorthodox and often paradoxical. He envisioned a commonwealth in which working people would receive their fair share of the nation's resources, and Woody did not seem to care whether the means for achieving this community came through communism, Christian socialism, populism, Jeffersonianism, or traditional American radicalism. But in these versions of collectivist radicalism, Woody was much more than the romantic individualist depicted in Ashby's *Bound for Glory*. His perception of humanity was grounded in an agrarian tradition of protest in his native Oklahoma, where a strong Socialist Party operated before the First World War; a Christian tradition that Jesus was the champion of the poor and was a meek person who would drive the money changers out of the temple; a tragic family history; and the experience of his generation with the Depression and Dust Bowl of the 1930s.

The Socialist Party often prospered in sections of Oklahoma where holiness sects opposed the materialism and modernism of established churches, and Woody was certainly a product of this milieu. While he never attended church on a regular basis, Woody was baptized into the Church of Christ, reading and quoting frequently from the Bible. When asked by leftist journalist Ed Robbin to name the people he most admired, Woody replied Will Rogers and Jesus Christ. Perceiving Jesus as a socialist outlaw, in songs such as "They Laid Poor Jesus Christ in his Grave," Woody described Jesus as a working-class carpenter who championed the rights of the common people until he was betrayed by the rich and their selfish interests.[5]

But Woody's family origins were not really so common. His father Charley Guthrie was a small-town real-estate entrepreneur who opposed the Socialist Party. During the oil boom of the early 1920s, Charley lost out to the big business rolling into the state, and the family became destitute. But even before the economic mishaps, personal tragedy struck the family. Woody's older sister Clara died after her dress caught fire. Many locals blamed Woody's mother, Nora, for the death. Whether the accusation was true or not, she did begin to behave in an eccentric fashion, wandering the streets in various states of undress. In June 1927, Charley was severely burned in another fire, this one definitely started by his wife. Nora was institutionalized and diagnosed as suffering from Huntington's chorea, a degenerative disease attacking the brain and central nervous system. Due to his family history, Woody, a physically small boy, was often ostracized by his peers. Woody's reaction was to perform poorly in academics and play the role of class clown. However, he did read avidly on his own and took pleasure in playing the guitar and harmonica.[6]

With the onslaught of the Depression in 1929, Woody joined his father in Pampa, Texas, where Charley found work managing a boarding house. Woody married Mary Jennings in October 1933. Two years later, Woody's first child was born, and he supported the family by painting signs, reading fortunes, drawing pictures, and playing music. Inspired by the dust storms engulfing the Texas Panhandle, Woody wrote tunes such as "Dusty Old Dust" ("So Long, It's Been Good to Know Yuh") proclaiming:

> So long, it's been good to know yuh
> This dusty old dust is a-gettin' my home
> And I've got to be driftin' along.

Leaving his family in Pampa, Woody headed to California in 1936 to see what "the great migration of Okies" really meant.[7] He was shocked at the prejudice with which many in California greeted the Dust Bowl refugees. Traveling by freight, he encountered many former members of the Industrial Workers of the World (IWW), and these old Wobblies introduced Woody to the music of the legendary Joe Hill. Woody began to carry around a copy of the Industrial Workers of the World's *Little Red Song Book*.[8] Eventually, Woody settled with relatives in Glendale, and he got a job with his cousin Jack Guthrie singing on radio station KFVD in Los Angeles. Woody soon replaced his cousin and established a popular singing duet with Maxine Crissman, whom he called Lefty Lou.

Woody's political contributions to the radio program were solicited by KFVD station owner Frank Burke. In fact, Woody did some reporting for Burke's progressive newspaper, *The Light*. Angered by how the capitalist system abandoned the unemployed living in Hoovervilles along the highways and underneath the bridges of America, Woody reported, "A drunk don't like his own vomit. And a dizzy Profit System don't like its own filth."[9]

Woody's anger about the mistreatment of Okies in California seemed to draw him into more radical circles. In 1938, Woody celebrated the pardon of radical labor leader Tom Mooney, who had served twenty-three years in prison for allegedly detonating a bomb during the 1916 Preparedness Day Parade in San Francisco, by composing "Mr. Tom Mooney Is Free." Ed Robbin, who was a correspondent with the *People's Daily World* and also provided radio commentary for KFVD during the Popular Front period, asked Woody to perform the song for a Communist Party function. When Robbin inquired as to whether the folksinger had any reservations about being associated with the Communist Party, Woody replied, "Left wing, right wing, chicken-wing—it's all the same thing to me. I sing my songs wherever I can sing ''em. So if you'll have me, I'll be glad to go." The crowd loved Woody's song, especially his last line: "and now let's free California too!"[10]

While Woody's ambiguous reply to Robbin indicates that the folksinger was not prepared to endorse Marxist-Leninist ideology fully, he seemed to find no fundamental conflict between the principles of communism and American radicalism grounded in concepts of Jeffersonianism, populism, and Christian socialism. To Woody, communism was simply common sense. Writing in one of his voluminous journals, Woody asserted,

> When there shall be no want among you, because you'll own everything in common. When the rich will give their goods into the poor. I believe this way. This is the Christian way and it is already on a big part of the earth and it will come. To own everything in common. That's what the Bible says. Common means all of us. This is old 'Commonism.'

Accordingly, Woody became a regular performer at Communist Party fund-raising activities, and he even commenced a column for the *People's Daily World*, which appeared on the editorial page under the heading "Woody Sez." The column, which eventually included 174 commentaries and ran from May 1939 until January 1940, featured Woody's cartoons and such down-home philosophy as, "I ain't a communist necessarily, but I been in the red all my life." The Communist publication tended to be less doctrinaire than its New York City equivalent the *Daily Worker* and enjoyed a circulation in the tens of thousands during the late 1930s.[11]

A close reading of these columns indicates that Woody was a great deal more complicated than the country bumpkin persona he sometimes assumed in his writing. Beneath the colloquialisms and the frequent misspellings is an intellectual whose writing articulated the suffering as well as the longing of the Dust Bowl refugees for a better life. Woody's columns do not rely upon quotations from Marx and Lenin, but they certainly indicate a strong sense of class consciousness and a disdain for what capitalism had accomplished for working people. While not a theoretician by any means, Woody's pieces also offer some evidence of party influence as the folksinger supported the shifting Communist Party line in 1939 and 1940 regarding the Molotov-Ribbentrop Pact. Nevertheless, Woody seemingly maintained his distance from the harsh dictates of party discipline, essentially envisioning the political organization as a voice for peace, equality, democracy, and justice.

In his first Woody Sez column, Woody introduced himself to readers in what he termed his "awgowbyografie." When describing his early years in Okemah, Oklahoma, and Pampa, Texas, Woody failed to mention the family tragedies that plagued the Guthries. Instead, Woody emphasized the exploitive nature of American capitalism by asserting that bankers had forced farmers off their land in the Southwest. Unable to make ends meet in Pampa, he headed to California hoping to find his relatives, "but I diden't know for shore wich r.r. bridge they was a livin' under, so you see I was a travelin' practically without a magneto. I mean a compast. I didne't know where the heck I was a goin'." Of course, Woody did find those relatives, although not living under a bridge, and they helped him put together his radio show. Woody indicated that he was happy to have an opportunity to write his column because he had "a Hillbilly's Eye-View of the hole Migratious Labor movement from the South to the Pacific Coast. An' because I figgered it wood be helpful to my people, the dustbowl refugees, I was tickled to get the chance."[12]

Woody chronicled and championed the common people with a strong sense of class-consciousness, often employing populist rhetoric. On May 18, 1939, he observed that the wealthy were concerned that providing relief to the poor might lower the standard of living. Woody defined the standard of living as a home, car, clothes, groceries, radio, an electric icebox, and a job with decent wages. Things that the people did not have because the wealthy "got it from you an me." He continued this theme of exploitation by describing Wall Street as the place where "the workers git worked on an the reapers get reaped—an the farmers get plowed under." Woody concluded that Wall Street speculators were rattlesnakes who made "easy street impassable" for the people.[13]

Normally, Woody tried to interject some humor into his denunciation of the grafters, but he had little time for levity when fellow migrants were attacked. Woody was angered by an article in the reactionary *Los Angeles Times* that asserted that the migrants were nothing more than gold diggers seeking to take advantage of the taxpayers and property owners by collecting relief. An incensed Woody wrote:

> Scenes of Life in a Trailer Camp City were painted to call your attention to the untold, inhuman suffering that these people are willing to go thru—just for some of that "easy relief money." How the Sheriff's Force cleaned out the jungles and drove the Shak dwellers out of the River Bottom, set fire to their cardboard Houses, and destroyed their patchwork shelters—was told about—not to make you feel in your heart a genuine sorrow for your brothers and sisters of our American Race that's got to live in such places, but to try to make you believe that these Underprivileged people are designing in their hearts to "Dig Some Easy Gold"—of your taxpayers.

In this defense of his fellow migrants, Woody drops many of his colloquialisms and writes in a more straightforward fashion. He maintained that all his people wanted was a chance to work and earn a living. The proud Oklahoman, however, did desert his collective approach for an individualistic conclusion to his piece, observing that he had been in California for more than two years, surviving on less than one dollar a day, but he had never applied for Relief. Although Woody would always struggle with holding down a regular job, he recognized the importance of work to the "Okie migrants."[14]

Woody also championed housing as a basic human right to which all were entitled. He described houses as places to "raise children in," but in Depression America corporations were using houses to "rob workin' folks" by charging exorbitant rents. In a refrain similar to his tribute to Oklahoma bank robber and folk hero Charles Arthur "Pretty Boy" Floyd, Woody concluded that working people could be robbed "with a gun 'er with a house." He continued this theme the following day by observing that policemen were employed to protect the property of the wealthy. Woody stated, "A policeman will jest stand there an' let a banker rob a farmer, or a finance man rob a workin' man. But if a farmer robs the banker—you wood have a hole dern army of cops out a shooting at him." Woody's ideas on social banditry may not have agreed with party orthodoxy emphasizing collective action and identity rather than individual adventurism, but they reflected the reality of many people in his native Oklahoma. As Woody wrote in "The Ballad of Pretty Boy Floyd":

> Now as through this world I ramble
> I've seen lots of funny men
> Some will rob you with a six-gun
> And some with a fountain pen,
> But as through this life you roam
> You will never see an outlaw
> Drive a family from its home.[15]

In addition to bankers and landlords who were supported by a corrupt legal system, Woody had nothing but contempt for loan sharks and private utilities earning immense profits at the expense of the poor. In several columns, he discussed widows, Native Americans, and veterans whose gas or electrical services were cancelled. An angry Woody proclaimed:

> Dear Gas Companies: Uneducated, unenlightened, and uninformed as I am, provides
> me with a magnificent opportunity, and elegant excuse to tell you right here and now
> that I oftimes have nightmares in which there go crawling and creeping species of crea-
> tures similar to those which are symbolized by the practices you use.

His venom was also apparent for furniture dealers who applied high rates of interest to purchases by working-class people, who could not afford to pay cash up front for their goods. Casting the creditors into the same circle of hell as bankers and utility companies, Woody wrote, "Dear Credit People: I have come to the conclusion, after long meditation, zealous forethought, and silent prayer, that you are a bunch of Low

Down Thieves . . . and I am unable to think otherwise." Personalizing the issue as he often did in his columns, Woody complained that it was difficult for his twenty-one-year-old brother George to get married because creditors were attempting to "enslave, degrade, depress, deprive, and otherwise 'rob' our young folks that's a falling in Love, and a getting married."[16] In this passage, Woody takes a rather traditional line of American protest that selfish interests were blocking the Jeffersonian pursuit of happiness.

Woody also addressed basic issue of health care in a column reporting that his family was expecting a baby. The singer understood that doctors, like everyone else, had to make a living, but he simply could not comprehend any way that a physician could charge as much for his services during one night of delivering a baby as a working man earned in six months of laboring. Woody contemplated, "Funny how one feller can hit a few licks of some sort of 'inspired work'—like a doctor, or a lawyer, and take all the inspiration out of you for a year." Celebrating the dignity and worth of all labor, Woody in his unique way appeared to call for a system of universal health care, writing, "I believe in a government wholesale price on babies, delivered to your house, 'cause they double the pressure, triple the increase, and quadruple the price at the hosspistol."[17]

In denouncing creditors and advocating for health care, Woody appears to fit within the reform tradition of the New Deal. The paradoxical Woody, however, also espoused more revolutionary sentiments in his Woody Sez columns. On June 24, 1939, he sounded like Marx proclaiming that the workers had nothing to lose but their chains. Stopping just short of calling for a revolution, Woody exclaimed, "Down with Wall Street. Down with salary loan sharks—down with the rape mad finance fiends—We are civilized to the brink of poverty, slavery, an' slaughter. If this be treason—make the most of it." In his unique fashion, Woody also sometimes used Marxist analysis regarding common ownership for the means of production. In discussing his trip to Redding, California, where workers had gathered in hopes of gaining employment on a dam project, Woody wrote, "When you get to where you perduce for Use instead of for a silly Profit—you'll have a cinch on 3 squares a day, on a job." The next day, however, Woody returned to more revolutionary rhetoric. He insisted, "Lots of the big money boys is a willin' to you a workin' for their Freedom—an' in persuit of their Happiness, but that is like a puttin' the constitution down in Pig Latin. To expect help, groceries, freedom and fair chance from a selfish, greedy, whole-hog, profiteer—is like milkin' a dead cow. It won't work."[18] Despite such a pessimistic forecast for reforming the American system, Woody did not totally depart from party orthodoxy regarding Popular Front cooperation with anti-Fascist democracies such as President Franklin Roosevelt's New Deal.

During the summer of 1939 before the signing of the Molotov-Ribbentrop Pact in August, Woody supported the New Deal and the reelection of President Roosevelt. Woody continued to denounce those exploiting the common people, but he appeared to tone down his rhetoric a bit, providing a less incendiary or revolutionary approach to the political and economic crisis of capitalism in the United States. Instead, Woody returned to extolling the virtues of the migrants and the poor. On July 7, he discussed his comfort level when walking down Skid Row in Los Angeles, asserting that he trusted hobos more than the "playfolks that populate our banks and hotels." In another piece about the migrants, Woody maintained that they were honest and true because they were forced to live in a state of nature with few possessions and empty bellies. Woody proclaimed,

> You Land Shirks, and other Friskers, listen to me, the hungrier you make us, the wiser
> we get . . . cause all of the good books on religion advice you to fast and think . . . and
> the fastest you can think is when youre right hungery.

Woody also had supportive remarks regarding how John Steinbeck portrayed the migrants in *The Grapes of Wrath*. Woody wrote:

> John's book is out to show you just exactly what th Arkies, an th Oakies, th Kansies, an
> th Texies, an-all of the farmers an workers has to go through—so's somebody can make a
> profit off of em. John's book was a little to poetry—like to ever take a holt among the real,
> genuine 'dusties'—but it will hit right where folks don't know what other folks has to go
> through—except by books.

And at three dollars, the singer concluded that the migrants would scarcely be able to afford Steinbeck's novel.[19]

As Woody reaffirmed his faith in the people, he also continued to defend the Communist Party and its supporters. On July 17, 1939, he reported that former party member John Leech was testifying before the House Un-American Activities Committee and denouncing communism. Woody labeled Leech as a Judas figure, observing:

> But thats the way it was when they nailed the carpenter to the cross—they took the word
> of the folks that didn't know anything a'bout him, and then—a feller named Judas, that
> deserted his party—sold out his teacher, an his own soule—for about 30 hunks of silver.

Woody often used Christian imagery in both his music and writings. When Woody was a young boy, the Socialist Party was an important political force in Oklahoma; however, the party in the Southwest did not champion a materialistic atheism. Instead, the socialist tradition in states such as Oklahoma embraced a millennial Christian tradition in which the meek would inherit the earth. Accordingly, the Socialist Party often did well in areas where such Pentecostal groups as the Church of Christ enjoyed popular support. In *Grass Roots Socialism*, James Green argues:

> In the early 1900s the new holiness sects of the Southwest clearly represented the primitive Christianity of the oppressed. The holiness movement was a "radical opponent" of materialism and modernism in the established churches, and in that sense it was a product of the same kind of class consciousness [*sic*] that led poor people to socialism.[20]

While Woody may have been a "red," he was certainly no atheist, maintaining a faith in Christian socialism led by a plain-speaking working-class carpenter who was opposed to vested economic and political interests. This somewhat simplistic belief in a Christian socialism allowed Woody to eschew the doctrinal disputes between Communists and Socialists.

Woody also defended labor leader Harry Bridges. The United States government wanted to deport the Australian-born leader of the longshoremen for his Communist connections. Woody asserted that Bridges believed that the union was Americanism, "and Abe Lincoln said the same thing." In a song written for Bridges, Woody proclaimed:

> Now that th song about Harry Bridges
> And the Union Battle he has fought—
> "Unionism is Americanism."
> And that's what I have all ways thought.

Woody believed that Bridges was in trouble because of the "red-baiting" pursued by William Randolph Hearst and his media empire. According to Woody:

> When a guy comes out a raisin' hell about the megertory workers, and hoboes, and poore folks, an worken people, an scares hell of em with cartoons and old storys in a newspaper—an tries to keep era ignerent—an rule em by fear—like th Hearst papers does—I ain't got no use for em.[21]

In this diatribe against Hearst, Woody was, as is often the case, more precise in denouncing the grafters than articulating how exactly change was to come about in the world. However, he maintained a simple vision in which a nation governed by the working people would usher in progress, while in a country "run by Money rule, you got rotten politicians, rotten banks, rotten crops, rotten clothing, rotten gangsters, and rotten ever thing." The vision of a workers' state, which ostensibly existed in the Soviet Union, appeared to describe Woody's ideal government. Yet, the ambiguous Woody spent little time and energy waxing poetically about the workers' paradise in the Soviet Union. While often defending communism and adhering to essential aspects of the party line, the singer was an American who wanted to create a people's government in the United States that would harken back to the founding principles of the Declaration of Independence that all men were created equal. Woody commented upon a Japanese family he encountered in his travels. They had migrated to the United States in search of freedom. Woody concluded:

> That's how come the U.S.A. to get started—And that's what has keep her a goin . . .
> Freedom. Folks is a lookin for Freedom. Here and hereafter, the best thing they ask for
> is Freedom. A Job of Work, a fair chance an Honest Share of the stuff they perduce . . .
> they got that much a comin to em, and they are dad-gum shure a goin to Get It. They'll
> cross oceans, fight wars, migerate like birds, go through hell's high waters, or anything
> else 1000 times—to get Freedom.[22]

This was Woody's paradise. An America where the common people could find fulfilling work and be free from exploitation. Woody placed little faith in organized religion. Instead, he believed in the millennial return of the working-class carpenter, who would bring peace, equality, and justice to the world. The folksinger envisioned an earthy paradise in which:

> Should the Master appear again on earth, that he would take a look at the churches, a
> look at the sinners, and associate himself at once with the sinners . . . as He did before.
> Religion is to forget yourself and work for the good of others. Outside of that there is
> no religion . . . no progress . . . no hope for you, your neighbor, your coming grand-
> children. Find out who is causing the Trouble here in this old World—remove the power
> from their hands—place it in the hands of those who ain't Greedy—and you can roll over
> and go to sleep.

Woody was more interested in ends than means, and if the Communist Party could usher in the commonwealth of equality called for by the Prince of Peace, then so be it.[23]

With the Molotov-Ribbentrop Pact followed by the invasion of Poland on the first of September

1939, it was a difficult time to be a Communist. The Popular Front policy of collective security against fascism was abandoned as Stalin, convinced after the Munich crisis of 1938 that the Western democracies would not stand up to Hitler, determined that the interests of the Soviet Union could best be served by forming a temporary alliance with the Nazi dictator. The shift in policy of the Communist Party in the United States made it apparent to many critics that American Communists were simply following the dictates of the Soviet Union and exercised no independence. Yet, Woody did not desert the party, shifting from the anti-Fascist Popular Front to a denunciation of capitalistic war as exploitive of the working class. Although he generally continued to support the New Deal and President Roosevelt for reelection in 1940, Woody downplayed the upcoming elections in his columns in the fall of 1939. He would not repudiate his leftist sympathies and increasingly focused his attention on questions of war and peace in his writings. A playful Woody commented upon his lost songbook, suggesting:

> Well you will find some of them songs to be putty dern left handed. They was so left wing
> I had to write em with my left hand and sing em with my left tonsil, an string my gittar
> up backwards to git eny harmony out of em.

He also wrote a column describing how he was sitting home, "buried about 6 foot deep in some dialecticle matternilisation, an it was a speakin a bout what was real, an what was just pure old imaginin," when his children wanted to play and eat, but they wanted real not imaginary oranges. For Woody, the future was always about the children and creating a better world for them.[24]

Woody increasingly wrote about the impact of war in Europe on the children, and he endorsed the Soviet policy of perceiving World War II as a capitalist conflict. He observed, "See where Hitler is a gonna jump on the wimmen & children, too, an everybody else says, if you jump on em, we'll jump on em too, which makes it look like theyre a goin to get jumped on." A few days later, Woody found the origins of the war to lie in the private ownership of scarce resources. He lamented, "Some war. Seems like theyre a fightin to see who owns what. . . . Well if th country belonged to ever body init they coodent no fights break out." War would be a problem as long as civilization was based on the profit system.[25]

In support of peace, Woody urged workers, who were strapped financially, to donate a day's pay to maintain the *People's Daily World* as one of the few voices against war and fascism. Taking on the persona of his new son Bill, Woody wrote, "But by the time I grow up to be a man, I want this old world to be, by dam, the people's world. Not just some chose few, but a world of working people of the working world."[26]

Despite Woody's plea for a peaceful world, war was a factor in Europe, and the singer commented on the conflict using football metaphors. Woody quipped:

Chamberlain kicked off an Hitler made a run thru Poland. Mussolini is on the side line. Warsaw got tackled behind the goal post, and lost the ball. Russia is in a huddle and seems to be gaining several yards. Every European radio is broadcasting the game, and every Dictator says his side is wining.

Never acknowledging that his analysis also supported Soviet self-interest, the columnist concluded that the war was a failure, squandering precious resources needed by the people. He denounced the European war in the most vehement terms, urging Americans to resist policies of conscription of aid to the British, which would draw the country into a war benefiting corrupt politicians and Capitalist grafters. Woody exclaimed:

War is a game played by maniacs, who kill each other. It is murder, studied and prepared by insane minds, and followed by a bunch of thieves. You can't believe in life, and wear the uniform of death. There are certain men who never think of any other thing besides slaughter. They are blood soaked butchers and they are believed to be heroes. Three fifths of the people decide to murder the other two fifths, who must take up killing in order to stay alive. Locate the man who profits by war—strip him of his profits and war will end.

In this analysis of the war in Europe before Hitler invaded the Soviet Union in June 1941, Woody voiced the Communist Party line. In his embracing of the Chinese people as victims of Japanese aggression, however, he also reflected a general American sympathy for the Chinese and condemnation of Japanese militarism. Departing from his earlier blanket denunciation of war in Europe with which the Soviets were most concerned, Woody wrote, "An'—I aint no prophet—but with a equal break, with powder an' shot, I wood not bet I red cent that Japan, or three more like Japan, cood conquer th' spirit of the August an Noble, Peace Worshipping China."[27]

Although in late 1939 the Woody Sez columns were focusing on issues of war and peace, Woody continued to rail against the exploitation of the working people by big business and profiteers, while calling for a more collectivist future. He envisioned a United States as one big union that everyone would join, concluding:

Now, if you an me an everybody all be longed to th same big union—an then th union was to guarantee you a job all of th time—why, heck—we cood all be richer then we by a dang sight.

And Woody persisted in his depiction of Jesus Christ as a model for organizing the people to drive the money changers and Capitalists from Wall Street. He concluded:

> Today we need to make a Whip of small organizations an small movements—an bind them and wind them into one great big "Whip"—an' drive not only the Money Changing Ideas and thoughts out of our own minds, and our bodily Temple—but all so to drive the Money Changers out of the Temple of our Nation.[28]

Steinbeck, much admired by Woody, tapped similar sentiments with Preacher Jim Casey and his idea of one big soul.

While embracing this collectivist vision, Woody was also unable to abandon his admiration for social outlaws. In an October column, he provided a rousing film review of *Jesse James* (1939), featuring Henry Fonda in the title role. Woody praised Frank and Jesse James as victims of the railroads who hired hoodlums to drive the farmers off their land. Even though the railroad bombed their home and killed their mother, the James brothers continued to fight the corrupt railroad interests. Woody insisted, "No wonder folks likes to hear songs about the outlaws—they're wrong allright, but not as dirty and sneakin' as some of our so called 'higher ups.'" Woody, however, remained an activist, not a film critic. He warned California vigilantes to "polish up your balls and chains," for he was coming to the cotton fields to monitor the progress of the cotton strike.[29]

In another column, however, Woody indicated that he was getting restless in California, speculating where as the "dirtiest of the Dustbowlers" he might migrate to next.[30] On January 7, 1940, Woody wrote his final Woody Sez column for the *People's Daily World*. As usual, he did not bid farewell to all his readers, friends, or family. Woody's adherence to the Communist Party line following the Molotov-Ribbentrop Pact had resulted in a parting of the ways between the radical folksinger and progressive KFVD radio station owner Frank Burke. With nothing to hold him in California and restless once again, Woody deposited his wife and children in Pampa before he headed toward a new promised land for migrants of the world, New York City.

A close reading of the Woody Sez columns in the *People's Daily World* provides ample evidence that the California years of the late 1930s were a crucial period in which Woody investigated the living conditions of the Dust Bowl refugees and formulated a radical hybrid political ideology which incorporated elements of Christian socialism, social banditry, populism, Jeffersonianism, collectivism, "commonism," and the ideology of the Communist Party. While the 1976 Ashby film based on Woody's autobiography attempted to strip the folksinger of his radicalism, Woody was already a committed leftist when he departed

California for New York City and composed "This Land Is Your Land" in early 1940. Nevertheless, this radical song continues to be defanged by ignoring the more radical verses that question private property.

> Was a big high wall there that tried to stop me
> A sign was painted said: Private Property
> But on the back side, it didn't say nothing—
> God Blessed America for me
> One bright sunny morning in the shadow of the steeple
> By the relief office I saw my people—
> And they stood there wondering if
> God blessed America for me.[31]

In New York City, Woody briefly authored a column for the *Daily Worker* and maintained his association with the Communist Party. Fading health—Woody was institutionalized for the last eleven years of his life, suffering from Huntington's disease, a degenerative disorder of the central nervous system—and thus spared the folksinger from suffering the full brunt of reactionary McCarthyism in the post–World War II period. He never recanted his Communist past and beliefs. As David Shumway suggested in an insightful essay on Woody's legacy, "If we are to understand Woody Guthrie's place in our cultural history, we can only do so by acknowledging his indigenous radicalism."[32] The Woody Sez columns for the *People's Daily World* illuminate the complexity of Woody's radicalism. His vision of a better world for all of God's children attempted to fuse elements of traditional American radicalism with Marxism. At times Guthrie's adherence to the Communist Party makes him appear as somewhat of a "Hillbilly Apparatchik" who slavishly followed the dictates of the party, but in his celebration of working people and the promise of American life he was very much a traditional left-wing American populist. In his profound way, Woody found room for Christianity, communism, populism, and Jeffersonianism in his own popular front, fighting for social justice during the late 1930s.

TOWNE FORUM
MEETINGS
DAILY
11AM 2PM
WE ELECT
Fay E.
ALLEN
Board of
Education
By Special Request.
Sun 2 PM
WOODY.
& HIS
Singing His Own
Songs of the Common
Dedicated
TO
SKID-ROAD
& Dust Bowl Refugees

Nine

WOODY AND SKID ROW IN LOS ANGELES

DARRYL HOLTER

During his years in Los Angeles from 1937 to 1941 Woody Guthrie spent a lot of time on L.A.'s Skid Row. He often worked there, frequently performing his songs for tips and drinks in the bars, coffee shops, and street corners on Main Street between Fourth and Fifth Streets or writing his Woody Sez articles for a daily newspaper with offices on Fifth Street between Main and Spring Streets. He sometimes slept in flophouses, twenty men to a room. These were the years of the Great Depression marked by high unemployment and grinding poverty, and Woody designated himself the voice for those whose voices too often went unheard: the working people, the Dust Bowl refugees, the poor, the homeless, and the people of Skid Row.

Woody's songs and writings expressed a clear and honest understanding of the Skid Row population. He wrote in a dry, folksy, humorous manner. In his early writing in Los Angeles, he deliberately misspelled words to give his writing a "Hillbilly" sound. His writings on Skid Row contain a sense of empathy that derived from his experiences in Oklahoma and Texas when, as a teenager, his middle-class, small-town family was torn apart: his father's business collapsed, his terminally ill mother was sent to an asylum, and his father was burned in an accident that forced Woody to live on his own or with friends or relatives for several difficult years. As the Depression deepened and the dark dust storms ravaged the towns of the Southwest, Woody learned to ride the rails and interact with migrant workers, the homeless, and hoboes. He arrived in Los Angeles in 1937 penniless and without a job or a place to live. As Woody

Opposite: Los Angeles, Spring 1941.

wrote in 1939, "Skid Row is generally where you land when you first hit Los Angeles on a freight train a'blowin' out of the Dustbowl."[1]

After landing a job hosting a daily fifteen-minute radio show on KFVD, Woody wrote a number of songs for his show that drew upon his experiences in Skid Row. In the song "Skid Row Blues," Woody describes how he has been "skiddin' around on Skid Row, the skiddiest street in town". In "Fifth Street Blues," Woody created a new set of lyrics for a traditional folk song called "Deep Ellum Blues." He tells the story of a soldier, a sailor, and a little girl from Hollywood—all of whom met a sad fate near Fifth and Main. Woody included "Fifth Street Blues" in a songbook he wrote entitled *On A Slow Train Through California*, compiled in Los Angeles in 1939. In the songbook, Woody dedicates the song "in respect and honor to 5th St., Los Angeles, California, for the Spirit that abides there, and for the people who go there, by the forces of an unbalanced social order, or by their own free will. . . . I love the Spirit and the people that walk there."[2]

Woody's use of the term "the forces of an unbalanced social order" lies at the heart of his assessment of the denizens of Skid Row. In a later passage he offers an explanation of why people stay in Skid Row:

> 5th St is one of the important places of the 20th Century Fix. When you see the folks of all nations crowded up down there, a goin' and a comin' and a millin' around and a pan-derin' around, up and down . . . you might ask why they don't leave. . . . Well, there are two schools of thought. One claims these folks "choose" to be there, and the other claims these folks is "caught" there, like rats in a trap of some kind. . . . I think both arguments is right. Some of the folks choose to be there. Some of 'em is caught down there. The world puts some of 'em on 5th St., and others just naturally like it there. . . . It is a natural growth of a natural society, and is not created by the people that's down there, but by the money grabbers that drove 'em down there."

While celebrating the Skid Row population in "Fifth Street," Woody does not glorify them but, rather, treats them like other human beings from other communities—noble and flawed, good and bad, honest and dishonest. He recognizes that different types of people, from many backgrounds, inhabit Skid Row or visit it for a variety of reasons. Woody's Skid Row is a loose, fluid community that includes people who have fallen into poverty, people who are trying to rise out of poverty, homeless people, visitors looking for cheap food or drinks or a pawn shop, alcoholics of all classes, people looking to buy or sell marijuana or cocaine, and struggling musicians playing for tips. "Two reasons why you hit Skid Row is something to eat, and somewheres to sleep," Woody wrote. "You can do both cheaper on Skid Row than you can in the more civilized sections of town. Besides the Police bother you too much in the classier sections."[3] In his autobiographical novel, *Bound for Glory,* Woody tells the story of how he and fellow folksinger Cisco Houston arrived on Skid Row on a cold and rainy December night in 1941 hoping to earn some coins singing for tips. In prose that works as poetry, Woody describes in unvarnished terms the wide variety of people who gather in Skid Row:

> This is where the working people come
> To try to squeeze a little fun
> And rest out of a buffalo nickel;
> These three or four blocks of old wobbling flop houses and buildings.
> I know you people I see here on the Skid.
> The hats pulled down over the faces I can't see.
> You know my name and you call me a guitar busker,
> a joint hopper, tip canary, kittybox man.
> Movie people, hoss wranglers, dead enders, stew bums;
> Stealers, dealers, sidewalk spielers;
> Con men, sly flies, flat foots, reefer riders;
> Dopers, smokers, boiler stokers;
> Sailors, whalers, bar flies, brass railers;
> Spittoon tuners, fruit-tree pruners;
> Cobber, spiders, three-way riders;
> Honest people, fakes, vamps and bleeders;
> Saviors, saved, and side-street singers;
> Whore-house hunters, door-bell ringers;
> Footloosers, rod riders, caboosers, outsiders;
> Honky tonk and whiskey setters, tight-wads, spendthrifts, race-horse betters;
> Blackmailers, gin soaks, comers, goers;
> Good girls, bad girls, teasers, whores; Los Angeles, Spring 1941.
> Buskers, corn huskers, dust bowlers, dust panners;
> Waddlers, toddlers, dose packers, syph carriers;
> Money men, honey men, sad men, funny men;
> Ramblers, gamblers, highway anklers;

Cowards, brave guys, stools and snitches;
Nice people, bastards, sonsabitches;
Fair, square, and honest folks;
Sneaking greedy people;
And somewhere, in amongst all these Skid Row skidders—
Cisco and me sung for our chips.[4]

While working at KFVD, Woody met Ed Robbin, a political activist who wrote for the *People's Weekly World*, the West Coast daily of the Communist Party. Robbin also had a show on KFVD that was on the air just before Woody's *Woody and Lefty Lou* show. Robbins befriended Woody and introduced him to the large group of political activists in Los Angeles. Soon Woody was writing articles for the *People's Weekly World*, which had its offices on Fifth Street between Spring and Main. One day Robbin took Woody, who as usual carried his guitar slung over his back, to Clifton's Caféteria, which was owned by Clifford Clinton who was active in a movement to reform the political system in L.A. and sometimes allowed unemployed people to pay whatever they thought the food was worth. Woody ate a big meal and then went to the cash register and laid down seven cents. The girl at the register called the manager who asked Woody if he didn't like the food. Woody said he liked it fine, but didn't have the "do, re, mi." The manager asked if Woody wanted him to call the police or ask him to work for a while in the kitchen. Woody chose the latter option and followed the manager into the kitchen. Robbin returned an hour later and went to Clifton's enormous kitchen. There he saw Woody perched on a tall chair singing some of his songs.

Take a seat, Ed, and make yourself at home. Some of these fellers are friends of mine. They listen to me on the radio. We probably did stoop labor in the same fields and ranches and drank in the same bars all the way from Texas to California. Ain't that right fellows? A man said, "Woody, whenever you want some grub, just slip in the back door over yonder. We've got plenty here."[5]

Woody also described his experiences in the skid rows of Stockton, San Francisco, and Redding, and visited several so-called "Hoovervilles," encampments of homeless people and migratory workers often located near railroad stations. In a song called "Hooversville," Woody described these encampments: "Ramblin' gamblin' rickety shacks, that's Hooversville. Rusty tin and raggedy sacks, that's Hooversville." He found that many of the Dust Bowl refugees were familiar with his radio show and were surprised to see him in the same dire economic situation as they were in. Wandering across the state as a roving reporter for an ephemeral liberal newspaper called *The Light*, Woody found himself stranded for two nights on the side of the road near Barstow, California, with a small army of unemployed men with nowhere to go. "These people," Woody reported, "are mostly the ones who have tired of marching with the starvation armies of wandering workers and grown weary of the smell of rotting fruit crops."[6] Woody began to refer to the homeless migrants as "my people" as he lived among them in ramshackle huts, leaky tents, with hunger and disease. He saw how badly his people were treated, not just by unemployment or poor working conditions, but by open discrimination: many hotels, retail stores and other establishments posted signs saying "No Mexicans or Okies."

By the time he left Los Angeles in 1940 bound for Oregon and then New York, the population of the city's Skid Row had left its mark on Woody Guthrie.

"HIS MASTER'S VOICE"
REG. U. S. PAT. OFF.   MARCAS REGISTRADAS

VICTOR

P 27-5   26621-A

TOM JOAD–Part 1

(Woody Guthrie)

Woody Guthrie

Singing with guitar and harmonica

Ten

"THE GHOST OF TOM JOAD"

BRYANT SIMON AND WILLIAM DEVERELL

The last shall be first and the first shall be last.
—Bruce Springsteen, "The Ghost of Tom Joad"

Holed up in a creaky cabin next to his Carmel, California, house, late on a series of deadlines, and pained over the breakup of his first marriage, John Steinbeck fretted over whether the book he was working on, *The Grapes of Wrath*, was any good. "I'm not sure anyone will read it," he worried in his diary. Of course, people would read the book, and it would become a touchstone for the last century and an inheritance for this one. Readers would take Ma Joad, Preacher Casey, and Tom Joad with them; they would turn these figures into frames of reference for what the Great Depression meant, and for their own politics and sensibilities.

Charting the history of *The Grapes of Wrath* and of Tom Joad is partly an experiment in what can be called the biography of a fictional character, following the real and representative lives that invented people—fictional characters—lived after they came on the scene. And it also traces the shifting cultural, political, and social meanings of Steinbeck's enduring and durable main character Tom Joad—the angry, scrappy, fictional Okie migrant who is beaten, but never licked. Why does he continue to resonate and to serve as an important and compelling figure more than seventy-five years after the publication of *The Grapes of Wrath*?

As unemployment lines once again snake around city blocks, Joad and Steinbeck are making yet another comeback. Today's wayward are compared to the Joads, but even more, we seek out Joad for some understanding. Fashion designers have marked the new normal by producing more austere, utilitarian clothing and place references to the Joads in their ad copy. *Business Week* recently reported that amazon.com sales of *The Grapes of Wrath* spiked with the onset of the New Recession. Bowery hipsters, at the same time, are going to Depression parties in loft apartments and showing up in wool hats like the one Joad—aka Henry Fonda—wore in John Ford's film version of *The Grapes of Wrath*. There is something new, which we will return to later, but invoking Joad is part of an American tradition.

Artists, filmmakers, documentarians, and politicians from Woody Guthrie in the 1940s to Studs Terkel in the 1960s to Bruce Springsteen in the 1990s to New York hipsters today, have invoked Joad in their various commentaries on the state of the American dream. In many ways, Joad has stood all these years for a deep and rich, though largely unrecognized, American political tradition. This tradition stresses the Declaration of Independence over the Constitution, New Deal intervention over free-market conservatism, cooperation over competition, the group over the individual, movement over staying put, and thoughtful dissent over blind patriotism. Really this a notion of communalism based not on socialism or liberalism, but on the social gospel, on ideas about mobility, community, second chances, and the possibilities of heaven on this earth. And its touchstone is the Great Depression—a moment when according to Steinbeck and to his Tom Joad the system failed the people, not one where the people failed the system.

Joad has retained his place in the American imagination, because of Steinbeck's emotive representation of the Great Depression. For him the Dust Bowl was not a natural disaster, but a man-made catastrophe brought on by greed and speculation. And again, for Steinbeck, the experiences of the wandering Dust Bowl Joads isn't unique—it is representative of a system that puts private gain ahead of people's lives, that privileges the few ahead of the many.

Joad's hold on so many for so long isn't solely due to the author's moving portrait or, for that matter, to the arresting drama of the dust storms, the trek along Route 66 (known to some as the Joad Road), the breakup of the family, and to the economic crisis of the 1930s—the underlying action of *The Grapes of Wrath*. Joad's dualities make him so compelling, everlasting, and even pliable—for he speaks to the complexity and realness, as opposed to simplicity and plasticity, of the American experience. He is tough and tender, a patriot and critic, a defender of place and man on the road, a dreamer and dissenter. Joad fervently believes in the promise of America, in the abiding faith that things can get better, but unlike those who chant jingoistic slogans, his faith in the nation does not blind him to its shortcomings. He wants to save the best features of America from its meanest and most selfish impulses. And that makes him the spirit of the American protest tradition, inherited from Tom Paine and Eugene V. Debs and passed on to Martin

Luther King Jr. and Steve Earle.

Tom Joad began as a nameless nonfiction character. Steinbeck, of course, was a child of California's Central Valley, the epicenter of America's agribusiness. From his hometown of Salinas, California, he never strayed very far, and neither did his best work. Fresh off the blockbuster successes *Of Mice and Men* and *In Dubious Battle*, Steinbeck was asked in the middle of the 1930s to write about the agricultural crisis taking shape in the farm fields near his parents' home. He got the story—by doing what we would today call immersion journalism. He went to the Hoovervilles and relief centers. He reminded himself as he went about his research: "Must take time in the description, detail, looks, clothes, gestures. . . . We have to know these people. Know their looks and their nature." Out of this research, he produced a seven-part series of newspaper articles, he called, "The Harvest of Gypsies." This detailed treatment of the Okies— the migrants or the "untouchables" of their day—at the hands of the growers, was Steinbeck's first take on the Great Depression. In his view, the growers were squeezing the people and making their lives an untenable hell. The series garnered a great deal of attention and added to Steinbeck's fame. This suggests something important about the broader culture of the Great Depression, something that is invoked whenever Joad is invoked.

The historian Jeff Cowie has written about how issues of "economic justice" were, in his words, "thick in the air in the 1930s." This led, as he and others have argued, to the "cultural enfranchisement of the working people." In other words, during the 1930s, the larger culture paid attention to the poor and their struggles—they saw them as central to the nation. Steinbeck, of course, both as a fiction writer and nonfiction writer, was one of the leading voices in this artistic and political movement.

"When I wrote *The Grapes of Wrath*," Steinbeck said in a 1952 interview, "I was filled with anger at people who were doing injustices to other people." What Steinbeck witnessed in his newspaper research had a profound effect on him and on *The Grapes of Wrath*. The details and feelings gave his novel a specific human context, a felt emotional quality, and a dramatic dimension that his earlier versions lacked. And the powerful emotion of anger—his impulse after following the Okies—never quite left the novel.

Tom Joad first appears to the reader when he is returning from prison. He exudes a meanness and a danger, a kind of smoldering aura. He is ready to do battle, against what it isn't clear. As the novel takes shape, so does the focus of his rage. He begins to direct his wrath at the faceless bankers and businessmen who are destroying his family, his Oklahoma community, and the way of life there. As he moves West, his ire is directed at the labor recruiters and growers who exploit his family and tear it apart. This points to one of the novel's main themes, one of the legacies of Joad—the idea of conversion, of change, and of moving beyond individualism and individual rage toward a larger collective vision.

Like so many Americans stories, *The Grapes of Wrath* is an inversion of *The Odyssey*. This is not an epic story about going home, but about leaving home. Steinbeck centers the Joads' journey and search for better days on the frontier and in California. For him and tens of thousands of others in the twentieth century, this is the modern American promised land, the westerly end of the continent, the place for second chances where redemption is possible. Yet, it also the cruelest of American places, a place of brutal Darwinian struggle where the mighty run roughshod over the many in the bright glare of celebrity and unending sunshine.

Out of that disappointment—a disappointment not in himself, but in his country—Joad's anger wells up again. He becomes a kind of everyman of the Depression. As Joad confronts the California shortcomings, he converts to a social gospel theology introduced to him by the itinerant preacher Jim Casey. Though Joad never loses his edge, anger, or capacity for violence, he moves with Casey away from individualism to a larger collective vision, the idea of connectedness as the solution to the problems of the Great Depression.

Joad, of course, delivers his invocation of this idea of the collective spirit of America in his final speech. Here we find out that he, like all American heroes, has changed—holding this possibility out to others. He tells his Ma (with a Jeffersonian hint):

> Whenever they's a fight so hungry people can eat, I'll be there.
> Whenever they's a cop beatin' up a guy, I'll be there. . . .
> I'll be in the way guys yell when they're mad an'—I'll be there in the way kids laugh
> when they're hungry an' they know supper's ready. An' when our folks eat the stuff they
> raise an' live in the houses they build—why, I'll be there.

Over the last seven decades, artists and public figures have continually reinterpreted Joad and his Depression-era collectivist message. Along the way, he has been turned into a symbol of conscience and suffering for others and for their own interpretations of the West, California, and the larger American past.

Shortly after the publication of Steinbeck's novel, John Ford directed a film version of *The Grapes of Wrath*. Played with simple grace and a smoldering anger by Henry Fonda, Ford's Joad follows Steinbeck's Joad west along Route 66 to California. By the end of this rough road, he too gives voice to a vague dream of American community. He says in the film's stirring climax that everyone is part of one big whole: if one person suffers, everyone suffers.

. Then there was Woody Guthrie. No single person exemplified, even personified, the character of Joad, better than Woody. Not long after the film version of the novel made its debut, Woody went from

California to New York to play at a benefit concert for what was called the John Steinbeck Committee for Agricultural Workers. With Gotham's literary left listening, Woody sang a few ballads and traditional songs accompanied by Huddie "Lead Belly" Ledbetter and Aunt Molly Jackson.

After the concert, Woody was not ready to call it a night. He told his friend Pete Seeger that the Victor record people "want me to write a song about *The Grapes of Wrath*." Woody wanted to get started right away. In search of wine and a typewriter—Woody's favorite tools for songwriting—the folksingers ended up in a Lower East Side apartment. Woody went right to work. Without notes, he typed verse after verse. Seeger dozed off as Woody walked in circles around the room, playing chords and singing in a muffled voice. When Seeger woke the next morning, he found Woody asleep on the floor, the wine jug empty, and seventeen verses of "Tom Joad" still in the typewriter.

Woody was tremendously proud of his new song. "I think the ballad of the Joads is the best thing I've done so far," he told a friend.

Woody's Joad was drawn from Ford's Joad, not, if the distinction matters, from Steinbeck's Joad. He never read the book, but he did say that the film was "Best cussed pitcher I ever seen."

Woody created his own lyrical version of *The Grapes of Wrath* and a Joad for the masses. There are people, he said, back in Oklahoma who haven't got two bucks to buy the book, or even thirty-five cents to see the movie, . . . but [my] song will get back to them." Set to the tune of the ballad of the West Virginia outlaw John Hardy, Woody's "Tom Joad" closely follows the action of Ford's film.[1]

"We got to git away Tom," Ma Joad says in an early stanza. Woody's Joads head west to the promised land, where "there was work for everything single hand." The road was hard. Once in California, the migrants find that the land of milk and honey is really a place of raw meanness: jungle camps, hungry kids, a vicious deputy sheriff, the barrel of a gun. California's false promises tested fragile faith. Minister Casey begins to preach a new gospel, telling "workin' folks to stick together." His this-world faith arouses the anger of a "vigilante thug," who clubs the preacher dead. "He laid preacher Casey on the ground," Woody sang. Outraged, Joad then kills the deputy and sets out for a life on the run. Quoting Ford's film almost verbatim, Woody's ballad ends with an homage to the communalist tradition. Tom tells his mother:

> Ever'body might be just one big soul
> Well it looks that-a way to me
> So everywhere you look in th' day or th' night
> That's where I'm a gonna be, ma
> That's where I'm a gonna be.

Wherever little kids are hungry and cry
Wherever people ain't free
Where men are fightin for their rights
That's where I'm gonna be, ma.
That's where I'm a gonna be.[2]

Even though it was seven minutes long and couldn't be pressed on a single side of a 78-rpm record, Woody's "Tom Joad" is a condensed version of the film and the book. It boiled down the action from the Steinbeck and Ford stories to essential details. And his Joad delivers the clearest political message yet.

In the novel, and again in the film, Joad vows to spend the rest of his life bearing witness to inequity and struggle. Woody's Joad does the same, but with an important twist. In this version, Joad becomes a fearless union organizer. Mirroring Woody's own down-home, left-wing politics, his Joad addresses the battle between the rich and the poor, and the need for working people to stick together in very specific ways—unions and political action—to end their hardships.

Like Ford's Joad, Woody's Joad will be there "wherever little kids are hungry" and "wherever people ain't free." But he will be there as a partisan voice "wherever men are fighting for their rights." Woody's Joad is closer to a Californian Joe Hill, the Joe Hill who told his followers, just before he was hanged, "Don't mourn, organize."

Woody did not simply cut scenes and imagery for his "Tom Joad" from the film version of *The Grapes of Wrath*. The singer knew something about Joad and his imagined family. Born in Oklahoma in 1912, Woodrow Wilson Guthrie spent the first few years of his life in relative comfort. His father was a real estate broker and local politician. Beginning in 1918, hard times hit the family. His father's business dried up and his political connections dissolved. Woody's mother, Nora, who had taught him how to sing, began a long and tortured battle with depression exacerbated by the debilitating, and undiagnosed, progression of Huntington's chorea. Mysterious fires plagued the family. Their house burned down. Nora scorched Charley with a kerosene lamp. Woody's baby sister Cathy burned to death doing chores. The family fell apart. Nora ended up in a rundown sanitarium, unable to recognize Woody. She died there in 1927. Broke, beaten, and robbed of "every illusion of hope," Charley left Oklahoma and settled in the Texas panhandle, barely eking out a small-farm living.[3] Woody moved in with him in 1929, but he did not stay long.

In the middle of the 1930s, as the dust storms blew, Woody crisscrossed the country, going from Texas to California and back again. Along the way, he ran into the "bum blockade" set up by the police along the California-Arizona border and he heard the well-to-do spit the word "Okie" at him. During this time, Woody never held a steady job. He picked fruit, painted signs, and sailed with the merchant marine. But mostly he got by singing traditional songs for the dislocated Okies in bars, on Skid Row, and in migrant camps.

In 1937, Woody moved to an L.A. suburb and started a radio show with his cousin Jack. Mixing folk ballads and homespun humor, their daily program quickly gained a loyal following among local Dust Bowl refugees. Soon the show became more political, more about the dust storms, the bitter plight of the migrants, and the injustices of the economic order.

In 1939, Woody appeared regularly at Communist Party rallies and tailored his songs to his new audience. He explained his politics as a product of his life. As Woody once boasted: "Most proud of anything . . . is the fact that I seem to have been born a shade pink, and didn't have to read many books to be a proletariat." As Woody's identification with the Left strengthened, his fame grew and that's what got him on the bill of that Steinbeck migrant-worker fund-raiser. Four months after the benefit, in July 1940, Victor Records released Woody's "Tom Joad." The song was part of Woody's famous collection *Dust Bowl Ballads*, which he dedicated to Steinbeck and echoed many of the themes in Steinbeck's novel and Ford's film.

Critics praised the collection not so much for Woody's voice or music, but because of its authenticity. *Dust Bowl Ballads*, the editors of a Brooklyn paper raved, "tell a moving story as only Singer Guthrie can tell it—with his true understanding of the plight of the 'Okies.'" Steinbeck's friend, actor Burgess Meredith, introduced Woody to a radio audience as "one of those Okies who, dispossessed from their farms, journeyed in jalopies to California."[4] One critic wrote, "Here is a wry-witted word-volcano, a prophet singer, who was *there* with the migratory workers in the California orchards, with the assembly-line robots trying to become men in the union organizing drives. . . . Guthrie was there—on the trains, and on the highways."[5] Woody was, in other words, both a real victim and an honest witness.

The strongest proof that Woody was real, though, was his resemblance to Joad. Observers repeatedly paired, and even confused, the songwriter with the Steinbeck character. It didn't matter that Joad was fictional. For many, he was the real, the most real and most recognizable emblem of the Great Depression. That remains the incredible power of fiction. A California radio producer's description of Woody could just as easily have been a description of Joad. Woody, he insisted, "had ridden . . . the jalopies," just like Joad. He had "worked the orchards and the fields," just like Joad. He had "faced the cops and the clubs of vigilantes," just like Joad. A press release for *Dust Bowl Ballads* boasted that Woody's songs, "document . . . the great contemporary scene so dramatically related by Steinbeck's *The Grapes of Wrath*." The *Daily Worker* went even farther, suggesting that Woody was a Joad himself. "He can tell you about the Dust Bowl, the original characters of the *The Grapes of Wrath*," it reported. What made Woody real, then, was not just growing up in Oklahoma or his experiences on the road or in migrant camps, but his resemblance to Joad.

Woody did what he could to strengthen the connection between himself and Joad. He even named his son from his second wife Joady Ben. Around the time of his birth, Woody wrote, "*The Grapes of Wrath*, you know, is about us a pullin' out of Oklahoma . . . and a driftin' around over . . . California, busted, disgusted, down and out, and a lookin' for work." Like the song "Tom Joad," the lesson of the story was to organize. "*The Grapes of Wrath*," Woody insisted, "says you got to get together, and raise hell till you get your job, and get your farm back and your house and your chickens and your groceries and your clothes, and your money back."[6] Working together, people could turn the world right side up, he declared.

In later years, Woody, sick with Huntington's chorea and unable to perform, kept coming back to the ghost of Tom Joad. Fifteen years after he typed out his Joad ballad, he wrote a short play about the Okie everyman. Joad still mattered, he still needed to face the vigilante man and not back down. And he still promised to stand by hungry and crying children, organize the unorganized, and stand up for, in the words of Guthrie's play for "folks . . . fightin f'r their rights."[7]

Woody was not the only one to come back to Joad. As the California economy went into its postwar boom phase, California boosters created their own portraits of the Joads. They were now prosperous residents of suburbs, testaments to American prosperity. But they were also, the "Beverly Hillbillies." Like the Joads, the Hillbillies loaded up their mattresses and bed frames on top of a jalopy and moved to California. Yet these new Joads of the American Century came not to seek jobs, but to spend newfound wealth—the wealth of a prosperous America. But while the Clampetts hang out by their cement swimming pool and had so much money they didn't need to work, they remained, like the Joads, a family, committed to each other and fighting off the schemes of the banker, Mr. Drysdale.

Even as some tried to depoliticize the Joads, though, and to tear them from the Great Depression, the family remained in the age of American prosperity, a link to hard times and a testament to faith in community. And they remained, like Joad, a voice of anger and disappointment. In the 1960s, social critic Terkel molded Joad—who in his telling was a sharecropper's son—into his American everyman, an ordinary, industrial worker, who plays by the rules, battles against long odds, and gains only a precarious hold on the American dream of prosperity. Around the same time, a Chicago playwright turned the Joads into an African American family battling slumlords and racism.

In the 1990s, singer/songwriter Steve Earle worried that the nation was "going straight to hell." In his rousing musical plea, "Christmas in Washington," Earle beseeched the spirit and conscience of Woody Guthrie to "come back" to an America irrevocably altered and yet somehow so reminiscent of the Depression era. At about the same time that Earle tried to rouse Woody, Bruce Springsteen also began a search for a way to explain and make sense of the yawning gap between the rich and the poor in America in the 1990s. Like Earle, he reached back to the 1930s as a touchstone. Springsteen went looking for the ghost of Woody Guthrie and found Tom Joad.

Springsteen's 1995 album, *The Ghost of Tom Joad*, is essentially a report on the vitality of the American Dream. Joad stands at the heart of Springsteen's ambivalent reckoning with poverty and powerlessness. It is Joad, this complex figure, not a film version of Abraham Lincoln, or some Horatio Alger hero, who is Springsteen's quintessential American. In the 1930s and 1940s, the written and sung Joad bore witness to the problems and possibilities of the nation, and in Springsteen's version, he continued to do so. As he sings in that familiar refrain at the end of his song, "The Ghost of Tom Joad":

> Now Tom said, "Mom, wherever there's a cop beatin' a guy
> Wherever a hungry new born baby cries
> Where there's a fight 'gainst the blood and hatred in the air
> Look for me mom I'll be there.
> Wherever somebody's fightin' for a place to stand
> Or a decent job or a helpin' hand.
> Wherever somebody's strugglin' to be free,
> Look in their eyes ma you'll see me."

In his concerts to support the recording, Springsteen demonstrated the importance of Joad for the 1990s by opening every show with the "The Ghost of Tom Joad." Speaking directly to his audience, he repeated Joad's famous soliloquy. He made clear that this speech embodied the real promise of American democracy, a vital spirit that America was losing touch with.

Joad became the symbol of Springsteen's emerging communalist vision for a just America. "The country," the singer said sounding like Joad, "is judged not by just its accomplishments, but by its compassion, by the health and welfare of its citizens."[8] On more than one occasion Springsteen declared:

"Nobody wins unless everybody wins; there ain't no party unless everybody's invited."[9] This is not an American Dream of acquisition, conspicuous consumption, or keeping up with the Joneses: it "ain't," in Springsteen's words, "about two cars in a garage; its about people living and working together without stepping on each other." In other words, when anyone in America is left out, the dream is a lie. "I don't think," Springsteen said, "there is any such thing as an innocent man; there is a collective responsibility."[10]

But why must Joad be brought back as a witness for America in the 1990s? In *The Ghost of Tom Joad*, Springsteen taps into the historical moment of the nation's deepest economic crisis. This is a meaningful reference, and the point is that the connections to the Great Depression (and Steinbeck and Woody) are important. Like his predecessors, he suggests that structural failures in the economy, not individual shortcomings, destroy community and make a mockery of the American Dream. In the Springsteen vision, too many people have been left out of the promise to justify the success of those who have made it. *The Ghost of Tom Joad*, like *The Grapes of Wrath*, is a tale of people on the road, wandering westward, living beneath railroad tracks, and "sleeping," in Springsteen's words, "on a pillow of solid rock" and "bathin' in the city aqueduct." The America Springsteen sees is stalked by the specter of the Great Depression. "Hot soup on a campfire under the bridge, shelter lines stretchin' round the corner, welcome to the new world order," Springsteen sings in the title song, telling us really that not much is new at all.

These notions about the past and these references to Joad represent more than a comparison of economic uncertainty in the Great Depression and in the 1990s. The singer's stark exploration about the continuities in westward wanderings and the realization of the limits of the American Dream also signify the artist's aesthetic ties to the great documentary impulse of the 1930s pioneered by Steinbeck, Ford, and Guthrie.

The documentary genre was the major artistic thrust of the 1930s. The basis of documentary is an idea or statement that what is being portrayed is real. It happened. It exists. The storyteller, like Steinbeck and Woody, says to the audience: "I was there. I saw it with my own eyes. Trust me." That eyewitness role is critical: Steinbeck lived in the Central Valley and wrote newspaper articles about it. We've seen how Woody embodied, or tried to embody, the Joad character. Springsteen deploys a similar documentary impulse. His stories, many derived from firsthand accounts by journalists, are meant to be trustworthy.[11] It is worth noting that Springsteen actually footnotes "The Ghost of Tom Joad," citing books, articles, and films.[12]

However, truth, whatever that may mean, is not exactly the point. In *Documentary Expression and Thirties America*, historian William Stott writes that the 1930s documentaries were not necessarily designed to reveal some sort of essential reality but tried to elicit emotion and empathy. Think of Dorthea Lange's

Migrant Mother. This is a photograph that triggers feelings of pain, sadness, and loss. Cultural historian Warren Susman, in an essay on the 1930s, writes that "the whole idea of documentary, not with words alone but with sight and sound, makes it possible to see, know, and feel the details of life, to feel oneself part of some other's experience."[13] No one can read *The Grapes of Wrath* and *not* imagine what it would be like to be a poor migrant worker without a home, working in the hot sun of California's Central Valley, and no one can*not* care about the people.

As Springsteen told an interviewer: "I start out to try and tell a good story . . . one where something is revealed, something happens, where I create characters that come to life, that are real, that are recognizable, they could be you, they could be me. And I ask the listener to walk in those shoes."[14]

These shoes take Springsteen, in the tradition of Steinbeck and Woody, to the edges and borders of the American experience. Here, in the shadows of the dream, Springsteen discovers that the mythology of American success was too often a lie.

Nowhere for Springsteen had the dream fallen harder than in California. Half the songs on the Joad album are about California, Springsteen's home through much of the 1990s (and the place where he sought personal retreat and a second chance in the wake of a very public divorce). This focus further ties the artist to the documentarians of the past; it is where many of them came to gather stories for their own versions of the state of the nation. And of course, it ties Springsteen back, once again, to Joad. Joad came west, as have countless millions of others in search of the American Dream before and since. But what many find, of course, is no dreamland but, instead, a shadow America. Pushing aside the triumphalism of frontier narratives, Springsteen and the earlier generation of documentarians tell stories of outsiders in the West—the sort of untouchables—like the Okies before them—who raise questions about the American promise. This takes Springsteen in the 1990s to the border between the United States and Mexico: to the Sierra Madre River, to San Diego, and to the flatlands around Tijuana, where he sees Mexicans looking and hoping for their chance at the American Dream.

These are the people Springsteen is most interested in, and the stories he tells are about Mexicans. Now the spirit of Tom Joad runs through their lives and bodies. Joad's West has become their North. Their American experience makes Springsteen uneasy, just like the Okie experience made Steinbeck uneasy.

Telling Joad stories, though, is not just about uneasiness and about witnesses, it is also about searching for solutions. "I'll be there," said Joad in the 1930s. But the 1990s were not the 1930s. What changed most dramatically was America's political culture. The New Deal and the Great Depression pushed concerns over economic morality and working people's lives to the center of the political debate. Throughout the 1930s, groups and individuals fought over fundamental questions about the distribution of wealth.

Steinbeck and Woody tried through their art, stories, and exposés, to shine spotlights on American problems. The solutions they proposed had everything to do with organizing and with government action.

However, the echoes of the 1930s that we hear in Springsteen's stories are in some ways mocking, simply because what was once central to the nation's political discourse was by the 1990s marginalized. In the New Deal era, social problems could best be handled by decisive, bold federal action. Equality of outcome became an important objective for a broad cross section of the country. Over the past generations, however, the terms of the debate have shifted dramatically, beginning with President Ronald Reagan's 1981 declaration that "Government is not the solution to our problem. Government is the problem," continuing with Bill Clinton ending welfare as we know it, and George W. Bush then pushing to privatize and deregulate as much of American life as possible.

Springsteen went to the edges and the borders for stories, but his message languished at the margins as well. Despite the political nature of Springsteen's music, despite presidential attempts to adopt him, and despite album sales in the tens of millions, he hardly made a dent in contemporary American politics. Political America doesn't debate Springsteen's stories or Springsteen's lyrics. Woody, Ford, and Steinbeck may not have won the day, but they were surely part of the larger discussion. Today, because the political debate in America has narrowed and moved sharply to the right, neither Joad nor Springsteen are in the contest.

But for Springsteen, like Woody before him, there continues to be hope in telling stories, hope epitomized by Joad, the scrappy fighter, beaten down, but never licked.

During the Barack Obama presidential campaign, Springsteen joined with Tom Morello of the leftist band Rage Against the Machine and played "The Ghost of Tom Joad" again. Their new version was no folk song; it was angry and urgent. Both singers almost screamed as they called out in the chorus, "to bring back the ghost of Tom Joad."

The legendary historian William Appleman Williams pointed out years ago that to talk about Steinbeck's America is to talk about the New Deal, and to talk about the New Deal is to talk about government action and talk about creating equality—equality of outcome—in America. That's true. That's not a myth, but there isn't much of this left in the Joad of today.

Today Joad is back—he is back in the way we dress, in the hats we wear, and in the lines of magazine copy we read. He's back, but he's back as a visual, and his message is losing its focus. The tragedy of the malleability and fame of Joad is that he may fall so deep into the image of Depression chic, that he will become more easily incorporated into the boho look of fashion's recent past, than into our political culture. Tragically, Joad will become an association, not to the 1930s or the New Deal or an angry response to post-Reagan inequality, but to westward wandering and wanderlust for wanderlust's sake and little more. That's the pernicious myth: that the Depression was a simpler time of khaki hues and untroubled All-American, stolid masculinity. That's the new myth of the consumer culture: that Joad is the independent, rugged westerner, scouting out the future in a land where looking good is more important than doing good. That's a dangerous, sad myth that has little to do with Springsteen, or Woody or Steinbeck.

But still these writers and singers would say, "Come back, Tom Joad," just one more time. Because Joad is, in the end, all about faith, faith in us all.

Eleven

WOODY AT THE BORDER

JOSH KUN

Not long after Woody Guthrie arrived in Los Angeles in 1937, he did a very Los Angeles thing. He took a trip to Tijuana, Mexico. Fresh off his radio successes at KFVD with the *Woody and Lefty Lou* show, Woody got an offer to do a show on Radio XELO, one of the many border-blaster radio stations that transmitted from just south of the U.S.-Mexico border to avoid FCC restrictions. Like all of the *equis* stations, XELO helped define the sound and style of American wireless pop culture—from the Carter Family to Wolfman Jack—and did so from beyond U.S. borders: the most American of sounds, direct from northern Mexico.

Woody and his family settled into a motel in Chula Vista, on the U.S. side of the line, and for the next three weeks would cross the border to Tijuana to do their show on XELO—a mix of songs, stories, and skits that, as Ed Cray tells it, never quite settled into the same groove as Woody's KFVD show. Woody's Tijuana trip ended like so many Tijuana tourist trips did: with bouts of heavy drinking and a visit from the Mexican cops who eventually ended Woody's south-of-the-border stay not by putting him in the Tijuana jail the Kingston Trio would sing about twenty years later, but by deporting him.

This seeming footnote to Woody's California story makes me wonder if his Tijuana broadcasts were the secret apolitical beginning of his politicized migrant aesthetics—what he famously called "the art and science of migratin"—the first time that Woody wasn't singing about borders but straddling them, immersing his songs and stories in a cross-border cultural economy of radio, tourism, and entertainment.

Opposite: **Woody, Lefty Lou, and, in front, Whitey McPherson, January 1938, Tijuana.**

He also sampled a cross-border political economy of immigration, empire, and inspection that from 1938 onward would become associated with his songbook and his legacy, even if he rarely returned there, even if the border and Mexican migrancy would become more pronounced in Woody's afterlife than they ever were when he was alive.

The principal connection between Woody and Mexican migrants, of course, comes not from his own cross-border trips, but the fatal trip of January 28, 1948, when a plane went down over Los Gatos Canyon killing the thirty-six people. Thirty-two of the thirty-six were Mexican farmworkers who had been brought north to work in the fields of the U.S. under the Bracero Program. As part of the program's mandate, the U.S. labor contractors would fly migrants in, and when their work was no longer needed, they would fly them back to the border. The plane was full of migrants on their way back to Mexico, and when Woody read newspaper accounts of the crash, he was outraged that only four names were published in articles—those of the non-Mexican plane staff and crew; the rest were listed solely as "Mexican deportees."

The incident inspired Woody's lyrics, which went far beyond a protest of making Mexican labor faceless and Mexican death inconsequential, and, by narrating from the point of view of a Mexican farm worker, became an indictment of the hypocrisy of U.S. immigration policy and by extension the anti-Mexican racism that was buried in the heart of U.S. agribusiness. "Six hundred miles to that Mexican border," he sang, imagining himself a Mexican migrant. "They chase us like outlaws, like rustlers, like thieves. We died in your hills, we died in your deserts. We died in your valleys and died on your plains. We died 'neath your trees and we died in your bushes. Both sides of the river, we died just the same." Woody gave the dead names, and reminded his listeners that the lifeblood of American nourishment pulses from Mexican corpses scattered in the valleys, canyons, and fields of the Southwest. But the song's accusations also pointed beyond the farming industry. By 1948, the focus on Dust Bowl migrants, Woody implied, had to shift south toward Mexico; the Dust Bowl had become the border, and Mexican migrants—deportees and immigrants alike—were the new Tom Joads.

No wonder, then, that the song has had a fierce return whenever anti-Mexican immigrant policy rears its head, showing up in the repertoires, for example, of bands like Los Super Seven, Quetzal, and Los Illegals. It has made a strong return in recent years, where the graveyard of Los Gatos Canyon has become the desert graveyards of Arizona and Sonora, and the political battleground over immigration policy has shifted to its current Arizona epicenter. The band Outernational, for example, made their version of the song a centerpiece of their album *Todos Somos Illegales* (*We Are All Illegals*), the title song recorded to protest SB1070, a song they play on their border tour, and a song they turned into a video designed to call attention to immigrant rights, in collaboration with Latino social-media-activist coalition Cuentáme.

What we might call the Mexicanization of Woody's migrant politics is most directly articulated in the evolution of the Tom Joad figure himself, an articulation most extensively put forth by Bruce Springsteen on his 1995 album *The Ghost of Tom Joad*. With his Dust Bowl migrant classic, "Tom Joad," Woody had given birth to a new pop-music archetype, a sung icon of dispossession and drift that still returns to us—in new guises, with new stories—whenever anybody is forced to hit the road, sweat in the sun for less than a living wage, and has become in Woody's words "busted, disgusted, down and out, and a lookin' for work." By the time Joad landed in Springsteen's hands, Woody's icon of the rugged white southern migrant blown west by dust and drought had become a ghost among a different set of the living. A family sleeping in their car. A man whose home is a cardboard box beneath a freeway underpass.

Dave Marsh once described Woody's Joads as "doomed figures of courageous sentiment." Springsteen's Joads—whether they turn out to be Mexican immigrants, ex-Marine INS agents, Vietnam vets, or the Vietnamese refugees they want to murder—all have some kind of hole in their belly and some kind of gun in their hand. The quiet, sour determination of Henry Fonda's celluloid Joad—who never gives up on the optimism of California—haunts Springsteen's "new world order" migrants precisely because it is not who they are. They've barely made it to California, and they've already been expelled from the Garden and left homeless or drug addicted or dead or worse: in love with things that will only hurt them. "The highway is alive tonight," Springsteen sings. "But nobody's kiddin' nobody about where it goes." Though the highways of Springsteen's Joads run in various directions, the direction they most frequently run is south-north, from the Mexican border on up, along highways covered in migrant shadows. A Mexican-born INS agent who drinks at a bar in Tijuana tells his partner: "They risk death in the deserts and mountains, pay all they got to the smugglers rings, we send 'em home and they come right back again. Carl, hunger is a powerful thing."

By placing Joad in a post-NAFTA songbook that includes songs about conflicted border patrol agents, migrants who end up in Fresno meth labs, Tijuana locals who smuggle cocaine balloons just to get across, Springsteen picks up the conversation that Woody's deportee has only just begun: the modern Tom Joad is not white and working class, the modern Tom Joad is from Jalisco or Michoacan or Zacatecas or Tijuana and is a deportee before he even makes it across the border—*if* he makes it across the border, *if* the highway doesn't eat him alive.

As powerful as Woody's migrant memes are, as powerful as tracking the dozens and dozens of cover versions of "Deportee" and "Tom Joad" can be, as a historical tool of critical thinking it has its limits—the vast majority of those covers are in English, and the vast majority are songs about Mexicans, not by Mexicans. Woody's migrant songs have in large part birthed a chain of influence carried out by singers who for the most part look like Woody and sound like him or at the very least come out of the U.S. folk music tradition. Lingering too much on this chain of influence, over-celebrating it, covers up the fact that decades before and decades after Springsteen spotted the ghost of Tom Joad, Mexican musicians were doing the same.

In fact, nearly eighteen years before the Los Gatos plane crash, Los Hermanos Bañuelos had already put the deportee into the cross-border songbook. In 1930, the duo entered a Los Angeles recording studio to cut "El Deportado" ("Deportee"), sung from the perspective of a migrant who was forced to leave Mexico during the revolution, is deceived by his employers in the North, and then eventually is repatriated as part of the repatriation wave that begins with the Great Depression. The song ends by making a direct connection to the Dust Bowl saga of Woody's migrants: "Today comes a large cloud of dust and with no consideration, women, children, and elders are being driven to the border. We are being kicked out of this country. Goodbye, beloved countrymen, they are going to deport us. But we are not bandits—we came to work hard."

The Dust Bowl devastation that drove so many Okies west to California, the Dust Bowl devastation that is the foundation for Woody's sung sagas of migrant dispossession and struggle, is the very same devastation that was used as justification to rid the U.S. of the "deportable aliens" whose jobs could be better used by "needy citizens." In fact, the same period that found Woody choosing to cross the border south to Tijuana was when so many Mexicans were still not choosing to return home and found themselves instead relocated against their will to Tijuana. It was those very years in the 1930s when Mexican deportees settled and founded La Libertad, the city's oldest residential neighborhood, which has the border as its backyard fence.

"El Deportado" is but one of countless examples of how Mexican *corridos*—those classic folk ballads turned alternative border media networks—have been giving voice to migrant stories ever since the border was created in 1848. In the late 1980s, for example, the Texas-based Los Terribles del Norte updated the Bañuelos "El Deportado" ode with one of their own, which starts with a phone call from a deported father to his son left behind in the United States. The spaces of the U.S.-Mexico borderlands that Woody traveled through, lived in, crossed, and portrayed in his songs, have always been sonic spaces, musical landscapes where the histories of Mexican ranchers, farmhands, *campesinos*, outlaws, mothers, and sons, have long been chronicled in the strummed stanzas of *corridos*. So central is music to the experience of migrant life in the borderlands that in Mexican anthropologist Manuel Gamio's pioneering 1927 migration study of two thousand Mexican immigrants returning from the U.S., he found that twenty percent of them brought back phonograph records. For every one hundred immigrants, 118 records returned to Mexico. Which is to say that moving back and forth across the border has always been, in part, a musical act, and that migrancy is a sonic practice as much as a spatial one.

Instead of treating the border—be it as line, monument, fence, wall—as a partition of silence where narrative does not exist, Mexican migrant music has always treated the border as something that, to borrow the title of Paul Botello's East Los Angeles mural "sings, speaks, and shouts," full of stories and brimming with narrative; the border as a living musical witness to the injustices and triumphs of Mexican life. Mexican scholar Gustavo López Castro has written extensively about Mexican *corridos* as forming a decades-spanning "songbook of migrancy," a mobile archive of everyday migrant life, of cross-border feelings and emotions that create communities of sentiment between Mexico and the U.S. and that lives in both formal and informal markets. The songbook of migrancy, he argues, will remain alive and valid as long it continues to function as "a cultural link between absences and anguish."

From songs about dishwashers to songs about cocaine smugglers, from songs about family reunions to songs about the border as a migrant tomb, the past century of *norteño* music is an archive of migrancy. In 2001, Los Tigres del Norte, the most prominent architects of Mexican migrant music, recorded "Paisano a Paisano" and imagined themselves in the middle of the Sonoran Desert, surrounded by the freedom of expanses and distances, the desert's limitless horizons and vistas, while singing about their limits in a time of border war:

> I have spent my life exploring other lands to give a better future to my children. . . . Because we've wanted to work, they have declared war on us, they are patrolling the borders, but they cannot tame us. . . . The nation hurts so much when my people cry—this is an international cry. From countryman to countryman, before I go on singing I ask the boss, who picks the harvest? Who cleans the hotels and restaurants and who kills themselves working construction while the boss scolds us while knitting in his luxurious mansion.

The song's video emphasized the border's convergence of transnational territory, state power, and cultural performance by cutting between the band performing alone against a sun-bleached desert-scape with images of Mexicans working and living on urban U.S. streets.

The songbook of migrancy is not just limited to *norteño* and *corridos*, but can be heard in the booming electronic sound systems of mobile Mexican DJs, the *sonideros* who mix *cumbias* and salsa together for dancing crowds on both sides of the border. *Sonideros* on both sides of the power have been overt in their support of migrant rights and frequently use their *sonido* performances and CD mixes to launch political commentaries on immigrant justice, employing sound system amplification as a form of migrant protest—decibels as politics. DJs don't just play tracks, they list off names in a continual avalanche of dedicatory shout-outs, to twenty-first-century Juans and Rosalitas.

In the wake of the landmark May 1, 2006 marches that filled the streets of states across the U.S. (in New York, California, Illinois, Georgia, Wisconsin, and Louisiana) with millions of marchers protesting against restrictive immigration laws, Sonido Condor collaborated with El Tigre Sonidero to weigh in by uploading a video to YouTube.com that mixed live performance footage, photo collage, original animation, and a *cumbia* soundtrack. It opened with a dedication: "For the immigrants of the United States. The First of May is the Day of the Immigrant. Immigrants are essential for this country because it gets rich off our sacrifices." Then as a Condor *cumbia* mix plays, the screen fills with images of giant white crosses in the desert sand labeled "*No Olvidado*" (Not Forgotten), homemade monuments to lost migrant lives in the "death-worlds"—what the video calls "the dangerous desert roads"—of the militarized borderlands. The video, which has garnered over 400,000 views, then cuts to a Condor performance that he begins with a speech about the urgency of immigrant protest. "This is for all of those who on May 1 did not go to work," he says, "and took to the streets to march peacefully to show the United States that we are not criminals. We are workers in search of immigration reform." He asks the crowd to cheer in their honor as the video moves through shots of immigration protests, Latino corner grocery stores, and white crosses. As the *cumbia* mix plays, we hear a sample of Aguilar saying "immigration reform" on a continual loop. It was the same May 1 marches that inspired Chicago's Sones de Mexico to connect the Mexican songbook of migrancy with Woody's. Not long after those same marches, they decided that his "This Land Is Your Land" needed a geographical reconfiguration: Why does this land that is our land stop at the California border?

In the contemporary moment, the music of migrancy isn't only about death, but about the sustenance of life—regional Mexican music in L.A. even when not expressly about the act of migrancy, is music for the migrant life, music of "migrant imaginaries" to borrow Alicia Schmidt-Camacho's concept—music about negotiating cultural worlds, about regional identities, about generational differences in suburban Los Angeles. It's about being a *paisa*, about riding in *jaripeos* on the weekend around the corner from a Wal-Mart, about all-night *bailes* at nightclubs in Whittier and Pico Rivera, about backyard *banda* parties in South Gate, about wearing ostrich boots and stenciling *mexicano hasta la madre* on the back window of your Tacoma. It's about driving to work while you listen to Don Cheto, the seventy-something immigrant wisecracking sage who doles out advice for new migrants, helps solve arguments between immigrant parents and their U.S. born kids, sings Vanilla Ice's "Ice Ice Baby" whenever there are immigration raids in L.A. County, and when he tells his son he's had it, we're moving back to Mexico, back to the rancho, his son says, in English, "I don't wanna leave L.A."

Tune in to L.A. stations like 105.5 La Que Buena and you'll hear Tom Joad's Mexican cousins, but also the ghost of Woody Guthrie himself, who if he wandered back to Los Angeles today, is probably somewhere singing along with a Mexican *banda* at the top of his lungs. The art and science of migratin' is alive and well in Los Angeles, and there's never been a better time for Woody Guthrie fans to start tuning in.

Twelve

WOODY GUTHRIE'S RECORDINGS 1939 TO 1949

DARRYL HOLTER

Woody Guthrie has acquired an iconic position in American popular culture and music, but his records were not widely distributed or sold during the years that he recorded, from 1940 to 1947.[1] Guthrie only became recognized as an important recording artist several years after he was sidelined with a terminal illness in the late 1950s.

KFVD RADIO (LOS ANGELES) "AIR CHECK" RECORDINGS

The earliest Guthrie recordings were discovered in 1999 by Peter La Chapelle in Los Angeles, in the course of research for his doctoral dissertation and subsequent book, as La Chapelle describes elsewhere in this volume.[2] A 350-pound Presto recording machine made these recordings. The recordings include two songs, "I Ain't Got No Home" and "Do Re Mi," both later rerecorded and distributed. Lyrics to "Big City Ways" (also called "Them Big City Ways") and "Skid Row Serenade," were found in some of Guthrie's notebooks, but the Presto disks are the only known recordings. These may have been "air checks" recorded for the Los Angeles radio station KFVD, where Woody conducted a daily show from 1937 to 1939. La Chapelle discovered the recordings in the Harry Hay Collection at the Southern California Library for Social Studies and Research.[3]

Opposite: **Woody Guthrie.**

LIBRARY OF CONGRESS RECORDINGS

Alan Lomax, a folk music collector, and the son of a folk music collector, produced the first set of Guthrie recordings in March 1940 and January 1941 in Washington, D.C. The younger Lomax promoted radio programs featuring American folk music for the Columbia Broadcasting System (CBS) and collected thousands of recordings for the Archive of American Folk Song. After hearing Woody perform at a benefit for Spanish Civil War refugees in New York City in February 1940, Lomax met Woody after the show and convinced him to come to Washington to record some of his songs.

The sessions took place over a three-day period and produced forty songs, about half of which were Guthrie originals. The Library of Congress initially housed the recordings, and they are now referred to as the Library of Congress Recordings. They were not for commercial distribution when recorded; scholars and others were to use them to learn more about how folk culture expressed the lives of American working-class people. One unusual feature of the recordings is that Lomax asked Woody to introduce his songs, providing a context for understanding the song. Lomax (as well as his sister, Elizabeth) posed questions that allowed Woody to expand on the origins and themes of the songs. In 1964, Elektra Records, and in 1988, Rounder Records, commercially released twenty-nine of the Library of Congress Recordings.

In both the songs and the conversations between Woody and Lomax, the listener learns a great deal about the music and social issues that influenced Woody's songwriting. We learn about the oil boom in Oklahoma and Texas in songs such as "Beaumont Rag" and "Texas Oilfields." Songs such as "Dust Bowl Disaster" and "Boll Weevil Song" expressed the brutal impact of the Dust Bowl on individuals and communities." The difficulties of being a migrant worker living on the road with little or no money are central in two Guthrie originals, "So Long, It's Been Good to Know Yuh" and "Do Re Mi." "Dust Pneumonia Blues" and "California Blues" portray the powerful lure of a new life in California. Another Guthrie original told the story of the New Year's Flood of 1934, when a deadly torrential rainstorm swept away homeless migrant families in encampments along the banks of the Los Angeles River.

DUST BOWL BALLADS

Lomax was so impressed with Woody's musical authenticity that he convinced RCA Victor to record the folksinger's first commercial recordings. *Dust Bowl Ballads*, recorded in Camden, New Jersey, on April 26 and May 3, 1940, consisted of twelve songs arranged in two sets of three 78-rpm records. With their focus on Dust Bowl experiences, many consider the Victor recordings one of the first concept albums. It opened with "The Great Dust Storm," one of Woody's earliest compositions, written in 1935 while he was still living in Pampa, Texas. Part of the song's appeal is its authenticity, enhanced by the fact that Woody writes in the first person. Commenting on the song, Woody wrote: "This actually happened in Pampa, Gray County, Texas, April 14, 1935. The storm was as black as tar and as big as the ocean. It looked like we were done for."[4] Woody wrote most of the songs during his years in Los Angeles, including "Do Re Mi," "Vigilante Man," and "Dust Bowl Refugee."

Woody was encouraged by RCA to write a song that could draw upon the popularity of John Steinbeck's novel, *The Grapes of Wrath*, which had had been made into a popular film. After an all-night, wine-lubricated writing spree, Woody produced "The Ballad of Tom Joad," a seventeen-verse, six-minute song that told the story of Steinbeck's protagonist. As is characteristic in many of his songs, Woody created new lyrics for a well known tune, in this case the Carter Family's "John Hardy."

"Talkin' Dust Bowl Blues" is one of the earliest examples of the talking blues style that Woody used for many songs during his career. Pete Seeger claimed to be greatly impressed with this form, which he defined as, "two lines that rhyme, two more that rhyme, then two or three irregular, free form lines followed as a comment, before the next stanza."[5] But Guy Logsdon points out that the form should be credited to Chris Bouchillon, who recorded the original "Talking Blues" in 1926. The song required a second take, but Woody accomplished each of the other songs in one recording. There was a humorous side to most of Woody's talking blues songs and "Talkin' Dust Bowl Blues" has a certain tall-tale aspect to it. Indeed, despite its vivid portrayal of the difficulties faced by the Dust Bowl refugees, Woody displayed a dry sense of humor in several of these songs that is also seen in his later work.

While the Library of Congress Recordings featured Woody as the unsophisticated "Okie," most of the songs on "Dust Bowl Ballads" reflected Woody's political evolution and his heightened consciousness of social and economic issues. The two albums were not widely reviewed; still, a critic at the *Los Angeles Daily News* described "Dust Bowl Ballads as "an epic story" that was "important and fascinating." The *Boston Post* claimed the songs underscored "the existence of true, rugged American pioneering spirit and indomitable will to survive."[6]

Although *Dust Bowl Ballads* was probably the most successful album Woody recorded, fewer than a thousand were sold and Victor declined to reissue it. Woody was paid $25 for each master disc, an amount totaling $300. Although Victor declined to reissue the album, Moses Asch rereleased it in 1948 (without license from Victor) and once again by Asch in 1964 on an LP album for his Folkways label, which added two songs not originally included, "Dust Bowl Blues" and "Pretty Boy Floyd."

COLUMBIA RIVER COLLECTION

Woody's next significant set of recordings took place when the Bonneville Power Administration (BPA) in Oregon hired him. The job involved writing a set of songs that to use in a documentary film, *The Co-lumbia* (1949), to promote the importance of hydroelectric power and electrification, especially in rural areas where jobs were scarce and economic development was limited. Although the job was initially supposed to last a year, BPA shortened it to a single month and Woody was given an emergency appointment that would not require a security check by the Civil Service Commission. BPA officials were afraid that Woody's political connections might create problems—and they were not wrong. J. Edgar Hoover's Federal Bureau of Investigation was on Woody's trail. The F.B.I. tried to prevent Woody from being hired, but he completed the work and moved on to the East Coast ahead of the bureau's efforts.[7] Woody needed the money and was excited by the beauty of the Oregon landscape, the huge scope of the electrification project, and its positive economic impact for the working people of the region. With only a month to finish his project, Woody worked prodigiously in what was probably the most productive month of his life and eventually completed twenty-six songs by the end of May 1941. He recorded the songs in the basement studio of the BPA, and the agency paid him $266 for his work.

Some of the songs from the BPA project became well-known Guthrie favorites, including "Grand Coulee Dam," "Hard Travelin," "Pastures of Plenty," and "Roll On, Columbia, Roll On," which Washington eventually designated as that state's official folk song. Set to the tune of "The Wabash Cannonball," which Woody undoubtedly learned from the Carter Family's recording of 1929, "Grand Coulee Dam" celebrated the massive construction project and links it to progress for humanity. The song also included some wonderfully poetic, tongue-twisting phrases: "In the misty crystal glitter of the wild and windward spray" and "Like a prancing, dancing stallion down her seaway to the sea."[8] In "Pastures of Plenty," Woody explored the relationship between the Columbia River, the new dam, and the workers who labor in the orchards, factories, and farms in the region. The song, narrated in the first person, began by describing the difficulties facing migratory workers who headed west looking for a new future. "We travel with the wind and the rain in our face," Woody wrote, "Our families migrating from place to place." But those days are behind us, he added, "One turn of the wheel and the waters will flow, 'cross the green growing field, down the hot thirsty row . . . the Grand Coulee showers her blessings on me, the lights for the city, for factory, and mill." "Pastures of Plenty is one of the most recorded Guthrie songs, having been sung by such luminaries as Tom Paxton, Ramblin' Jack Elliot, Dave Von Ronk, Harry Belafonte, and Holly Near.

In the end, however, the documentary included only three of the songs, and the master recordings were lost or destroyed. In 1987, BPA employees discovered copies of the original recordings, and seventeen of these songs were issued by Rounder Records in an album entitled *Columbia River Collection*.

THE ALMANAC SINGERS

In 1941, after his monthlong job in Oregon, Woody returned to New York and collaborated with Seeger, Millard Lampell, Lee Hays, Peter Hawes, and others in a loosely organized group called the Almanac Singers. The members of the Almanac Singers were acoustic folk musicians who performed topical songs, usually for left-wing, liberal, and union audiences. They played informally together after Woody met Seeger in March 1940 and the two men embarked on a trip to Texas, Oklahoma, and California, playing mostly at rallies organized by labor unions.

The Almanac Singers first albums of three 78-rpm records, *Songs for John Doe*, did not include Woody or any of his songs. The recordings were notable for their advocacy of nonintervention in the World War II, a view that conformed to the controversial position of the Communist Party at that time. The group recorded two 78-rpm albums with Alan Lomax for the independent General label in June and July 1941 in New York, *Deep Sea Chanties and Whaling Ballads* and *Sod Buster Ballads*, generally nonpolitical folk songs. Members of the group traded off the vocals, with Woody doing lead on "Blow the Man Down," "House of the Rising Sun," "Hard, Ain't It Hard," and "I Ride an Old Paint." The group recorded more political songs for the Keynote label in 1941, with Woody participating in two songs, "Babe O'Mine" and "Song for Bridges." After the German armies invaded the Soviet Union, in July 1941, the Almanac Singers dropped their noninterventionist posture and became advocates for an all-out war against the Axis Powers. Woody recorded "Reuben James," a song about the sinking of a U.S. ship by German submarines, on an album called *Dear Mr. President* in 1942.

Despite talent and commitment, the Almanac Singers were not able to overcome the negative reviews and gossip in the tabloid press that emphasized the group's affinities with the Communist Party. As the war effort deepened, Woody enrolled in the merchant marine, Seeger joined the army, and the group disbanded. However, the influence of the Almanac Singers, especially their belief that music could be a powerful tool for social and political change (note the message scrawled in large letters on Woody's guitar: "This Weapon Kills Fascists") continued with the formation of a new group, The Weavers (which did not include Woody) in the early 1950s, and the creation of the organization People's Songs in 1946, founded by Seeger, Woody and other prominent members of the folk community to promote songs about labor and the American people.

THE ASCH RECORDINGS

Nearly all of the remaining Woody recordings were done by Moses Asch between 1944 and 1947. Asch was a recording engineer who had become interested in folk music, especially after recording Huddie "Lead Belly" Ledbetter in 1941. Asch recorded a number of emerging musicians in the small, but growing New York folk music scene including Pete Seeger, Josh White, Sonny Terry, Brownie McGhee, Les Paul, and several others. Woody visited Asch's office in 1944 while on leave from the Merchant Marine, and the two men entered into a professional and personal relationship that continued until Woody's health deteriorated and he could no longer record. Asch first recorded "Hard, Ain't It Hard" and "More Pretty Girls than One" in April 1944. Woody and fellow folksinger Cisco Houston recorded more than 160 songs for Asch in a six-week period. They made additional recordings in 1945. This massive amount of recording resulted in what the Smithsonian's Jeff Place called the mother lode of Woody's recorded legacy, including traditional songs and Guthrie originals. A variety of labels issued the recordings and compilations over the years, beginning with Asch, Asch-Stinson, Disc Records, Folkways, and Verve/Folkways. Eventually the Folkways catalogue of recording was donated to the Smithsonian Institution to become the Smithsonian Folkways label.

The large number of songs, the multiplicity of themes, Asch's disorganized record keeping, and the ever-changing labels and releases made the Asch recordings almost too unwieldy to organize. But when Place, archivist for the Smithsonian Institution's Center for Folklife Programs and Cultural Studies, listened to all the songs as he transferred the fragile old master discs to digital tapes and compact discs, he began to envision the compilation of most of them into a single, multithemed collection. The result was the four-CD collection, *Woody Guthrie: The Asch Recordings*, issued between 1997 and 1999. The collection benefited further from detailed introductions for each volume written by Guthrie expert, Guy Logsdon. Logsdon and Place prepared annotations for songs.

Many of the recordings, which total 105 in all, include Houston, whose vocals provided a more finished sound to Woody's unvarnished country-based voice. Moreover, the addition of guitar and vocals on some tracks by Lead Belly and harmonica work by Sonny Terry added a new dimension. Seeger's banjo and vocals appear as well on a few songs. Listeners also get a chance to hear Woody's rudimentary violin and a good deal of his harmonica work as well.

The four volumes are organized in broad themes, all of which represent the multiple origins and influences in Woody's music. Volume I is entitled "This Land Is Your Land" and contains three versions of what is often considered to be Woody's best-known song. Originally written by Woody in February 1940, and entitled "God Blessed America," the song began as an "answer song" (or a critical response) to Kate Smith's tremendously popular, "God Bless America," which had been written by Irving Berlin. Woody offered an alternative, more critical perspective on American society. While extolling the natural beauty of America with lyrical imagery ("From the redwood forest to the Gulf Stream waters," and "In wheat fields waving, and the dust clouds rolling"), Woody criticized an economic system which leaves behind the poor and jobless. In its original version (not recorded), Woody juxtaposed a high wall with a big sign that is painted "Private Property" against an image of hungry people lined up at the Relief Office in the shadow of a steeple. Until Place found this version in the Asch recordings, no one had known that Woody had actually recorded the "Private Property" version of his most well-known song.[9]

In 1944, preparing to record the song for Asch, Guthrie changed the title by crossing out "God Blessed America" and substituting "This Land Is Your Land." He also changed the first verse into a chorus, deleted the last verse, and altered the lyrics of other verses. Volume I opens with the most familiar version of "This Land," but it also includes a second version, which contains the two more politically charged verses from the original version.

Ironically, Woody's best-known song was not regarded as important at the time it was recorded.[10] Seeger was not particularly impressed when he first heard it, but he began to sing it after it was released in 1951. More than anyone else, it was Seeger who popularized the song, singing it for church groups and schools during the 1950s when he was blacklisted and could not find regular music work. It also seems significant that Woody decided not to include "This Land Is Your Land" when he, Lomax, and Seeger compiled the massive songbook, *Hard-Hitting Songs for Hard-Hit People* in 1946, although the compilation included more than 200 songs and dozens of Woody compositions.[11] Woody's son, Arlo, tells the story of hearing the song for the first time as a grade school student at a "progressive" school in New York only to learn that it was written by his father.[12]

Another well-known Guthrie composition, "Philadelphia Lawyer" (originally entitled "Reno Blues"), told the story of a jealous cowboy from Reno who shot a lawyer who was trying to steal his girl. Woody wrote it for his radio show in Los Angeles in 1937. Other songs from the Los Angeles period include "Do Re Mi," "Going Down the Road Feeling Bad," "Pictures from Life's Other Side," and "Hard, Ain't it Hard." "Lindbergh" was a criticism of Charles A. Lindbergh, the American aviator who sympathized with the Nazis and urged wartime American neutrality. "Hobo's Lullaby," written by Goebel Reeves, was rumored to be Woody's favorite song. "Pastures of Plenty," probably recorded in 1947, derived from Woody's experiences in Oregon, as did "Grand Coulee Dam." In "New York Town," Woody used an African-American blues style similar to that used by Blind Lemon Jefferson in "One Dime Blues," a song

Woody had recorded for Lomax. "Gypsy Davy" is a Texas and Oklahoma version of a British ballad that predates the eighteenth century. One of the first songs Woody wrote when he arrived in New York in February 1940 was "Jesus Christ," a song that implied that if Jesus came back to earth he would be so appalled by the poverty, gambling, and social inequality that he would protest and be jailed by the authorities.

In years spent in Oklahoma, Texas, and Los Angeles, Woody learned hundreds of songs from radio shows, listening to records, and song sharing with other musicians. These songs derived from a wide range of sources: traditional, country, gospel, tin-pan alley, parlor songs, and African-American blues. Woody often memorized these songs; he incorporated them into his performances and used them on his radio show on KFVD in Los Angeles.

Many of the songs on Volume 2 were songs Woody learned from the Carter Family recordings, including "Little Black Train," "Baltimore to Washington," "Sowing on the Mountain" (one of the few songs where Houston sings the lead and plays while Woody provides backup vocals), and the oft-recorded "Worried Man Blues." "Take a Whiff on Me" is a song that references cocaine use. "Stackolee" (also called "Stagger Lee") is the well-known story of a big, tough, bad man who shot and killed Billy de Lyons in an argument over a Stetson hat. Woody picks up the fiddle and tries to make it sound like a cackling hen in "Hen Cackle," one of the few instrumentals in the Asch recordings. Likewise, Woody plays fiddle in another breakdown called "Rye Straw."

The Carter Family recorded "Johnny Hart" (also called "John Hardy"), the story of a man who killed another man over a gambling debt. Woody utilized the same melody for his seventeen-verse song, "Tom Joad." In "Train 45" (sometimes called "900 Miles"), Woody leaves the guitar to Butch Hawes, while Bess Lomax Hawes plays mandolin.

Volume 3 is entitled "Hard Travelin'," which is an appropriate title for this collection of songs, many of which were written and rewritten as Woody, often with Seeger and members of the Almanac Singers or Houston, crisscrossed the country to sing his songs at political events and union rallies in Pittsburgh, Cleveland, Chicago, Milwaukee, Duluth, Denver, San Francisco, Los Angeles, and Oklahoma City.

Woody wrote the song "Hard Travelin'" during his stint in Oregon in 1941, but he updated it for his recording for Asch in 1947 by adding information about steelworkers, miners, and farmworkers. Like most Guthrie compositions, this song has a catchy melody. He uses wordplay by means of repetition as the narrator describes his "hard travelin'" experiences, "hard ramblin'," "hard gamblin'," "hard-rock minin'," laying in a "hard rock jail" for vagrancy, and "looking for a woman that's hard to find." Woody wrote the up-tempo "Farmer-Labor Train" to the melody of "Wabash Cannon Ball" for the Henry Wallace campaign for the presidency on the Progressive ticket in 1948.

Within the trade union community, Woody's "Union Maid" has become one of the most widely heard songs and its popularity grew throughout the 1970s and 1980s as more and more women entered the workforce and became union members. According to Seeger, Woody banged out the song on a typewriter in the local office of the Communist Party in Oklahoma City in June 1940. To make sure that the crowd would join him in singing the song, Woody used the familiar melody from "Red Wing." Unlike most of the Asch recordings, "Union Maid" is a live performance at a union or political rally. Unfortunately, only a fragment of the song remained in the Asch recordings and all but part of the last verse is missing. However, the chorus is a rouser as the crowd joins in on the easy-to-sing chorus. The recording reveals how well Woody could connect with his audience.

Two other well-known Guthrie songs were narrations of early twentieth-century strikes that resulted in deadly violence aimed at strikers. "1913 Massacre" recounts the tragic story of the copper miners of Calumet, Michigan, mostly of Italian and Finnish heritage, who went on strike in 1913. Woody skillfully takes his listeners into the story, climbing a high staircase to join the strikers and their families as they celebrate around a tall Christmas tree on the second floor of a large building called Italian Hall. Woody introduces the listener to the strikers, who describe their reasons for striking. Suddenly, someone (Woody suggests the "copper boss thugmen") yelled "Fire!" and the children tumbled down the steep staircase to doors that opened to the inside and could not be opened because of the tangled bodies at the bottom of the staircase. In the panic, seventy-three children died, most smothered to death. "1913 Massacre" is surely one of Woody's most powerful songs and was later recorded by his son, Arlo. "Ludlow Massacre" tells the grisly story of the deaths of eleven children and ten adults by volunteer militia units (mostly mining company employees) in the midst of a seven-month-long strike by Colorado coal miners. Forced out of company housing, the miners set up a tent city outside of Ludlow. Faced with gunfire from the militia, the miners dug pits beneath their tents for safety. Bombs and shots were fired into the tent city and at one point the miners returned gunfire. The militia doused the tents with kerosene and set them on fire.

"Miner's Song" initially sounds like a children's song with its rapid tempo and repetitive phrasing of "dig-dig-dig-a-dig-dig-dig," but once the words are understood it becomes clear that the song reflects the drudgery of mine work and the tall tales and stories miners tell to pass the time away. And as the narrator notes, "I'm gonna dig my life away-o."

Volume 3 of the Asch recordings also includes several songs that urge the defeat of Hitler and the Fascist forces and support for the American allies, especially Britain and the Soviet Union. One of the most interesting Guthrie compositions is called "What Are We Waiting On?" Woody notes that "London (is) in ruins, Paris (is) in chains" and the Soviets are fighting on the Eastern Front. Woody asked "Good people, what are we waiting on?" The song was written in 1942 and Woody's question is the same one that many people were asking at the time as they waited for the U.S. and British to launch the "second front" or "western front" in Europe.

"When the Yanks Go Marching In" utilized the familiar melody that everyone recognizes, but substitutes "yanks" and "tanks" for "saints." Woody adds new lyrics to express the desire to win the war. Sonny Terry plays the harmonica and Houston does backup vocals. "Ship in the Sky," tells the story of a young child who proudly points to an airplane flying above and says to a friend, "My daddy rides that ship in the sky." Another child announces that his father works in a plant that makes planes that can fly through the sky: "My daddy keeps your daddy up in the sky." Additional children chime in to make the point that the war effort needs everyone's cooperation to be successful. It is a children's song, perhaps, but one with a powerful wartime message for everyone.

"Miss Pavlichenko" is interesting because it is another rare example of Asch recording a live performance. Lyudmila Pavlichenko was a Ukrainian lieutenant and sniper in the Soviet Army who had been honored with an award for having killed 257 German soldiers. She received a hero's welcome in the U.S. during the war years when a great deal of attention was being paid to the bloody siege of Leningrad and many Americans appreciated the fact that the Russian armies were doing the heaviest lifting in the fight against the German Wehrmacht. The song was written in 1942, but probably not recorded until the live performance at the first People's Songs "Union Hootenany" at Town Hall in New York City on May 9, 1946. The song, and the audience participation, underscores Woody's ability to motivate his listeners.

Woody wrote a version of "Sally, Don't You Grieve" as early as 1938 in Los Angeles, but this version was recorded by Asch in April 1944 and was reshaped to suit the effort to win the war. Receiving his papers to report for active duty, the narrator rushes down to the army office telling Sally "not to grieve" and to get a job and "help the USA." Woody was probably familiar with a 1927 recording with the same title by Ernest Phipps and "His Holiness Quartet."

In 1945, after being drafted into the army, Woody heard a recording of a song he had written eight years earlier in Los Angeles. The song, "Oklahoma Hills," Woody wrote for his radio show, *Woody and Lefty Lou*. The song had been slightly rewritten and recorded by Woody's cousin, Jack Guthrie in 1945 and it very quickly soared to the top of the country charts.[13] This encouraged Woody to write more country and western songs and many of these songs, as well as others that were not his compositions, are included in Volume 4 of the Asch recordings.

The album's title track is "Buffalo Skinners," the lyrics of which Woody took from a song called "Boggy Creek" that had appeared in a collection of cowboy songs that John and Alan Lomax had issued in 1938. Woody set the lyrics to music, offering up one of the very few cowboy protest songs that has ever been written. Woody sang about a jobless young cowboy who accepted an offer to work on a cattle drive on the condition that he would receive good pay and edible food. But when the drive was completed, despite overcoming dangers and dire problems, the drover/employer refused to pay the cowboys. They retaliated by killing the drover and leaving his bones to bleach in the sun. Woody wrote a number of songs with a similar narrative where a "little guy" who is wronged by someone much more powerful than he retaliates and triumphs, including "Philadelphia Lawyer" and "East Texas Red" (recorded by Arlo Guthrie).

Volume 4 also includes songs about outlaws, including "Pretty Boy Floyd" and "Billy the Kid," a song written by Andrew Jenkins. Woody's interest in outlaws had been enhanced by his experiences on the road and riding the rails, where local police, railroad guards, and company thugs meted out rough and capricious justice against train hoppers and hoboes.

Several of the songs reflect Woody's opposition to racism, especially "Slipknot," a song written in 1940 and recorded in 1944 which tells the story of the lynching of a black teenager and his mother. Woody's adaptations of "Dead or Alive (Poor Lazarus)" and "Cocaine Blues" (originally recorded as "Bad Lee Brown") derived from African American songs. "Train Blues" features the harmonica master, Sonny Terry. It is interesting to compare Terry's harmonica work in the Asch recordings with Woody's own harmonica playing in the Library of Congress recording of the same song, "Lost Train Blues." "Along in the Sun and the Rain" is an apt summary of Woody's lifetime of experiences, the good times and hard times, happiness and sadness. He sings that he has seen many towns, kissed many lips, had many fights, and shaken many hands. The recording is somewhat unusual in that Woody sets it in a minor key. "The Return of Rocky Mountain Slim and Desert Rat Shorty" is notable as an example of "country humor" that was frequently heard on live radio stations and tent shows in rural towns in the southwest. Woody and Cisco ham it up as a couple of good old cowboys who are trying to sell their songbook to an audience. The song is spoken against a guitar backdrop of talking blues chord progressions.

In 2003, a number of metal-plated masters of Asch recordings from 1944–45 were retrieved from a basement in Brooklyn. As previously noted, because of wartime shortages of certain types of materials, Asch had no access to blank acetate discs needed for recording. However, Herbert Harris of the Stinson Trading Company possessed such discs and thus a partnership formed. Later, when Asch closed Asch Records and the collaboration with Stimson ended, some of the metal-plated masters from the Asch recordings went with Stimson and these were the ones that were found in 2003. The story of this discovery, written by Guthrie biographer Ed Cray and Rounder Records' Bill Nolin, was published in a booklet and a uniquely packaged set of CDs called *Woody Guthrie: My Dusty Road*, issued by Rounder Records in 2009.

Asch recorded all fifty-four of the songs in the *Woody Guthrie: My Dusty Road* collection—so they were not a separate set of recordings.[14] Six of the songs are listed as "previously unreleased" but "Tear the Fascists Down" is the same recording as "What Are We Waiting On?," which is found in Volume 3 of the Asch recordings. Likewise, "Sonny's Flight" is the same recording as "Train Blues," which was released on Volume 4 of the Asch recordings. One of the songs that Asch never released commercially, "Harriet Tubman's Ballad," is a powerful narrative of a truly remarkable woman. However, Smithsonian-Folkways released the recording in 1994 on *Long Ways to Travel: The Unreleased Folkways Masters, 1944–1949*. As Tubman's life was huge, Woody's songs required two recordings lasting more than six minutes.[15]

NURSERY DAYS

In 1947, Woody recorded two sets of children's songs for Asch's new label, Disc Records (Asch Records had gone out of business in 1945). Although Woody had always made up songs while playing with his children (from his first marriage), most of the children's songs recorded in 1946 were written for his daughter, Cathy (from his marriage to Marjorie Maia), who Woody had playfully nicknamed "Miss Stack bones." Woody played the songs for Cathy, her friends who lived in the Coney Island neighborhood where the Guthrie family lived, and the children of Lomax and other family friends. In 1947, Disc Records issued "Songs to Grow On: Nursery Days," and then "Songs to Grow On: Work Songs for Nursery Days" a year later. In the liner notes to a 1956 release, Woody wrote: "I don't want the kids to be grownup. I want to see the grown up folks be kids."[16] Sixteen of the songs were issued by Smithsonian-Folkways as *Woody Guthrie: Nursery Days*, in 1992.

The songs involved word games ("How dido" and "Jaggy Bum") and subjects that are part of daily parent-child interaction such as waking up ("Wake Up") and cleanliness ("Clean-O"). "Don't You Push Me Down" encourages kids to have fun playing with each other without hurting each other. "Sleep Eye" is a go-to-sleep song. "Put Your Finger in the Air" is a sort of Simon-says or "follow the leader" game song. Probably the most well-known song from these recording is the "Car Song" (also called "Riding in My Car") where Woody imitates the sounds of the car's engine and its horn. Guy Logsdon wrote that the "Car Song" is "one of the best examples of Woody's ability to put himself in the role of a child and create songs; he was an adult child."[17] According to Ed Cray, the songs were an immediate success in left-wing book and record stores.[18]

BALLADS OF SACCO AND VANZETTI

In 1946, Asch suggested that Guthrie write a set of songs regarding the case of Sacco and Vanzetti, two Italian immigrants and anarchists who were convicted of killing two men in an armed robbery in Massachusetts in 1920. Following a controversial trial, failed appeals, and a campaign by left-wing groups, the state executed the two men in 1927. Woody grew interested in the topic, read up on the case, and traveled to Boston to gain material for the songs. But unlike his previous compositions, which were written in astonishingly short periods of time, Woody found it difficult to complete the Sacco and Vanzetti songs. Nearly a year passed before Woody finally wrote the songs a few days before he and Houston entered Asch's small recording session in January 1947. The results were not promising. "Listening to these songs," wrote Jeff Place, "one can hear some hesitation in the voices of both Woody and Cisco, as if they were still reading from the printed lyrics."[19] Woody was not satisfied with the results and dropped the project. In 1960, Asch released eleven songs in an album called *Ballads of Sacco and Vanzetti* on the Folkways label.

By 1947, Woody's illness, still not properly diagnosed, had begun to erode his ability to concentrate and perform his music. His recordings tapered off accordingly. He spent weeks and months dreaming up ideas for new albums of songs and continued to write, but he could not maintain a sustained focus on his material. Still performing in left-wing and union venues, often for little or no pay, Woody's audiences noticed that he often forgot the lyrics or was unable to complete a song. Always interested in religion, he wrote and recorded a few children's songs about the Jewish faith for Asch.[20] The songs were not released until the Asch Recordings were compiled in 1998. Woody also recorded some songs with Cisco Houston regarding the work of Omar Khayyam, but they were also never released. In 1951, after a fall-out with Asch, Woody found a new music publisher in the Richmond Organization. Howard Richmond lent Woody a tape recorder for him to document his recordings, but none of these were released, either. The songs now reside in the Woody Guthrie Archives. In 1952, Woody recorded two more unreleased songs for Decca Records. In a final recording in 1954, Woody, accompanied by Sonny Terry, Brownie McGhee, Ramblin' Jack Elliott, and Alonzo Scales, dropped in on Asch to record a few songs. But the session was a failure, marred by heavy drinking and Woody's inability to remember the lyrics to the songs. Woody Guthrie would never record again.

THE LIVE WIRE

In 2001, two "wire recordings" of an unusual Guthrie concert in 1949 were discovered in a storage closet in the Florida home of Paul Braverman. Braverman was a student at Rutgers University who was interested in folk music. He heard that Woody was playing at an event sponsored by the Jewish Community Center in Newark, New Jersey, so he brought his wire recorder, an early recording mechanism that was soon displaced by more modern tape recorders, to the concert and recorded it. The wire recordings were donated to the Woody Guthrie Archives. After working through the various technical aspects of converting the wire recordings to digital formats, the ten songs as well as introductions and commentaries by Woody and his wife, Marjorie, were released as *The Live Wire: Woody Guthrie in Performance, 1949* by Woody Guthrie Publications, in 2007.

Woody's live performance lasts seventy-four minutes and includes songs that span the length of his performance career, from "The Great Dust Storm," written in 1935, to "Goodbye Centralia," a song written sometime around April 1947. Although the sound quality is poor and some of the songs are incomplete, the live wire recordings are important because they capture Woody's unique and spontaneous performance style in a way that eludes professional recordings. The listener hears rough-edged Guthrie vocals that reflect many years of "hard travelin'" and living hard. Knowing what we now know about Woody's health condition, the listener may detect a sense of disappointment in the voice, but not resignation. In book notes for the publication, Jorge Arevalo Mateus suggests: "On the wires, we hear an even harder-edged Guthrie than is usually associated with the 'Dust Bowl Balladeer.' One hears the unraveling of a man's life, and his unflinching determination to face it. Guthrie's always dry vocals are more caustic and terse, the guitar playing leaner, with a slicing attack that suggest Blues attitude, perhaps even frustration, as survival instincts kick in."[21] The wire recordings also offer another unique value as they reveal something of the relationship between Woody and his wife, Marjorie. This aspect is articulated beautifully by Nora Guthrie, Woody and Marjorie's daughter, in her prologue to the book/album: "With this recording, we hear their very real mutual desire to reach out and to relate to people. . . . She makes sure he keeps it moving in the right direction, timing his stories, trying to shepherd his verbal ramblings. The dynamic between them is sometimes as comical as it is serious with mom helplessly giggling at his outpourings, while at the same time desperately trying to rein him in."[22]

WOODY'S RECORDING LEGACY

From our vantage point in the twenty-first century, it may seem strange that Woody's influence could have been so great given that none of his recordings sold well during his working career and most of his performances were usually small, often unpaid, events. However, it is his rich trove of recordings that artists have drawn upon for more than a half century that has cemented his musical legacy. Pete Seeger, blacklisted by the Red Scare in the 1950s, learned to sing "This Land Is Your Land" and kept his career going by singing for small liberal groups and in schools and churches. Jack Elliot modeled himself after Woody and built a career as a cowboy folksinger primarily on the strength of Woody's songs. Bob Dylan's first experience with Guthrie recordings was transformative:

> All these songs together, one after another made my head spin. . . . It made me want to gasp. It was like the land parted. . . . Guthrie had such a grip on things. He was so poetic and tough and rhythmic. . . . I listened all afternoon to Guthrie as if in a trance and I felt like I had discovered some essence of self-command. . . . I could sing all these songs, every single one of them and they were all that I wanted to sing.[23]

Dylan seemingly *became* Woody for a period in his early career, performing his songs almost exclusively, adopting Woody's accent by dropping g's and adding a's, performing with a harmonica rack around his neck, and dressing in battered boots and tattered clothing. Dylan's first album contained only two original compositions, "Song to Woody" and "Talkin' New York" with its famous line: "You sound like a Hillbilly. We want folk singers here." While Dylan soon found his own voice, he served as a powerful conduit for the Guthrie recordings as the folk-revival mushroomed in the 1960s and folk-rock emerged as a new musical category genre in the 1970s. A deluge of recordings of Guthrie songs followed by artists such as Country Joe McDonald, Arlo Guthrie, Odetta, John Mellencamp, the Byrds, Bruce Springsteen, Willie Nelson, Emmylou Harris, U2, Billy Bragg, Wilco, Alison Krauss, Janis Ian, Jonatha Brooke, and others.

More than a century after his birth, Guthrie recordings continue to be an important musical source for emerging artists in the twenty-first century. In what is now called "Americana," a genre of popular roots music formed by the common and diverse traditions of American folk, country, and blues, Woody Guthrie stands as the towering figure, tall and unbowed.

Telephone
DRexel 2391

338 South Western Avenue
LOS ANGELES, CALIFORNIA

TO WHOM IT MAY CONCERN:

     Mr. W. W. Guthrie was employed by
the Standard Broadcasting Company during the
following periods of time: May, 1937 to Feb.,
1938 - January, 1939 to November, 1939.

     During this time Mr. Guthrie
travelled through Northern California and
reported on migratory labor conditions for
the newspaper "Light", edited at that time by
Mr. J. Frank Burke, the "Editor of the Air."

Frank Burke

127

SELECTED BIBLIOGRAPHY

Albert, Carl Bert, and Danney Goble. *Little Giant: The Life and Times of Speaker Carl Albert*. Norman, Oklahoma: University of Oklahoma Press, 1990.

Archer, Seth. "Reading the Riot Acts." *Southwest Review* 91, no. 4 (September 22, 2006).

Atwood, Rudy. *The Rudy Atwood Story*. Old Tappan, New Jersey: Revell, 1970.

Briley, R. "'Woody Sez:' Woody Guthrie, the *People's Daily World*, and Indigenous Radicalism." *California History* 84, No. 1 (2006): 30-43.

Buhle, Mari Jo, Paul Buhle, and Dan Georgakas. *Encyclopedia of the American Left*. New York: Oxford University Press, 1998.

Cotton, Gordon A., and Jeff T. Giambrone. *Vicksburg and the War*. Gretna, Louisiana: Pelican Publishing Company, 2004.

Cray, Ed. *Ramblin' Man: The Life and times of Woody Guthrie*. New York: W.W. Norton, 2004.

Davidson, Donald. "Current Attitudes toward Folklore." *Tennessee Folklore Society Bulletin* 6 (December 1940): 44-51.

Dochuk, Darren. *From Bible Belt to Sunbelt: Plain-folk Religion, Grassroots Politics, and the Rise of Evangelical Conservatism*. New York: W.W. Norton, 2011.

Dunaway, David King. *How Can I Keep from Singing: Pete Seeger*. New York: McGraw-Hill Book, 1981.

Dylan, Bob. *Dylan Chronicles*. London: Simon & Schuster, 2002.

Eberts, Mike. *Griffith Park: A Centennial History*. Los Angeles: Historical Society of Southern California, 1996.

Flamming, Douglas. *Bound for Freedom: Black Los Angeles in Jim Crow America*. Berkeley: University of California Press, 2005.

Franklin, Jimmie Lewis. *Journey toward Hope: A History of Blacks in Oklahoma*. Norman, Oklahoma: University of Oklahoma Press, 1982.

Fuller, Daniel P. *Give the Winds a Mighty Voice: The Story of Charles E. Fuller*. Waco, Texas: Word Books, 1972.

Garman, Bryan K. *A Race of Singers: Whitman's Working-class Hero from Guthrie to Springsteen*. Chapel Hill: University of North Carolina Press, 2000.

Gilmour, Michael J. *Call Me the Seeker: Listening to Religion in Popular Music*. New York: Continuum, 2005.

Goff, Philip. "Early Christian Radio and Religious Nostalgia." In Colleen McDannell, Ed. *Religions of the United States in Practice*, 305-15. Princeton, New Jersey: Princeton University Press, 2001.

____. "'We Have Heard the Joyful Sound:' Charles E. Fuller's Radio Broadcast and the Rise of Modern Evangelicalism." *Religion and American Culture* 9, no. 1 (1999): 67-95.

Gordon, Linda. *Dorothea Lange: A Life Beyond Limits*. New York: W.W. Norton & Company, 2009.

Green, James R. *Grass-roots Socialism: Radical Movements in the Southwest, 1895-1943*. Baton Rouge: Louisiana State University Press, 1978.

Gregory, James N. *American Exodus: The Dust Bowl Migration and Okie Culture in California*. New York: Oxford University Press, 1989.

Grossman, James R. *Land of Hope: Chicago, Black Southerners, and the Great Migration*. Chicago: University of Chicago Press, 1989.

Guthrie, Woody. *Bound for Glory*. New York: E.P. Dutton, 1968.

Guthrie, Woody, and Maxine "Lefty Lou" Crissman. *Woody and Lefty Lou's Favorite Collection of Old Time Hill Country Songs: Being Sung for Ages, Still Going Strong*. Gardena, California: Spanish American Institute Press, 1937.

Guthrie, Woody, and Moses Asch. *American Folksong: Woody Guthrie*. New York: Oak Publications, 1961.

Guthrie, Woody, and Robert Shelton. *Born to Win*. New York: Macmillan, 1965.

Guthrie, Woody, Dave Marsh, and Harold Leventhal. *Pastures of Plenty: A Self-portrait*. New York: HarperCollins, 1990.

Guthrie, Woody, Marjorie Guthrie, and Guy Logsdon. *Woody Sez*. New York: Grosset and Dunlap, 1975.

Guthrie, Woody, Nora Guthrie, and Steven Brower. *Woody Guthrie: Art Works*. New York: Rizzoli, 2005.

Hampton, Wayne. *Guerrilla Minstrels: John Lennon, Joe Hill, Woody Guthrie, Bob Dylan*. Knoxville: University of Tennessee Press, 1986.

Healey, Dorothy, and Maurice Isserman. *California Red: A Life in the American Communist Party*. Urbana: University of Illinois Press, 1993.

Horton, Carol A. *Race and the Making of American Liberalism*. Oxford, England: Oxford University Press, 2005.

Hurewitz, Daniel. *Bohemian Los Angeles and the Making of Modern Politics*. Berkeley: University of California Press, 2007.

Isserman, Maurice. *Which Side Were You On?: The American Communist Party during the Second World War*. Middletown, Connecticut: Wesleyan University Press, 1982.

Jackson, Mark Allan. *Prophet Singer: The Voice and Vision of Woody Guthrie*. Jackson: University Press of Mississippi, 2007.

Joyce, Davis D. *An Oklahoma I Had Never Seen Before: Alternative Views of Oklahoma History*. Norman: University of Oklahoma Press, 1994.

Kaufman, Will. *Woody Guthrie, American Radical*. Urbana: University of Illinois Press, 2011.

Kempton, Murray. "The Curse of the Guthries." *New York Review of Books*, February 14, 1981, 9.

Kirby, John B. *Black Americans in the Roosevelt Era: Liberalism and Race*. Knoxville: University of Tennessee Press, 1980.

Klehr, Harvey. *The Heyday of American Communism: The Depression Decade*. New York: Basic Books, 1984.

Klein, Joe. *Woody Guthrie: A Life*. New York: Knopf, 1980.

La Chapelle, Peter. *Proud to Be an Okie: Cultural Politics, Country Music, and Migration to Southern California*. Berkeley: University of California Press, 2007.

Larrowe, Charles P. *Harry Bridges; the Rise and Fall of Radical Labor in the United States*. New York: L. Hill, 1972.

Litwack, Leon F. *Trouble in Mind: Black Southerners in the Age of Jim Crow*. New York: Knopf, 1998.

Logsdon, Guy. "Jack Guthrie: A Star That Almost Was." *Journal of Country Music* 15, no. 3 (1993): 32-38.

Lomax, Alan, Woody Guthrie, and Pete Seeger. *Hard Hitting Songs for Hard-hit People*. Lincoln: University of Nebraska Press, 2012.

Maharidge, Dale, and Michael Williamson. *Journey to Nowhere: The Saga of the New Underclass*. Garden City, New York: Dial Press, 1985.

Marsh, Dave. *Glory Days: Bruce Springsteen in the 1980s*. New York: Pantheon Books, 1987.

McWilliams, Carey. *Factories in the Field; the Story of Migratory Farm Labor in California*. Boston: Little, Brown and Company, 1939.

Noble, Donald R. *The Steinbeck Question: New Essays in Criticism*. Troy, New York: Whitston Pub., 1993.

Old Fashioned Revival Hour Quartet Songbook. Waco, Texas: Word Publishing, 1952.

Place, Jeffrey, and Robert Santelli. *Woody at 100: The Woody Guthrie Centennial Collection*. Washington, D.C.: Smithsonian Folkways Recordings, 2012.

Prothero, Stephen R. *American Jesus: How the Son of God Became a National Icon*. New York: Farrar, Straus, and Giroux, 2003.

Reuss, Richard A. "Woody Guthrie and His Folk Tradition." *The Journal of American Folklore* 83, no. 329 (1970): 273.

Robbin, Ed, and Will Geer. *Woody Guthrie and Me: An Intimate Reminiscence*. Berkeley: Lancaster-Miller Publishers, 1979.

Santelli, Robert, and Emily Haas Davidson. *Hard Travelin': The Life and Legacy of Woody Guthrie*. Hanover, New Hampshire: Wesleyan University Press, 1999.

Santelli, Robert, and Nora Guthrie. *This Land Is Your Land: Woody Guthrie and the Journey of an American Folk Song*. Philadelphia: Running Press, 2012.

Seeger, Pete, and Marjorie Guthrie. *Woody Guthrie Folk Songs: A Collection of Songs by America's Foremost Balladeer*. New York: Ludlow Music, 1963.

Seeger, Pete, Phil Ochs, Gordon Friesen, and Josh Dunson. *Woody Guthrie: A Tribute*. New York: Guthrie Children's Trust Fund (reprinted from *Mainstream*, August 1963), 1963.

Shindo, Charles J. *Dust Bowl Migrants in the American Imagination*. Lawrence: University Press of Kansas, 1997.

Starr, Kevin. *Endangered Dreams: The Great Depression in California*. New York: Oxford University Press, 1996.

Taylor, Paul. "From the Ground Up." *Survey Graphic* 27, no. 7 (September 1936).

———. *On the Ground in the Thirties*. Salt Lake City: Gibbs Smith, 1983.

Timmons, Stuart. *The Trouble with Harry Hay: Founder of the Modern Gay Movement*. Boston: Alyson, 1990.

Whitfield, Stephen J. *The Culture of the Cold War*. Baltimore: Johns Hopkins University Press, 1991.

ENDNOTES

One. WOODY GUTHRIE IN LOS ANGELES, 1937–1941

1. Ed Cray, *Ramblin' Man: The Life and Times of Woody Guthrie* (New York: W.W. Norton, 2004): 12.
2. Woody Guthrie, "Railroad Blues: conversation," *Library of Congress Recordings*, (Rounder Records, 1988) Disc 1, Track 2.
3. Cray's biography is indispensable on Woody's early years; see especially pp. 51–55.
4. See Joe Klein, *Woody Guthrie: A Life* (New York: Knopf, 1980), 97; and Mark Allen Jackson, *Prophet Singer: The Voice and Vision of Woody Guthrie* (University Press of Mississippi, Jackson), 7.
5. Jackson, *Prophet Singer*, 71.
6. Guy Logsdon and Arlo Guthrie, Interview with Maxine Crissman, December 13, 1983, author's copy.
7. "This program was in the nature of a hillbilly act featuring 'Woody and Lefty Lou' and during the time they were on this station they received the greatest mail response of any act on the station," Letter of reference from Frank Burke, president of Standard Broadcasting Company, June 18, 1938. Guy Logsdon Collection.
8. Peter La Chapelle, *Proud to Be an Okie: Cultural Politics, Country Music, and Migration to Southern California* (University of California Press, Berkeley, 2007), 51, and James N. Gregory, *American Exodus: The Dust Bowl Migration and Okie Culture in California*, (Oxford University Press, Oxford, 1989), 41.
9. Logsdon and Guthrie, Interview with Maxine Crissman.
10. Maxine Crissman, from an interview with Joe Klein, ca. 1980. WGA Accession 2000-38.21, 38.22.
11. Richard Reuss, "Woody Guthrie and His Folk Tradition," *The Journal of American Folklore, v. 83, July–September, 1970: 273–303*.
12. La Chapelle, *Proud to Be an Okie*, 56.
13. See Logsdon and Guthrie, Interview with Maxine Crissman.
14. Woody Guthrie, *Woody and Lefty Lou's Favorite Collection*, collection of author, (Los Angeles, 1937 and 1939).
15. La Chapelle, *Proud to Be an Okie*), 48.
16. Guthrie, *Woody and Lefty Lou's Favorite Collection*.
17. Woody Guthrie, "Fifth Street Blues." WGA Notebook Series-1, Item-5, 123. ©2002 WGP, Inc.
18. See Logsdon and Guthrie, Interview with Maxine Crissman.
19. Maxine Crissman interview with Joe Klein.
20. Woody Guthrie, "Downtown Traffic Blues." WGA Notebook Series-1, Item-4, page 92. ©2001 WGP, Inc.
21. Woody Guthrie, "Them Big City Ways." Notebook Series-1, Item-4, 124. ©2004 WGP, Inc.
22. Woody Guthrie, "Stay Away from that Home Brew." WGA Notebook Series-1, Item-4, 49. ©2004 WGP, Inc.
23. Woody Guthrie, "Reno Blues," in *On a Slow Train through California* (Los Angeles, 1939). WGA Notebook Series-1, Item-89, n.p. ©1976 WGP, Inc.
24. Woody Guthrie, "California! California!" WGA Notebook Series-1, Item-4, 15. ©2001 WGP, Inc. Will Kaufman, in his fine book, *Woody Guthrie, American Radical*, takes issue with this interpretation of the song, contending that Guthrie's song "bitterly mock(ed) the exploitation of the migrant's hope." (University of Illinois, Urbana, 2011, 15). Kaufman may be right, and certainly Guthrie was capable of contradictory sentiments, and he often juxtaposed the beauty of the land with the unfairness of the economic and social system.
25. See Logsdon and Guthrie, Interview with Maxine Crissman.

26. Woody Guthrie, *A Poem*, October 10, 1937, from Maxine Crissman, in the collection of Guy Logsdon.

27. Maxine Crissman interview with Joe Klein.

28. See Logsdon and Guthrie, Interview with Maxine Crissman

29. See Logsdon and Guthrie, Interview with Maxine Crissman.

30. From *The Light,* in Cray, *Ramblin' Man,* 120.

31. Woody Guthrie, "A-Watching the World Go By." WGA Notebook Series-1, Item-5, 75. ©2002 WGP, Inc.

32. On discrimination against "Okies," see Kevin Starr, *Endangered Dreams: The Great Depression in California* (Oxford University Press, Oxford, 1996), 239–242 and Linda Gordon, *Dorothea Lange: A Life Beyond Limits,* (Norton, 2009), 226.

33. Charles F. McGovern, "Woody Guthrie's American Century," in Robert Santelli and Emily Davidson, *Hard Travelin': The Life and Legacy of Woody Guthrie* (Wesleyan University Press, 1999), 117.

34. Woody Guthrie, *Woody Guthrie: American Folksong,* (Moe Asch, Disc Co. of America, 1947).

35. Gordon, *Dorothea Lange,* 227–228 and Mercer G. Evans, "Housing for Migratory Agricultural Workers," *Public Welfare News* 7 (1936), 2–4; see also Paul S. Taylor, "From the Ground Up," *Survey Graphic* 25, no. 7 (1936).

36. Dorothy Healy, from an interview with Joe Klein, ca. 1980. WGA Accession 2000-38.56.

37. Cray, *Ramblin' Man,* 132.

38. Woody Guthrie Business Card, the Collection of Barry Ollman.

39. Guthrie replaced the old Woody and Lefty Lou theme song with a new one called "Old Lone Wolf." Pete Seeger, ed. *Woody Guthrie Folk Songs,* Ludlow Music, New York, 1963, 36.

40. Pete Seeger and Robert Santelli, "Hobo's Lullaby," in Santelli and Davidson, Op. Cit., 22.

41. Ed Robbin, *Woody Guthrie and Me: An Intimate Reminiscence* (Lancaster-Miller, Berkeley, 1979), 50–53.

42. Maxine Crissman interview with Joe Klein.

43. Robbin, *Woody Guthrie and Me,* 28.

44. Woody Guthrie, *On a Slow Train through California.* WGA Notebook Series-1, Item-89.

45. Robbin, *Woody Guthrie and Me,* 32.

46. Robbin, *Woody Guthrie and Me,* 34.

47. Reuss, "Woody Guthrie and His Folk Tradition," 282.

48. Robbin, *Woody Guthrie and Me,* 35.

49. Daniel Hurewitz, *Bohemian Los Angeles and the Making of Modern Politics* (University of California Press, Berkeley, 2007), 176–177.

50. Klein, *Woody Guthrie,* 131.

51. Stuart Timmons, *The Trouble with Harry Hay, Founder of the Modern Gay Movement* (Alyson, Boston, 1990), 124.

52. Klein, *Woody Guthrie,* 137.

53. Reuss, "Woody Guthrie and His Folk Tradition," 295.

54. Jackson, *Prophet Singer,* 97.

55. Woody Guthrie, "Them Big City Ways." Notebook Series-1, Item-5, page-77. ©2004 WGP, Inc.

56. Woody Guthrie, "I'm Goin' Back to the Farm." WGA Notebook Series-1, Item-4, 70. March 14, 1939. ©2002 WGP, Inc.

57. Woody Guthrie, "I'm Goin' Back to the Farm." WGA Notebook Series-1, Item-5, 218. October 10, 1939. ©2002 WGP, Inc.

58. Woody Guthrie, "Railroad Blues: Conversations," *Library of Congress Recordings,* Disc 1, Track 2.

59. Woody Guthrie, "Goin' Down the Road Feeling Bad: Conversations," *Library of Congress Recordings,* Disc 3, Track 1.

60. Jackson, *Prophet Singer,* 139.

61. Guthrie, *On a Slow Train through California*.

62. Alan Lomax, Woody Guthrie, and Pete Seeger, *Hard Hitting Songs for Hard-Hit People* (Oak Publications, New York, 1969), 115.

63. Woody Guthrie, *Woody Sez*, 37.

64. Woody Guthrie, *Dust Bowl Ballads*, (RCA Victor Records, 1940) Track 2.

65. Woody Guthrie, "I Ain't Got No Home in this World Anymore." Woody Guthrie Papers, Moses and Frances Asch Collection. Ralph Rinzler Archives, Center for Folklife and Cultural Heritage. Box 1, Folder 1.

66. Guthrie, *Woody and Lefty Lou's One Thousand and One Laffs*, May, 1938. Document from Maxine Crissman, in Guy Logsdon Collection.

67. Guthrie, *On a Slow Train through California*.

68. Stephen Whitfield, *The Culture of the Cold War*. (Baltimore., Johns Hopkins University Press, 1991), 201–203.

69. Guthrie paid a heavy price for his defense of the Communist Party. J. Edgar Hoover and the FBI were on Guthrie's trail by the time Guthrie had completed his highly productive month-long job writing songs for the opening of the Columbia River Dam system in 1941 (U.S. Department of Justice, Federal Bureau of Investigation, Memo to John Edgar Hoover, Director, June 9, 1941, WGA, Personal Papers, Box 2 Folder 48). By the time the agency tried to prevent Guthrie from being hired, he had already completed the work and moved on to the East Coast (Ibid. Memo from John Edgar Hoover, October 17, 1941, WGA, Personal Papers, Box 2 Folder 48). A few years later, the Almanac Singers, including Guthrie, Pete Seeger, and others, achieved great commercial success before being destroyed by anti-Communist hysteria. The wonderful songbook by Guthrie, Alan Lomax, and Pete Seeger, *Hard-Hitting Songs for Hard-Hit People*, was prepared and ready for publication in 1942, but there was no publisher until 1967, when the political atmosphere had grown hostile. Like many artists, musicians, and actors, Guthrie saw his professional options narrow decisively during the Cold War years.

70. Guthrie started his Cornbread Philosophy column, which prefigured his Woody Sez articles. "I'm trying to elect Olson for governor. I heard he was for the Little Man. And I am not but 5 feet 6 inches, and weigh a hundred and twenty with a bowl of chili." *The Light*, July 1, 1938.

71. *Hollywood Tribune*, July 21; August 7; August 14; August 21, 1939.

72. Guthrie, *Woody Sez*, xvi.

73. Steinbeck wrote this in 1940 as the introduction to *Hard-Hitting Songs for Hard-Hit People*, still despite his name, no publishers were willing to publish it until 1967.

74. Klein, *Woody Guthrie*, 135.

75. Seeger and Santelli, "Hobo's Lullaby," in Santelli and Davidson, 31.

76. Klein, *Woody Guthrie*, 136.

77. Guthrie, *On a Slow Train through California*.

78. *People's Songs Bulletin*, vol. 3, no. 8, September, 1948, cited in Reuss, "Woody Guthrie and His Folk Tradition.".

79. David King Dunaway, *How Can I Keep from Singing: Pete Seeger* (McGraw-Hill, New York, 1981), 67.

80. Reuss, "Woody Guthrie and His Folk Tradition," 285.

81. Reuss, "Woody Guthrie and His Folk Tradition," 281.

82. Bob Dylan, *Chronicles*, Volume I (Simon and Schuster, New York, 2004), 244.

83. Robbin, *Woody and Me*, 61; see also Cray, *Ramblin' Man*, 206.

84. Guthrie, *Woody Guthrie American Folksong*.

Two. RAMBLIN' IN BLACK AND WHITE

1. The authors would like to thank William Deverell, Darryl Holter, and the other organizers of the "Woody at 100" symposium, held at the University of Southern California in spring 2012. The conference allowed us to express our preliminary ideas about Woody and race in a singularly creative and supportive environment.

2. Maxine (Crissman) Dempsey interview by Richard Reuss, June 14 to June 18, 1968, Box 3, Richard Reuss Papers, Indiana University, Bloomington. Hereafter cited as RRP.

3. That New Deal liberals privileged class uplift and orderly capitalism over racial problems, and that racial liberals were a small minority within mainstream liberalism, is illustrated in John B. Kirby, *Black Americans in the Roosevelt Era: Liberalism and Race* (Knoxville: University of Tennessee Press 1979). Carol A. Horton, *Race and the Making of American Liberalism* (New York: Oxford University Press, 2005) considers the full twentieth century and a broad definition of "liberalism" that includes both classical liberalism (what today would be considered neo-conservatives) and welfare state liberalism; either way, racial egalitarianism was not promoted by white-mainstream liberals during the Guthrie era.

   Although the American North and West were also clearly racist (e.g., Flamming, *Bound for Freedom*; and Grossman, *Land of Hope*), the violent and suffocating racism of the American South was a different animal. Doubters in this regional distinction should begin with Leon F. Litwack, *Trouble in Mind: Black Southerners in the Age of Jim Crow* (New York: Vintage, 1999). On Oklahoma, see Jimmie Lewis Franklin, *Journey toward Hope: A History of Blacks in Oklahoma* (University of Oklahoma Press, 1982). For the story of another poor-white child who grew up in Oklahoma's "Little Dixie" and eventually became a champion of civil rights in the U.S. Congress, see Carl Albert, with Danney Gobel, *Little Giant: The Life and Times of Speaker Carl Albert* (Norman, University of Oklahoma Press, 1990).

4. Woody Guthrie, *Bound for Glory* (Plume [a division of Penguin Books USA]: New York, 1983), p. 19. This and all subsequent citations to *Bound for Glory* are from the Plume edition. Originally published by E.P. Dutton: New York, 1943.

5. Guthrie, *Bound for Glory*, 30.

6. Guthrie, *Bound for Glory*, 30-31.

7. Guthrie, *Bound for Glory*, 31.

8. Guthrie, *Bound for Glory*, 33-34.

9. Guthrie, *Bound for Glory*, 33.

10. Will Kaufman, *Woody Guthrie: American Radical* (Urbana: University of Illinois Press, 2011), 145-148.

11. Ed Cray, *Ramblin' Man: The Life and Times of Woody Guthrie* (New York: W. W. Norton, 2004), 5.

12. Joe Klein, *Woody Guthrie: A Life* (New York: Delta, 1980), 12.

13. For details of the Canadian River Bridge lynching, see: "Mother and Son are Lynched at Okemah," *Tulsa Daily World,* May 26, 1911, Box 3, RRB; Kaufman, *Woody Guthrie*, 145.

14. Richard Reuss, "Field Notes, Okemah, Oklahoma," August 15-18, 1966, Box 3, RRP.

15. Ibid.

16. *California Eagle*, November 15, 1919.

17. Richard Reuss, "Field Notes, Okemah, Oklahoma," August 15 to August 18, 1966, Box 3, RRP.

18. Steven Brower and Nora Guthrie, *Woody Guthrie Art Works* (New York: Rizzoli, 2005), 16.

19. Guthrie, *Bound for Glory*, 253-255.

20. From Woody Guthrie and Maxine Crissman, *Woody and Lefty Lou's Favorite Collection, Old Time Hill Country Songs: Been Sung for Ages, Still Going Strong*, published by KFVD (n.d., n.p). Box 3, RRP. Originally titled, *Old Time Hill Billy Songs: Been Sung fer ages Still goin strong!!*

21. Ibid.

22. Interview with Maxine (Crissman) Dempsey by Robert Klein (n.d.), Woody Guthrie Center, Tulsa, Oklahoma.

23. Ibid.

24. Maxine Crissman interviewed by Richard Ruess, June 14 to June 18, 1968, Box 3, RRP.

25. Ibid.

26. Ibid.

27. Jeff Guthrie, interviewed by Richard Reuss, December 12, 1967, Box 3, RRP.

28. Reprinted from Maxine Crissman interviewed by Richard Ruess, June 14 to June 18, 1968, Box 3, RRP.

29. Klein, *Woody Guthrie*, 238-239.

30. Al Richmond interviewed by Richard Reuss, July 10, 1967, Box 3, RRP.

31. "Woody Sez," Box 3, RRP.

32. Woody Guthrie, *Woody Guthrie Folk Songs: A Collection of Songs by America's Foremost Balladeer* (New York: Ludlow Music, 1963), 183.

33. Cray, *Ramblin' Man,* 261.

34. Kaufman, *Woody Guthrie*, 155-158.

35. Guthrie and Crissman, *Woody and Lefty Lou's Favorite Collection,* n.p.

36. Woody Guthrie, "Stewbally: My Version of an Old Folk Song," (n.d.), Box 3, RRP.

37. Woody Guthrie to Harold Ambellan and Elisabeth Higgins, June 10, 1941, Box 3, RRP.

38. Richard Reuss interview of Alan Lomax, Box 3, RRP.

39. Quoted in Cray, *Ramblin' Man,* 194.

Four. THE GUTHRIE PRESTOS

1. Woody Guthrie, "Songs, People, Papers," typed manuscript, 6, in manuscript set 1, box 4, folder 31, Woody Guthrie Foundation and Archives, New York (hereafter WGFA), (this collection has since been moved to the Woody Guthrie Center in Tulsa); Bryan Carman, *A Race of Singers: Whitman's Working-Class Hero from Guthrie to Springsteen* (Chapel Hill: University of North Carolina Press, 2000), 117; Quotation from "Woody Sez," *People's World,* June 12, 1939, 4.

2. Woody Guthrie, *$30 Wood Help!,* (Los Angeles: self-published pamphlet, 1939), in Woody Guthrie Papers (hereafter WGP), Ralph Rinzler Archive, Center for Folklife and Cultural Heritage, Smithsonian Institution, Washington, D.C.; "Saga of Ham and Eggs Caravan," *People's World,* May 20, 1939, 1,3.

3. See 1939 runs for both newspapers.

4. Woody Guthrie, "Woody Sez," *People's World,* June 17, 1939, 4; Cray, *Ramblin' Man,* 139.

5. Gregory Alan-Kingman Horn, "The Southern California Library for Social Studies and Research: An Independent Home for the Left," paper, UCLA Graduate School of Education and Information Studies, n.d., accessed July 25, 2013, http://pages.gseis.ucla.edu/faculty/maack/Documents/Hom.pdf.

6. Stuart Timmons, *The Trouble with Harry Hay: Founder of the Modern Gay Movement* (Boston: Alyson Publication, 1990); Harry Hay, interview by author, February 16, 1999, West Hollwood, California.

7. Harry Hay, interview by author, February 16, 1999, West Hollwood, California.

8. Presto expert Alan Graves maintains an excellent website documenting this history: http://www.televar.com/grshome/Presto.htm. Also see Michael Biel, "The Making and Use of Recordings in Broadcasting Before 1936," (Ph.D. dissertation, Northwestern University, 1977).

9. Guy Logsdon, "Jack Guthrie: A Star That Almost Was," *Journal of Country Music* 15, no. 2 (1993): 32-38; Maxine (Crissman) Dempsey, interview by Richard Reuss, field notes, June 14 to June 18, 1968, Richard Reuss, Indiana University, 3, 5, 6; George Sanders, "Hollywood Hoedown Lowdown," *Country Song Roundup* 1, no. 8 (October 1950), 16.

10. Maxine (Crissman) Dempsey, interview by author, November 11, 1999, Carson City, Nevada.

11. Cray, *Ramblin' Man*, 36.

12. Woody Guthrie and Maxine Crissman, *Woody and Lefty Lou's Favorite Collection of Old Time Hill Country Songs: Being Sung for Ages, Still Going Strong* (Gardena, California: Spanish American Institute Press, 1938, 20; Woody Guthrie, "Woody Sez," *People's World* (San Francisco), May 27, 1939, 4.

13. "New Year's Flood," in Guthrie, "Songs of Woody Guthrie," 98, in Woody Guthrie Manuscript Collection (hereafter WGM), American Folklife Center, Library of Congress, Washington, D.C. On the 1934 flood see: "Thirty-Seven on Death List in Record Deluge," *Los Angeles Times*, January 2, 1934; "Seventy-Five on Missing List of Tragic Storm, *Los Angeles Times*, January 3, 1934, 1; Myrtle Esther Silver, "Medical Care for Families on Relief in Glendale District of Los Angeles County," (M.A. thesis, University of Southern California, 1937), 23-24; Gretchen Palmatier Couch, "An Analysis of School Attendance and Child Welfare Services in Glendale City Schools," (M.S. thesis, USC, June 1939), 144; "Flood Clean-Up Speeded Through Coordination," and "Storm Lesson Pointed Out," *Los Angeles Times*, January 5, 1934, pt. 2, 1. A similar flood hit in the same area in 1938, which may have piqued Guthrie's interest in the subject of the 1934 flood. See for instance: "Known Deaths Reach Seventy as Storm Flood Waters Recede," *Los Angeles Times*, March 4, 1938, 1; and Kevin Roderick, "Deadly Flood of 1938 Left Its Mark on Southland," *Los Angeles Times*, October 30, 1999, B6.

14. See Guthrie, "Songs of Woody Guthrie," WGM, 98, and Guthrie, "Songs, People, Papers," WGFA, 2. Also see Mike Eberts, *Griffith Park: A Centennial History* (Los Angeles: The Historical Society of Southern California, 1996) 155, 171-81.

15. Guthrie, "Songs of Woody Guthrie," WGM, 39, 82. The song fragment "bound to get lousy in the Vickburg jale" appears to stem from a poem, "The Vicksburg Jail," that was later set to music. That song was a Union prisoner of war's complaint about the conditions in a Confederate jail in Mississippi. See Gordon A. Cotton and Jeff T. Giambrone, *Vicksburg and the War* (Gretna, La.: Pelican Publishing, 2004), 60.

16. Guthrie, "Songs of Woody Guthrie," WGM, 80, 111.

17. Guthrie, "Original Songs," WGFA, 93. Also see Woody Guthrie, letter to Alan Lomax, April 1941.

18. Versions of "(Them) Big City Ways" appear in Guthrie, "Songs of Woody Guthrie," WGM, 64 and in Guthrie, "Songs, People, Papers," WGFA, 124.

19. Guthrie, "Dust Bowl Blues," 12, in "Songs of Woody Guthrie," WGM.

20. Handscript inventory of fan letters, in "Original Songs," WGFA, 176-77.

21. See chapters 3 and 7 of this book.

22. Guthrie described skid rows on Fifth Street and Hollywood Boulevard in the *Hollywood Tribune* on July 31 and August 7, 1939.

23. Seth Archer, "Reading the Riot Acts," *Southwest Review* 91, no. 4 (September 2006): 507-509, 512-513.

24. Archer, "Reading the Riot," 513.

25. Guthrie and Crissman, *Woody and Lefty Lou's Favorite Collection*, 1, "Do-Re-Me" in fact appears to have been penned Guthrie even earlier in 1937. See Woody Guthrie, "Do Re Mi," 30, in "Songs of Woody Guthrie," WGM.

26. Guthrie and Crissman, *Woody and Lefty Lou's Favorite Collection*, 1; Woody Guthrie, "Do Re Mi," in "Songs of Woody Guthrie," WGM, 30; Woody Guthrie, "Do Re Mi," notebook 1, folder 5, p. 43, WGFA.

27. See for instance H.R. Stoneback, "Rough People . . . Are the Best Singers: Woody Guthrie, John Steinbeck, and Folksong," in *The Steinbeck Question*, Donald R. Noble, editor, (Troy, New York: Whitson Publishing, 1993), 161-62.

28. Woody Guthrie, "Desert Sun, Rr. 'Bulls' Harass Workers," *Light: Democratic Leader* (Los Angeles), September 9, 1938, 1, 9.

29. The first of these was [Woody Guthrie], "Cornbread Philosophy," *Light: The Democratic Leader*, September 1938, 4. "Woody Sez" ran in the *People's World* and later the East Coast *Daily Worker*.

30. Gregory, *American Exodus*, 11-13.

31. Harry Hay, interview by author; Guthrie, "Songs, People, Papers," 6; Will Geer, interview by Victor and Judi Wolfenstein, audio recording, ca. 1970; Guthrie, "High Balladree," 2E, WGFA; Guthrie, "Woody Sez," June 17, 1939, 4.

32. Woody Guthrie, "This Baby Must Grow," cartoon, *California Progressive Leader* 1, no. 3, (November 10, 1939), 1; Woody Guthrie, "Production for Use Will Save the Taxpayer," cartoon, *California Progressive Leader*, 1, no. 2, October 18, 1939, 1; Woody Guthrie, "Woody Sez" column, *People's World*, July 1, 1939, 4.

33. See an explanation of the Presto disc product lines in the company's 1940 catalog, *Presto Instantaneous Sound Recording Equipment and Disc* (New York: Presto Recording Company), p. 1035 A.

34. Cray, *Ramblin' Man*, 120.

35. Woody Guthrie, "Songs, People, Papers," WGFA, 6; Carman, *Race of Singers*, 11.

36. Notes at the bottom of "California! California" in Guthrie and Crissman, *Woody and Lefty Lou's Favorite Collection*, 15.

37. Donald Davidson, "Current Attitudes toward Folklore." *Tennessee Folklore Society Bulletin* 6 (Dec. 1940), 44-51.

Six. IN THE SHADOW OF THE STEEPLE I SEE MY PEOPLE

1. Cray, *Ramblin' Man*, 72-3. On Harmonialism, see Peter W. Williams, *America's Religions: From their Origins to the Twenty-First Century* (Urbana and Chicago: University of Illinois Press, 2002), chapter 41.

2. Klein, *Woody Guthrie: A Life*, 75-77.

3. Klein, 58-59.

4. Jack Guthrie quoted in Cray, 100.

5. Cray, 107.

6. Quoted in Klein, 93.

7. Cray, 121.

8. Klein, 99.

9. Rudy Atwood, *The Rudy Atwood Story* (Revell, 1970).

10. "A Hint to Better Things," recording of the Little Country Church, n.d. (internal evidence suggests 1935 or 1936). Billy Graham Historical Center, Wheaton College, Wheaton, IL. Transcribed by Philip Goff with permission.

11. History of "The Little Country Church," see Philip Goff, "Early Christian Radio and Nostalgia," in *Religions of the United States in Practice*, volume 2, Colleen McDannell, ed. (Princeton, NJ: Princeton University Press, 2001), 305-315.

12. Daniel P. Fuller, *Give the Winds a Mighty Voice* (Waco, TX: Word Books, 1972).

13. For a history of the rise of the Old Fashioned Revival Hour in the 1930s and 1940s, see Philip Goff, "We Have Heard the Joyful Sound: Charles E. Fuller's International Broadcast and the Rise of Modern Evangelicalism," Religion and American Culture: A Journal of Interpretation 9:1 (Winter 1999), 67-95.

14. "This World Is Not My Home," *Old-Fashioned Revival Hour Quartet Songbook* (Waco, TX: Word Publishing, 1952).

15. Klein, 470.

16. "I Ain't Got No Home," words and music by Woody Guthrie, © 1961 and 1963 WGP, Inc.
17. Liner notes, *Hard Travelin'*, vol. 3 of The Asch Recordings, 19.
18. Klein, 128.
19. James Knight, "I Ain't Got No Home in This World Anymore': Protest and Promise in Woody Guthrie and the Jesus Tradition," in Gilmour, *Call Me the Seeker*, 28.
20. Hampton, *Guerilla Minstrels*, 130.
21. Klein, 163.
22. Guthrie, *Bound for Glory*, 251.

Eight. WOODY SEZ

An earlier version of this essay was published in *California History*. The editors of this book thank the University of California Press.

1. For Hal Ashby's film *Bound for Glory* see Vincent Canby, "Bound for Glory," *The New York Times*, December 6, 1976, 46; Judith Crist, "Bound for Glory," *Saturday Review*, December 11, 1976, 78; and Janet Maslin, "Bound for Glory," *Newsweek*, December 13, 1976, 104.
2. Ed Cray, *Ramblin' Man: The Life and Times of Woody Guthrie*, 138-140; Joe Klein, *Woody Guthrie: A Life*, 113-135; Dorothy Ray Healey and Maurice Isserman, *California Red: A Life in the American Communist Party*; and Harvey Klehr, *The Heyday of American Communism: The Depression Decade*.
3. Bryan K. Garman, *A Race of Singers: Whitman's Working-Class Hero from Guthrie to Springsteen*, 169-170; and Woody Guthrie, *Bound for Glory*, 399.
4. Ronald D. Cohen, "Woody the Red?," in Santelli and Davidson, *Hard Travelin'*, 150.
5. James R. Green, *Grass-Roots Socialism: Radical Movements in the Southwest, 1895-1943*, xiii and 368; Stephen Prothero, *American Jesus: How the Son of God Became a National Icon*; Klein, *Woody Guthrie*, 125; "Jesus Christ Was a Man," Lomax, Guthrie, and Seeger, *Hard Hitting Songs for Hard-Hit People*, 336-337; and Guthrie, Marsh, and Leventhal, *Pastures of Plenty*, 35.
6. Harry Menig, "Woody Guthrie: The Oklahoma Years, 1912-1929," in Joyce, *An Oklahoma I Had Never Seen Before*, 162-190.
7. "So Long It's Been Good to Know You," in Lomax, Guthrie, and Seeger, *Hard Hitting Songs*, 226-227.
8. Moses Asch, ed., *American Folksong: Woody Guthrie* (New York: Oak Publications, 1961), 22-23.
9. Cray, *Ramblin' Man*, 126-132.
10. "Tom Mooney Is Free," in Lomax, Guthrie, and Seeger, *Hard Hitting Songs*, 356; Richard H. Frost, *The Mooney Case* (Palo Alto, California: Stanford University Press, 1968); and Robbin, *Woody Guthrie and Me*, 30-33.
11. Woody Guthrie, *Woody Sez* (New York: Grosset & Dunlap, 1975); Guthrie, Marsh, and Leventhal, *Pastures of Plenty*, 163; Paul Richards, "People's World," in Mari Jo Buhle, Paul Buhle, and Dan Georgakas, *Encyclopedia of the American Left* (Urbana: University of Illinois Press, 1992), 573-574; and "Woody Sez," *People's Daily World* (PDW), June 17, 1939, 4.
12. "Woody Sez: A New Columnist Introduces Himself," PDW, May 12, 1939, 4. To maintain the flavor of Guthrie's writing, the misspellings and grammar employed by Guthrie are maintained.
13. "Woody Sez," PDW, May 18, 1939, 4; and "Woody Sez," PDW, May 19, 1939, 4.
14. "Woody Sez: Migratious Workers Take Lots of Abuse," PDW, May 23, 1939, 4.
15. "Woody Sez: House," PDW, May 31, 1939, 4; "Woody Sez," PDW, June 1, 1939, 4; and "Pretty Boy Floyd," Asch, ed., *American Folksong*, 27.

16. "Woody Sez," PDW, June 3, 1939, 4; "Woody Sez," PDW, June 6, 1939, 4; and "Woody Sez," PDW, June 19, 1939, 4.

17. "Woody Sez," PDW, June 23, 1939, 4.

18. "Woody Sez," PDW, June 24, 1939, 4; Woody Guthrie, "Roving Reporter Covers Hunger by a Dam Site," PDW, June 27, 1939, 4; "Woody Sez," PDW, June 28, 1939, 4; and "Woody Sez," PDW, July 3, 1939, 4.

19. "Woody Sez," PDW, June 24, 1939, 4; Woody Guthrie, "Roving Reporter Covers Hunger by a Dam Site," PDW, June 27, 1939, 4; "Woody Sez," PDW, June 28, 1939, 4; and "Woody Sez," PDW, July 3, 1939, 4.

20. "Woody Sez," PDW, July 17, 1939, 4; on James Leech see Klehr, *The Heyday of American Communism*, 463; James R. Green, *Grass Roots Socialism*, 173; Klein, *Woody Guthrie*, 125; and "Jesus Christ Was a Man," in Lomax, Guthrie, and Seeger, *Hard Hitting Songs*, 336-337.

21. "Woody Sez," PDW, August 3, 1939, 4; "Woody Sez," PDW, August 4, 1939, 4; "Woody Sez," PDW, August 7, 1939, 4; and Larrowe, *Harry Bridges*.

22. "Woody Sez," PDW, July 31, 1939, 4; and "Woody Sez," PDW, September 6, 1939, 4.

23. "Woody Sez," PDW, August 15, 1939, 4; and "Woody Sez," PDW, October 27, 1939, 4.

24. "Woody Sez," PDW, September 12, 1939, 4; and "Woody Sez," PDW, September 15, 1939, 4.

25. "Woody Sez," PDW, September 22, 1939, 4; "Woody Sez," PDW, September 26, 1939, 4; "Woody Sez," PDW, September 27, 1939, 4; and Isserman, *Which Side Were You On? The American Communist Party During the Second World War*, 198a.

26. "Woody Sez," PDW, October 6, 1939, 4; and "Woody Sez," PDW, November 20, 1939, 4.

27. "Woody Sez," PDW, November 14, 1939, 4; "Woody Sez," PDW, November 22, 1939, 4; and "Woody Sez," PDW, November 30, 1939, 4.

28. "Woody Sez," PDW, October 18, 1939, 4; "Woody Sez," PDW, December 1, 1939, 4; and "Woody Sez," PDW, December 5, 1939, 4.

29. "Woody Sez," PDW, October 10, 1939, 4; and "Woody Sez," PDW, October 26, 1939, 4.

30. "Woody Sez," PDW, December 14, 1939, 4.

31. Guthrie, Marsh, and Leventhal, *Pastures of Plenty*, 149.

32. David R. Shumway, "Your Land: The Lost Legacy of Woody Guthrie," in Santelli and Davidson, eds., *Hard Travelin'*, 157.

Nine. WOODY AND SKID ROW IN LOS ANGELES

1. Woody Guthrie, *Woody Sez*, 56.

2. Guthrie, *On a Slow Train through California*, WGA Notebook Series-1. Item 89, n.p.

3. *Woody Sez*, 58.

4. Guthrie, *Bound for Glory*, 258.

5. Robbin, *Woody and Me*, 75-76.

6. *The Light*, in Cray, *Ramblin' Man*, 120.

Ten. "THE GHOST OF TOM JOAD"

An earlier version of this essay was published in *California History*. The editors of this book thank the University of California Press.

1. Klein, *Woody Guthrie: A Life*, 163.

2. Typescript of "Tom Joad," from the Woody Guthrie Papers, Moses and Frances Asch Collection, Smithsonian Folkways, Library of Congress.

3. Murray Kempton, "The Curse of the Guthries," *New York Review of Books* (February 1981): 8-11; quoted at p. 9.

4. Shindo, *Dust Bowl Migrants*, 175.

5. Guthrie, *Born to Win*.

6. Guthrie, Woody Sez, 133. Interestingly, similar claims of authenticity had been made about Henry Fonda. Filmmaker Pare Lorentz, in a review of the film version of *The Grapes of Wrath*, wrote that Fonda was so believable in the role that "you may think he is ... one of the actual migrants." Review cited in a filmography mss. in the John Ford Papers, Lilly Library, Indiana University; see box eleven, folder four.

7. "Tom Joad," typescript, Woody Guthrie Archives, New York.

8. From CBS Television, *60 Minutes*, January 21, 1996.

9. Marsh, *Glory Days*, 278, 364.

10. Ibid., 284-285; and Corn, "Bruce Springsteen Tells the Story of a Secret America," *Mother Jones*, March/April 1996, beginning at p. 23.

11. Taylor, *On the Ground in the Thirties*, and McWilliams, *Factories in the Field*.

12. The California songs spring from pieces in the *Los Angeles Times*. See, for instance, Mark Arax and Tom Gorman, "California's Illicit Farm Belt Export," March 13, 1995 [about "Sinaloa Cowboys"]; Sebastian Rotella, "Children of the Border," April 3, 1993 [about teenaged male prostitutes in Balboa Park]. As David Corn has written in *The Nation*, "Springsteen is not *of* his subjects, but he reads the newspapers—damn well—and he gives hoot." See "Guthrie's Ghost," *The Nation*, December 11, 1995, p. 733. Another extremely important influence on the recent album is Dale Maharidge's book *Journey to Nowhere: The Saga of the New Underclass*. On this, see Tom Schoenberg, "Professor's Research Inspires a Rock Star," *Chronicle of Higher Education*, January 19, 1996: A7. In Maharidge's words, Springsteen "is a musical Steinbeck. The people he's writing about don't have a voice, so the songs are important, they talk about what's going on in our society today." See Richard Harrington, "Steelworker's Song," in *Washington Post*, December 5, 1995.

13. Stott, Documentary Expression, 8.

14. CBS Television, *60 Minutes*, January 21, 1996.

Twelve. **WOODY GUTHRIE'S RECORDINGS**

1. Guy Logsdon, *Woody Guthrie: A Biblio-Discography* (Revised August 25, 2011). The best summary of Guthrie's recordings is by Jeff Place, "Woody Guthrie's Recorded Legacy," in Robert Santelli and Emily Davidson, ed., *Hard Travelin': The Life and Legacy of Woody Guthrie*, Wesleyan University Press, Hanover/London, 1999, 56-67. I have deliberately chosen not to list or discuss Guthrie recordings that have been reissued, often by foreign companies, without permission from the owners of the original recordings, from those who hold copyrights or from the Woody Guthrie estate.

2. La Chapelle, *Proud to Be an Okie*.

3. Harry Hay was an actor who was active in the Communist Party in Los Angeles in the 1930s and 1940s. Hay also taught musical appreciation courses in the People's College, a local, alternative "college without walls" and may have used the recordings in his courses. In his introduction to "Big City Ways" Guthrie makes a reference to "college."

4. Woody Guthrie Publications (WGP) Box 1, Folder 2.

5. *Talkin' Union* 6, April 1983, 4.

6. Cray, 182.

7. U.S. Department of Justice, Federal Bureau of Investigation, Memo to John Edgar Hoover, Director, June 9, 1941 and October 17, 1941, WGA Personal Papers, Box 2 Folder 48.
8. Ed Cray and Bill Nowlin, *Woody Guthrie: My Dusty Road*, Rounder Records, Burlington, MA, 2009, 41.
9. Guy Logsdon, "Notes on the Songs," Woody Guthrie, the Asch Recordings, Volume 1, Smithsonian Folkways, 1997.
10. For a wonderfully detailed analysis of the song, see Mark Allan Jackson, *Prophet Singer: The Voice and Vision of Woody Guthrie*, University Press of Mississippi, Jackson, Mississippi, 2007, 9-47.
11. *Hard Hitting Songs for Hard-Hit People*, Oak Publications, New York, 1967.
12. Arlo Guthrie, Concert at Woodyfest, Okemah, Oklahoma, July 14, 2010.
13. Guy Logsdon, "Jack Guthrie: A Star That Almost Was," The Journal of Country Music, volume 15-2, 1993, 32-38.
14. If we compare the matrix numbers identifying each song in the Asch Recordings and the Dusty Roads project we see they are identical. See Logsdon, 29-33.
15. Cray and Nowlin, 56. The Smithsonian/Folkways recording of "Harriet Tubman's Ballad" is track 4 on *Long Ways to Travel: the Unreleased Folkways Masters, 1944-1949*, Logsdon, 64.
16. *Woody Guthrie: Nursery Days*, Liner Notes, Smithsonian Folkways, 1992
17. Guy Logsdon, *Woody Guthrie: This Land is Your Land: The Asch Recordings*, Volume 1, Annotation, Smithsonian Folkways, 1997, 11.
18. Cray, 299.
19. Place, "Woody Guthrie's Recorded Legacy," 65.
20. "The Many and the Few" and "Hanukkah Dance" in *Woody Guthrie: Hard Travelin': The Asch Recordings*, Volume 3, tracks 26, 27,
21. *The Live Wire: Woody Guthrie in Performance, 1949*, Woody Guthrie Publications, 2007, 54.
22. Ibid., 5.
23. Dylan, *Chronicles, Volume I*, 244.

CONTRIBUTORS

DARRYL HOLTER is the author of *Workers and Unions in Wisconsin: A Labor History* and *The Battle for Coal: Miners and the Nationalization of Coal-Mining in France*. He is a musician and singer-songwriter, a former labor leader, an urban developer, an adjunct professor of history at the University of Southern California, and a member of the Professional Musicians Union Local 47 in Los Angeles.

WILLIAM DEVERELL is professor of history and director of the Huntington-USC Institute on California and the West at the University of Southern California. He is the author of numerous studies of the nineteenth- and twentieth-century American West, including *Whitewashed Adobe: The Rise of Los Angeles and the Remaking of Its Mexican Past*.

RON BRILEY has taught history for almost forty years at Sandia Prep School in Albuquerque, New Mexico, where he also served as assistant head of the school. He is the recipient of national teaching awards from the Organization of American Historians, American Historical Association, National Council for History Education, and the Society for History Education. He is the author of several books and numerous scholarly articles on the history of sport, music, and film, and is a frequent contributor to the History News Network. His interest in Woody Guthrie stems from an identification with the folksinger's political commitment to social justice. He was born, raised, and picked cotton in the Texas Panhandle near Guthrie's adopted home of Pampa, Texas.

DANIEL CADY is an associate professor of history at California State University, Fresno. He specializes in twentieth-century migration to California with an emphasis on religious and musical cultures. His scholarly work is especially focused on the lives of African Americans in 1920s Los Angeles and their battle to establish venues for elite recreational activities.

TIFFANY COLANNINO oversaw the Woody Guthrie Collection in her role as archivist at the Woody Guthrie Foundation in New York City, where she collaborated on a variety of award-winning Guthrie projects, including documentary films, audio productions, book publications, and museum exhibits. She has lectured internationally on the life and legacy of Woody Guthrie, as well as contributed to the development of the Woody Guthrie Center in Tulsa, Oklahoma. A native of Montreal, Canada, she received her masters of science degree in Library and Information Science with a concentration in Archival Management from Simmons College in Boston.

ED CRAY, now professor emeritus at the University of Southern California, is the author or editor of twenty books, including a comprehensive biography of Woody Guthrie entitled *Ramblin' Man.*

DOUGLAS FLAMMING, a Guggenheim Fellow and winner of Georgia Tech's prestigious Geoffrey Eichholz Teaching Award, specializes in the social and political history of the United States since the Civil War. He is the author of *Creating the Modern South: Millhands and Managers in Dalton, Georgia*; *Bound for Freedom: Black Los Angeles in Jim Crow America*; and *African Americans in the West.*

JAMES FORESTER reviewed a mimeographed copy of a book by Woody Guthrie in a 1939 edition of the *Hollywood Tribune*, all because he thought the author had something important to impart.

PHILIP GOFF is the director of the Center for the Study of Religion and American Culture and professor of Religious Studies and American Studies at Indiana University-Purdue University, Indianapolis. Author or editor of nearly two hundred books, journal volumes, articles, and papers, his research focuses on the relationship of religion to other aspects of American culture. His edited books include *Religion and the Marketplace in the United States* and *The New Evangelical Social Engagement.*

JOSH KUN is associate professor in the Annenberg School for Communication and Journalism at the University of Southern California. He is the author of *Audiotopia: Music, Race, and America; Songs in the Key of Los Angeles*; and *To Live and Dine in L.A.: Menus and the Making of the Modern City*; as well as a co-editor of several volumes, including *Tijuana Dreaming: Life and Art at the Global Border* and *Black and Brown in Los Angeles: Beyond Conflict and Coalition.* He co-edits the book series Refiguring American Music for Duke University Press, and his curated exhibitions and installations have appeared at the Los Angeles Central Library, GRAMMY Museum, and Autry National Center, among many others.

PETER LA CHAPELLE is professor of history at Nevada State College where he has taught U.S. Cultural and Political History and Oral History since 2006. La Chapelle is the author of *Proud to Be an Okie: Cultural*

Politics, Country Music, and Migration to Southern California which received an honorable mention for the Urban History Association's Kenneth Jackson Award for Best Book in Urban History. He is also the faculty supervisor of the Nevada State College Undergraduate Oral History Project, a Library Services and Technology Act grant project which involves students in collecting oral histories of residents of Henderson, Nevada, a blue collar satellite community of greater Las Vegas.

ED ROBBIN was a labor activist who broadcast a nightly news commentary on KVFD in Depression-era Los Angeles advocating workers' rights and supporting union formation in Los Angeles industries. When Woody Guthrie played a new song he had written, "Tom Mooney is Free" Robbin was impressed and invited him to sing at a political rally in downtown Los Angeles. Robbin was instrumental in introducing Woody Guthrie to the local left by way of rallies, meetings, and readings. He was also the Los Angeles bureau chief for the San Francisco-based *People's World,* the West Coast equivalent of the Communist Party's *Daily Worker* (New York), which soon featured Guthrie's own regular "Woody Sez" column.

BRYANT SIMON is professor of history of Temple University. He earned his B.A. and Ph.D. at the University of North Carolina at Chapel Hill. He is the author of *A Fabric of Defeat: The Politics of South Carolina Millhands, 1910-1948*; *Boardwalk of Dreams: Atlantic City and the Fate of Urban America*; and *Everything But the Coffee: Learning about America from Starbucks.* His research and teaching have been honored by the Organization of American Historians, New Jersey Historical Commission, Urban History Association, Fulbright Commission, and the Humboldt Foundation.

ACKNOWLEDGMENTS

The co-editors of this volume express warmest thanks to the following people for their special assistance: Nora Guthrie; Anna Canoni; Tiffany Colannino; Bob Santelli; Marcie Booth, Chris Sampson; Tara McPherson; Ali Stuebner; Guy Logsdon; Pete La Chapelle; Will Kaufman; Mark Allan Jackson; Daria Yudacufski; Kim Matsunaga; Mary Megowan; Elizabeth Logan; Simone Bessant; Tom Zimmerman; Erin Chase; Stephanie Smith; Kate Blalack; and Leslie Chang. Our thanks as well to graphic designer Amy Inouye, for her creative approach to helping us tell the stories of Woody in Los Angeles, and to publishers Paddy Calistro and Scott McAuley, of Angel City Press, for their exuberant support from the very beginning.

IMAGE CREDITS

The authors and publisher gratefully credit the Woody Guthrie Estate for its generous cooperation during the assembly of this book and for its permission to use the works created by Woody Guthrie that appear in this book. Many institutions work as part of or with the Estate to preserve the legacy of Woody Guthrie. The Woody Guthrie Center in Tulsa, Oklahoma, is the educational center opened in 2013 that holds the Woody Guthrie Archive, which houses many of the original works of Woody Guthrie. Woody Guthrie Publications, Inc, is the copyright holder for all works created by Woody Guthrie (paintings, artwork, illustrations, handwriting, photographs, etc.). Woody Guthrie Publications and TRO are the publishers of all songs written by Woody Guthrie. The authors have worked with each of these institutions to honor the work and legacy of Woody Guthrie and to share our academic study with our readers. We especially appreciate the efforts of Woody Guthrie's granddaughter, Anna Canoni who gave of her time and knowledge, always with kindness.

We are also grateful to the following institutions and individuals for supplying the images on the pages listed:

Stephen Deutch, photographer/Chicago History Museum, via Getty Images: 65

Fuller Theological Seminary Archives: 108

Philip Goff: 98

Woody Guthrie Archive / Woody Guthrie Center: 5, 6, 12, 15, 16, 48, 51, 56, 62-63 (Original handwritten lyrics "Hangknot, Slipknot" by Woody Guthrie © Woody Guthrie Publications, Inc. Used by permission. WGP/ TRO © Copyright 1963 (renewed) Woody Guthrie Publications, Inc. & Ludlow Music, Inc., New York, New York administered by Ludlow Music, Inc. International Copyright Secured. All Rights Reserved.), 68, 87-97, 146, 152, 166, 174, 207

The Huntington Library, San Marino, California: 30, 31 (center left)

Peter La Chapelle: 73, 84

Research Center of the Oklahoma Historical Society: 54

Ralph Rinzler Collection, The Center for Folklife and Cultural Heritage, Smithsonian Institution, Washington, D.C.: 64

Stanford University, Department of Special Collection and Archives, Seema Weatherwax Photographs: 8, 28, 31 (except center left)

Jon Stich: cover, 2

Tom Zimmerman: 130